KEY STEPS TO BUILDING
YOUR FAMILY TREE ONLINE

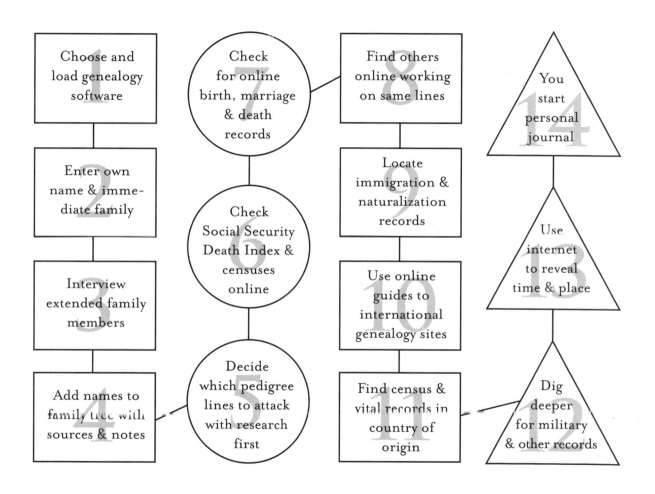

1. Choose and load genealogy software

2. Enter own name & immediate family

3. Interview extended family members

4. Add names to family tree with sources & notes

5. Decide which pedigree lines to attack with research first

6. Check Social Security Death Index & censuses online

7. Check for online birth, marriage & death records

8. Find others online working on same lines

9. Locate immigration & naturalization records

10. Use online guides to international genealogy sites

11. Find census & vital records in country of origin

12. Dig deeper for military & other records

13. Use internet to reveal time & place

14. You start personal journal

FINDING
YOUR FAMILY
ON THE
INTERNET

The Ultimate Guide to
Online Family History
Research

Michael Otterson

SILVERLEAF
PRESS

Silverleaf Press Books are available exclusively
through Independent Publishers Group.

For details write or telephone
Independent Publishers Group, 814 North Franklin St.
Chicago, IL 60610, (312) 337-0747

Silverleaf Press
8160 South Highland Drive
Sandy, Utah 84093

CONTENTS

FOREWORD

The Internet is a dynamic environment. Web sites and web pages come and go and change constantly. No book can hope to keep up with the multitude of site changes that take place daily on thousands of genealogical sites. That's why I've emphasized how to access and mine those sites which have already proved they can endure, or which are backed by significant organizations such as governments, major commercial operations, international volunteer groups, or genealogical professionals that are here to stay.

Keep this in mind when accessing the many Web links that are given in these pages:

- Enter the Web address in the address box at the top of your Web browser screen, where it's labeled "Address"—*not* in the search box of your search engine, which is what a surprising number of people do.

- Type the Web address *exactly* as it appears in the text. Don't add spaces, hyphens, or anything else, or the link won't work. For ease of reference, I have made all letters in most Web site addresses and page links appear as lower case. Capitalization makes no difference in most URLs, or Web addresses. On the few occasions where it does make a difference, I have pointed that out.

- If you encounter a "Page not found" message, as you may occasionally, it usually just means that the information has moved to another part of the site. Try entering just the stem of the Web address—i.e. the part that will take you to the home page. Then look at the on-site menus or site search engine to locate the topic you're looking for.

I have used another convention in the book which will make things easier. Whenever I have listed an active link *within* a site, it is set in bold. You can therefore quickly distinguish those items on a page that link you to the key information you want.

The inconveniences of changing Web sites are simply that—a minor inconvenience. As you begin to explore the Web for its rich potential, none of this will detract from the amazing world of Internet family history that awaits you.

ACKNOWLEDGMENTS

Every family history enthusiast who has volunteered countless hours to transcribe data and share it on the Internet deserves thanks from the rest of us. Indeed, without the growing army of volunteer contributors across the world, much of the data now available online would be found only on paper or microfilm at public libraries, government archives, or family history centers. The valued contributions of volunteers of all ages, cultures, and nationalities are amply demonstrated in these pages.

Dozens of images appear in this book. They include photographs, screen captures from genealogy software programs, graphics from numerous private and commercial Web sites, reproductions of forms and data from the archives of various county and national governments in the United States and around the world. I'm grateful for the willingness with which these site owners have granted approval to reproduce them. Great care has been taken to acknowledge copyright and ownership in each case.

Special thanks go to Elaine Hasleton, in the U.S., and Margaret Seabourne, in Britain, for their review of the entire manuscript and for helpful suggestions. Of particular note, Alan Mann's depth and professional expertise in Internet family history and his suggestions relating to the United States sections have significantly strengthened the book and made it more useable.

Where the phrase "used by permission" appears in the captions or text, it does not imply any endorsement or sponsorship by any organization of all or part of the book. I take full and sole responsibility for the accuracy of the text, the opinions expressed, and the recommendations made.

—Michael Otterson

1
THE INTERNET BOOM

Building your family tree just got a whole lot easier.

A few decades ago, the would-be family tree enthusiast would sooner or later end up in some library or other, peering into an artificially lit microfilm reader while laboriously turning a handle that advanced the film of a two-hundred-year-old document frame by frame. Because most of the names were not indexed alphabetically, it was a tedious process that, to be sure, often yielded results for the patient searcher. But often, it didn't. All but the serious researchers easily became discouraged; and the world today is full of people who once started their family trees but then gave up because it just seemed too hard.

Then came advances like microfiche—hundreds or even thousands of alphabetically sorted names packed onto a filmcard a few inches wide, each one viewable on a special reader available at certain libraries. That helped, but still the vast majority of data was not indexed or was otherwise difficult to find.

It was not until the late 1990s, or even the first few years of the twenty-first century, that things really took off. The soaring number of Internet users helped drive the creation of increasingly sophisticated software and powerful search engines. New technologies allowed extensive scanning and indexing of original records that once could be read only by a trip to a library, or even to another coun-

Microfiche cards allow easy access to indexed names but need a library with a reader to be viewed.

try. Companies that specialized in putting genealogical data on the Internet sprang up, offering users access to census and other records for a fee.

What's Available?

Today, countless groups of volunteers transcribe data to put on Web sites so it can be free for everyone. These volunteer efforts vary from a handful of people independently transcribing headstone inscriptions in a village cemetery to huge coordinated efforts involving the transcription of millions of birth, marriage, and death indexes for entire continents.

Because of such efforts, along with the actions of governments and archivists at many levels, the amount of family history data on the Internet today is truly staggering, and it is growing every day. People are often amazed to find they have to travel no further than their own keyboard at home to find the marriage date of their grandparents or the names of their great grandparents. Scanned, perfectly readable images of census pages, written by hand a century and a half ago, can be retrieved in seconds. There is something almost magical about looking on your own computer screen at a handwritten record from the 1700s that was originally scratched with a quill pen, possibly by the light of an oil lamp.

Sample of United States census entries, 1900. (Image copyright 2005 MyFamily.com, Inc., and reproduced from Ancestry.com. Used by permission.)

Want to see the name of that immigrant ancestor who passed through New York's Ellis Island, the Gateway to America, at the end of the nineteenth century? It's likely you can do it. But would you also like to see a picture of the ship he came on? It might well be there, too. Lists of the names on headstones in obscure cemeteries, records of military service, land records and wills, photographs of war memorials, parish records showing the passage of families through birth, marriage, and death—these are all part of the treasure trove on the Internet for those willing to explore from the comfort of their own homes. The treasure has amassed to literally hundreds of millions of searchable names, and we are only at the beginning. In the next few years, the amount of searchable data, scanned images, and records that will be posted to the Web will dwarf what we have today.

Pluses and Minuses

Can you do all your family tree research on the Internet? Definitely not. That day may arrive—when there is massive international cooperation to make the world's records accessible to everyone—but it is not here yet. There is a bedrock collection of online data readily available, such as United States census records spanning many decades. But the picture is less complete when looking for a marriage or death certificate or some evidence of an ancestor's arrival at a dockside from Europe. There is always a substantial element of luck when researching family history, and the same is true of the Internet.

What the Internet has done is deliver four big things to the family history enthusiast:

1. A rapidly increasing amount of primary source material, such as online census data or the Social Security Death Index. In the case of census records, these are the digital scans of original documents, so what you are seeing is what was written back in the day of the event.

2. Massive amounts of secondary material—this is often information from important records transcribed by volunteers that can be helpful at crucial moments in your search. The records do contain transcription errors, but they are still helpful and can lead you to original source material.

3. The indexing of much of the material, providing the ability to search such sources at high speed. While using search engines to track down data effectively is an art in itself, such searches allow discoveries to be made in minutes rather than days, weeks, or months.

4. The chance to team up more easily with others searching the same family lines.

These advantages are significant, and, together with the more traditional search methods and some other tips we'll include in this book, they help account for why so many Internet users are online searching for their ancestors.

Coordination and Collaboration

One of the most striking features of this frenzy of activity is the surge in collaborative efforts. People are helping each other like never before. Some of the most popular Web sites are those that bring together people who are searching the same family lines. Kids barely in their teens as well as retired couples have joined a massive, global, and quite amazing hunt for people long since dead.

In the process of searching, families have been reconnected. If the Internet and email are sometimes criticized for making the world impersonal, this is one field where that doesn't apply. I can count numerous second, third, and fourth cousins that I now include in my family circle whom I didn't know existed until we met on the Web. A few years ago I came across a first cousin whom I hadn't seen since I was nine years old when she lived in a tiny Scottish village. Nearly fifty years later, unknown to each other, we were both searching the same family lines, a half a world apart—she on one side of the Atlantic, me on the other. Now, we write, cooperate, and share information regularly.

One World

International boundaries have tumbled and are hardly relevant any more. Take the case of Jim Wiltsher. Jim lives in a tiny rural community in New Zealand, about a half-hour's drive south of Auckland. He and his wife, Gay, run a little shop and are close to retirement. I became aware of Jim when he wrote to me through a popular British Web site called GenesReunited. He had seen my list of surnames posted on that site and had written because one of them contained the name Wiltsher, an unusual spelling. Jim was right at the start of his quest to discover his family tree.

The people emailing each other on such sites often have no idea where the other person lives. Jim assumed that since he was writing to a British site, and about British ancestors, that I was responding from England. It wasn't until we exchanged private email addresses later that he realized I was in the United States, and I discovered he was at the other end of the world in New Zealand. Jim, by the way, is a good example of the millions of people who have caught the family history bug. When he first contacted me, he was unsure of the name of his paternal grandfather. With a single evening's work on the Internet, we had pushed his lines back to five generations and found the butcher's shop owned by his great grandfather, next to an English pub called the Wagon and Horses. We'll pick up Jim's story again later, because it's people like Jim who truly illustrate the miracle of Internet genealogy.

Motives and Passion

What is it that drives people to spend their time finding connections to people long since dead? There are probably lots of answers, but I like the one from Alex Haley, written in the mid-1970s. Haley was the African-American journalist who wrote the stunningly successful story *Roots*. It told the epic tale of Haley's family, including the capture of his African ancestor Kunte Kinte by slave traders, Kinte's journey to America, and the terrible hardships suffered by the family and descendants for the next several generations. *Roots* became a television phenomenon, transformed into a mini-series that dominated American television ratings for weeks. It also gave genealogy as a hobby a huge boost. About his motivation for writing an epic family history, Haley said:

> In all of us there is a hunger, marrow deep, to know our heritage—to know who we are and where we came from. Without this enriching knowledge, there is a hollow yearning. No matter what our attainments in life, there is still a vacuum, an emptiness, and the most disquieting loneliness.

Haley's story also suggests something else. This passion for seeking out ancestors is not just about names and dates and places. They may be the sinews that bind the family tree together, but what people really want is the *stories*—especially stories of their own kin. A commonly made distinction is that genealogy is the science of researching family lines (the names and dates and places); family history is the flesh on the bones, the stories and events that make these long-dead people come alive and render their life's experience not only interesting but motivational and even inspirational.

In this the Internet has been a huge help. My own father died when I was only a few months old, so I never knew him personally. The most valuable, tangible thing I have of him is a logbook he kept while a British POW in Italian and German prison camps during World War II. In one journal entry, he records his forced evacuation from Libya on a prison ship headed for Italy. It makes great reading for his descendants. But it was on the Internet that I found photographs of the ship, including scale models that showed the very hatch under which he sat cramped for three miserable days with his dysentery-stricken mates. It was on the Internet that I found the

Page from World War II log of author's father. Some such journals can now be found on the Internet.

photographs of the gates to Stalag IVB, the German prison camp near Mühlberg on the Elbe River where he spent the last Christmas of the war. And it was to the Internet that I turned to post his story so that anyone interested could read about it and share the experience. No living family member knew of these details. Possibly he shared them with no one else during his short lifetime.

Some Initial Cautions

This book is primarily for the people who are just starting out, or have dabbled in research for a few years but don't consider themselves experts, or who want to use the Internet for family research but don't know how. There are countless people all over the world who would start or continue work on their family trees if they knew it didn't demand skills and resources beyond their reach. Some people have launched into Internet searches with the best of intentions, but have promptly drowned in the bewildering and rapidly expanding mass of genealogy Web sites and data. For some such people, it can be a long time before they venture back onto the Web to search for family roots.

And so, you may have picked up this book because you feel like Alex Haley, or because you are just mildly curious. You may be trying to solve a long-standing family puzzle, or your search may be driven by religious convictions to identify your past family. Whatever the reasons, it's my purpose to help you reach the next level by using methods available within your own home. Or, if you've already started and have become lost and overwhelmed by the mass of information out there, I'd like to help you thread your way through it.

The truth is that family history calls for some common sense, good judgment and reasoning skills, and a little imagination. But it doesn't necessarily require the sleuthing skills of a Sherlock Holmes or a fat bank account. We all like to get maximum returns for the least monetary investment; I won't advise spending anything if there are free alternative sources or unless the cost is worth it.

If you get to the end of this book and begin to enjoy some success with your family tree, you can decide for yourself where you want to take it after that. There are literally hundreds of good books available that will take you through the next steps or guide you through specialized areas. Necessarily, this book focuses mostly on what's available online. It isn't a comprehensive guide to tracing your family tree using more traditional methods. Hopefully, you'll get to the point where you want to get into substantial research beyond the Internet. But that will be up to you.

We also need to be clear that Internet research has its major down side. While millions more people today are tracing their family trees, an avalanche of beginners has cascaded across the World Wide Web, leaving questionable data and false leads strewn across the path of those who follow. It's impossible to estimate how many thousands of people have downloaded the wrong family tree just because it seemed to fit what they expected. Some of the so-called world family trees that are now easily available on the Web are filled with erroneous data to trap the unwary.

The most common starting point for beginners using the Internet is a range of collaborative Web sites or large databases. People love to get online and type in a couple of surnames on a "surname list" or a common family tree of millions of names in the hope that they will illuminate the dark recesses of their family history in a few hours. Certainly that's possible. However, it's a course that experienced genealogists strongly recommend against. What might look like your ancestor could be someone else entirely. Or, the information that others have built around your ancestor could be a tangle of inaccurate data with wrong names and dates and places. There will be a time to check out these Internet sources and to evaluate them carefully, but it isn't the first thing you should do. And you will have to know what you're doing.

So, how do you know what's right and what isn't? How do you know which databases are reliable and which ones should be avoided? How can you test and check information so you don't make the same mistakes?

Because anyone today can post anything, this book will take you step by step through the processes that will help you recognize what's questionable and avoid common mistakes. I will introduce you to some good habits so that you first build a solid foundation and post only accurate information. Caution, discipline, and patience are vital if your research is to be worth anything. Eventually, you will want to sit back and look at your family history as something you and your descendants can be proud of.

So, have this book open as you sit down in front of your computer, and let's get started.

2
CHOOSING YOUR SOFTWARE

....

Overview

To benefit from what you'll learn in the coming pages, you'll need easy access to a computer, at least an elementary working knowledge of basic software programs, an Internet connection, and the ability to send email with attachments.

As we lay out the step-by-step approach to building your family tree, I'll err on the side of simplicity rather than complexity. At various points, I'll break out some hints for ease of reference while allowing the more proficient or confident reader to stay with the main text. By the end of this chapter you'll have genealogy software loaded on your computer free of charge, and the program will be set up for your use.

Downloading Free Software

If you don't have a family history program on your computer, there are lots of good ones to choose from of varying degrees of sophistication. Among the most popular in a long list of options are Family Tree Maker, Personal Ancestral File, the Master Genealogist, Legacy, Ancestral Quest, and RootsMagic. All of these are pretty good, and some are excellent. They vary from each other in the way their screens look, and each has whistles

TIP: Using the Address Bar

Surprising at it may seem to frequent users of the Internet, not everyone who uses Google or other search engines finds the on-screen instructions intuitive. According to Web monitoring services that analyze where site visitors come from, large numbers of users type the web address in the search box, not into the address bar at the top of the screen. Putting a Web address in the search box will result in a long list of search results, and possibly in utter confusion. Whenever an address is given in this book beginning with "www" or "http," type the address exactly as shown into the **Address Bar,** not in the box where you would enter text for a search.

and bells that may be absent from rival programs. Some offer unique report variations, others link to online searches, and still others offer features such as historical timelines as background to any life being researched. For a more complete list of programs, including those in less-used languages, go to www.cyndislist.com and from the home page type **software** in the search box.

If you have already invested in a family history program for your computer, by all means stick with what you've got. Since you are probably already familiar with it, you should be able to follow along with your program's equivalent menus and options as we work through the next few chapters.

If you don't yet have a program, save yourself some money and, for the time being, download a free copy of Personal Ancestral File from the Internet. It has everything you will need to get started; and if you get hooked on family history and want to invest in a program later with a few extra features, you can easily switch. You will be able to import all of your data to your new program without losing anything.

Some of the other programs I've mentioned also offer free downloads of reduced versions from the Internet or free trial periods, but Personal Ancestral File is one of the quickest to learn and easiest to use. Some people like it so much that they stick with it.

Several good software programs are on the market, including those shown here. (Legacy is a registered trademark of Millennia Corporation; Family Tree Maker is a registered trademark of MyFamily.com, Inc; RootsMagic copyright 2001–2005 RootsMagic, Inc; Personal Ancestral File is a product of The Church of Jesus Christ of Latter-day Saints, copyright Intellectual Property Reserve, Inc. All Rights Reserved. Used by permission.)

Avoid Non-genealogy Programs

One thing you should *not* do is try to create your tree and keep your notes in some software program not dedicated to that purpose. I am often surprised when exchanging emails that even though there are free programs for family history readily available on the Web, many people choose to type up lists or create their own trees in word processing or spreadsheet software. Sure, if you intend to stop at a few dozen names that might serve you. But dedicated genealogy programs come with a host of valuable and sophisticated features that will deliver benefits again and again.

One of the big benefits of working on the Web is the ability to exchange large amounts of data in files that can be read by any family history program. No one wants to have to retype dozens of names and dates, along with notes and source details. So, if you have your information typed in something other than a dedicated genealogy program, bite the bullet now and plan to transfer it to something much more useful. The same goes for hard-copy records. By all means keep printed pages of your family tree's major lines as extra insurance, but don't plan on working from paper and cluttering your desk or table with notes on scraps of paper. That makes as much sense today as keeping a diary by chiseling it out in stone.

Don't Build Your Tree Exclusively on a Generic Web Site

Some genealogy Web sites offer their visitors the facility to build their trees directly online using the host site, instead of a genealogy program loaded on their home computers. Such Web-based programs are sometimes quite unsophisticated, difficult to navigate, or worse, they don't allow the user to download GEDCOM files. GEDCOM files use a common genealogical language that makes them transferable between many different programs. Cutting-edge technology and expected innovations may well make working directly online with your family tree an option before much longer (see Chapter 17), but even then you'd be best served also to keep your data in your own software program. Off-line programs will always have more sophisticated features. Also, if you use a laptop, you won't always have Internet access when you're on the road, and at times you will want all your data at your fingertips.

Step 1: Download Personal Ancestral File

Let's work through the process of downloading a free copy of Personal Ancestral File and setting it up for your personal use. Because software packages are upgraded frequently and some details may change, don't be alarmed if the screen doesn't react precisely as indicated here. It should be fairly easy to figure out from the screen what is needed if you read the steps below.

1. Log on to the Web and type **www.familysearch.org** in the address bar. We'll talk in much more detail about this important site later.

2. Click **Order/Download Products,** found on the top menu bar. That will take you to another menu called Software Downloads—Free. *Free* is the magic word. Often, *free* doesn't really mean free. In this case it does. You won't get annoying follow-up emails and there is no down side. The owners of this site want to promote family history research among as many people as possible, so everyone benefits. Other sites that offer free downloads or free trials are helpful; but almost invariably some of the advanced features will be disabled or the trial will last only a month or so before you have to buy the full version. That's not the case with Personal Ancestral File.

3. Click **Software Downloads—Free**.

4. Choose your software. This will be the top item from the list on the next screen—**Personal Ancestral File 5.2**—if you want to work in the English language. If you're more comfortable in another language, this page offers several variations, including Spanish, Portuguese, French, and German. When you have decided which one you want, click the **Download** button next to your choice and follow the on-screen instructions until the program has loaded onto your computer.

You now have a powerful program that will help to manage and display what we hope will be a steadily growing amount of valuable data. If, later on, you decide you want to try a program with more sophisticated features, you can easily download a trial version, make the comparisons, and decide if it's worth the cost of switching. Any information you enter in PAF will be easily transferable to another program.

Step 2: Set Up Your Personal Preferences

The first time you open the Personal Ancestral File (PAF) program, you will be presented with a welcome screen and a list of options. If this is the first time this program has been used on your computer, select **New** to create a new file. You will be asked to create a file name, and you should also specify a folder on your drive to keep it in. So, for example, you might want to create a new folder under PAF 5.2 called "Data" or "Family Trees"—whatever you like. Your file name might by your own surname plus "family," or your family name plus the family name of your spouse. Again, it doesn't matter as long as it's descriptive and you can distinguish it from other family trees or branches you might create later.

Once you have specified your file name, you should be presented with a Preferences screen to enter your personal information, such as name, address, and phone number. Do it. This contact information will identify you when, at a later stage, you begin to exchange information with others. This way, you only have to type in your details once.

If you do not see this screen automatically, you can access it later from the Tools menu item under Preferences (see below).

Many people like to start playing with new software as soon as it's loaded, and that's not a bad way to get to know Personal Ancestral File. For the most part, PAF is fairly intuitive, and you'll get the hang of the basics after a few minutes of experimenting with it. But resist the temptation to start adding names for the moment, and let's take care of a couple of preliminaries that will tailor the program to your use.

Choices for configuring software are commonly found under a Preferences or an Options tab. These may be a stand-alone menu item or are sometimes found under the File or Tools menus.

In PAF, select **Tools**, then **Preferences**. As with any software, these choices are mainly about how your information is displayed, and have no significance beyond convenience of use. They will not affect your data and you can change them later if you want. For instance, do you want your surnames to appear in capitals? Do you want your place names to be listed largest to smallest, or the other way around? What screen colors do you want? How big do you want your type to be on the screen, and how do you want your reports to look?

For now, I recommend you accept the program's default settings with the exceptions found in the Tip box on page 13. Selecting the options in the box will make navigating around your screen easier to begin with.

Step 3: Set Up the Folders on Your Hard Drive

If you haven't done so already, this is a good time to set up the various folders on your hard drive so you can access them easily, logically, and consistently. In addition to your data files—and you may have several—you also need a place to put files that you will receive and send to others, and a place to keep reports and backups. In addition to the suggestions here, you should also create folders for images such as document scans and photographs.

Use the Preferences window within PAF to set up the folders as shown on this

TIP: Recommended Preference Settings in PAF

Most settings are just a matter of taste. But the following will prove useful initially. From the PAF menu across the top of the screen, select **Tools**, then **Preferences**, and then the choices indicated below:

General tab:

If you are a member of The Church of Jesus Christ of Latter-day Saints, check the **Use LDS data** box. If not, leave this box blank so that unnecessary labels and options don't clutter your screen.

Set the number in the **File Backup Prompt Frequency Box** to **1**. This will prompt you to back up your data every time you exit the program—highly recommended (see Tip box, page 35, "Back Up Every Time You Exit").

Names tab:

In the **Append to names** box, click the circle next to **RIN (Record ID Number)**. You will come across the letters RIN in various software programs. They stand for Record Identification Number (MRIN stands for Marriage Record Identification Number). Each individual in your family tree will be assigned a sequential number that is unique to that person, so even if two people have the same name and even the same birth date, the computer will always identify them separately. Once assigned, a RIN can't be edited.

File tab:

Look under the box labeled **RIN of Home Person on File Open**. Click the circle next to **Use** and enter the number 1 in the box next to it. This setting means that your own name and details will be the first thing you see when you open the program. This makes navigation a little easier when starting out. You can change this option later when you start to work consistently on certain lines and have more names in your database.

page (using your own choice of names). For instance, you might want to have a main folder called Family History, and use your computer's built-in software such as Microsoft Explorer to create additional sub-folders for photographs and scans of important documents such as certificates and census pages.

Spending a few minutes on these preliminaries will help you organize your information properly and avoid complicating your work with unnecessary clutter. The advantages will soon be obvious.

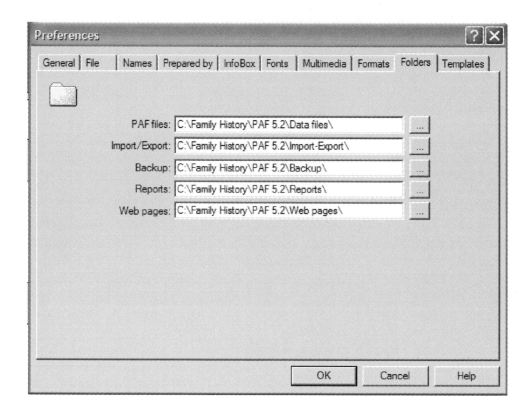

PAF preferences screen. (Personal Ancestral File, image copyright 1999, 2002 by Intellectual Reserve, Inc. Used by permission.)

3
ENTERING YOUR
FIRST NAMES

Overview

Once your preferences are set, you'll want to start entering names. This chapter will take you through the process and introduce you to the online forms you will use to interview your living family members and transfer their information to your computer program. It will also warn you about accepting information from family members without corroboration.

Step 1: Enter Your Own Name First

Let's take a look at what a typical Personal Ancestral File screen display looks like. The various genealogy software programs look a little different from each other, but they all share common features. For most people, it takes only a little practice to switch comfortably from one to another. If you are using a different program, just follow along with the equivalent commands. We'll start by reviewing how to add yourself to the screen.

1. Since you already created your file, you should now be looking at a screen with some empty boxes in it. PAF puts the primary individual—the person on whom you are working—at the top left of the screen, with the parents to the right and the spouse and children below.

2. Enter your personal information. There are two ways to enter data in PAF. From the menu, click **Add, Individual.** Alternatively, just right-click on the big empty box at the top left of your screen and select **Add Individual.** Enter your given names and surname.

3. Click the dropdown arrow in the box labeled **Sex** and select the correct gender.

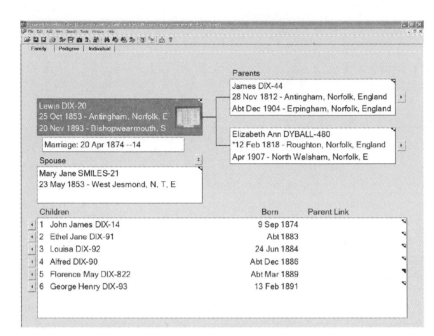

PAF family view (Personal Ancestral File, image copyright 1999, 2002 by Intellectual Reserve, Inc. Used by permission.)

4. Click on the birth box and enter your full birth date and birthplace. The place should be specific—at least the town or city, the county, the state (if applicable), and the country. Don't assume from the name of a county or town that the place is obvious to someone else just because it's obvious to you. Is New South Wales an obvious location? It is if you live in Australia. If you live elsewhere, you could be forgiven for thinking it has something to do with South Wales. Do you mean Cambridge in Middlesex County in the state of Massachusetts, USA, or Cambridge in Cambridgeshire, England? Is that Middlesex in Massachusetts or the county of Middlesex in Eng-

TIP: Entering Dates

Unlike most of the rest of the world, Americans generally write dates with the month first, followed by the day. Europeans reverse the two. Either way is fine, since computer programs ask you to specify which style you are using, and will render it correctly with a three-letter abbreviation for the month. However, it's a good habit to always write months in full or with the three-letter abbreviation and never with numbers, since failing to do so in emails and other correspondence between individuals in different countries can lead to misunderstandings.

land? Don't use place-name abbreviations, and always add the name of the *country*.

5. Click the **Save** button. You've just entered your first name. We'll go back and enter more details soon.

Did You Notice the S?

It's likely that you noticed the "S" alongside some of the boxes in the Add Individual window. This stands for **source** and is very important. However, to keep things simple I'm going to ask you *for this one time only* to set that aside for now while you are just adding your immediate family. We'll come back to the topic of sources in our next chapter and treat it in detail. Normally, you would *never* enter a name without entering the source—that is, where you got the information. Other programs, including Family Tree Maker and Legacy, use icons rather than letters for entering or retrieving sources.

Step 2: Enter the Names of Your Spouse, Children, and Parents

The order in which you enter your family names makes no difference to the program, but each name you create will be allocated the next sequential RIN or unique number by the computer, and that number will be permanently associated with the name. Some people like to add their wife or husband and the kids first so the numbers are in sequence, but it makes no difference whatsoever to anything you'll be doing later.

Each time you add a name, the computer creates the relationship you specify according to whether you are entering a husband, wife, father, mother, or child. Once it has the names in the correct relationship to each other, your program will be able to display them for you by family, by pedigree, or in a helpful list of all your names, sorted in a variety of ways. These family history programs are also intelligent enough to recognize certain errors. If you accidentally enter a birth date that is later than a death date, for instance, you will be prompted to correct your mistake. When you have added all the information that you, personally, are absolutely sure about for your immediate family, you have enough to take the next step.

How to Enter Additional Names

To enter additional names, right click on the spouse, children, or parent boxes, then select the **Add** option to enter information for that individual. If you are creating a spouse relationship, the program will prompt you for marriage details. Click **Save** in the new window when complete.

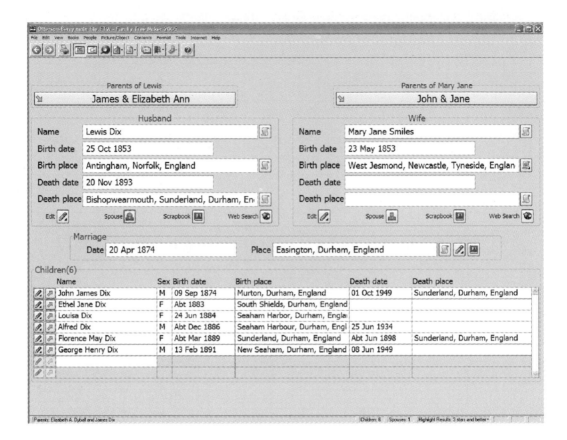

Family Tree Maker (FTM) is reportedly the biggest-selling family history program in the world. The family view puts the husband and wife side by side in the top half of the screen with equal information about each. Their parents are placed at the top and their children below. This three-generation view shows considerable data on the screen at one time. Photos are displayed by clicking on a camera icon under the name. FTM uses a Web icon to trigger Web searches on Ancestry.com, with which the program is affiliated. Some competing programs have parallel Web searching functions. (Image copyright 2005 MyFamily.com, Inc., and reproduced from Family Tree Maker software. Used by permission.)

Step 3: Talk to Living Relatives

Most genealogy books suggest that the first step for beginners is to talk to living relatives. However, creating something on your computer first—even a simple file with your own immediate family, as we have done—is an advantage before you start talking to family. You now have at least an elementary sense of the key information you want, and you will "think" in terms of this information when you start to have conversations with your family. You will also be more likely to enter the information promptly when you come home from a visit, and not keep it in sheaves of paper or in a box somewhere.

Ask for the basic information first. The next step is to plumb the depths of knowledge of living relatives—brothers and sisters, parents, aunts and uncles, cousins, grandparents, and great uncles and great aunts—everyone.

Of course, you can do this any way you want, but whether you use the phone or email, a letter or a personal visit, use a *system*. Just asking relatives for everything they know isn't a good idea. You'll end up with lots of gaps and as many questions as answers. Be specific. What you want first is full birth dates and places (day, month and year, city, county, state), and the same for marriages and deaths. You need full names, including multiple given names or nicknames when they are known. Without a fairly good idea of where your forebears lived and when, your task will be much more difficult when you come to online research.

Get it in writing. If the information is written down somewhere, such as in a family Bible, so much the better. If not, to reduce the chance of mistakes, it's best to get your relatives to write down the information they know by filling out a form, or fill it out yourself when talking to them. You will need two types of forms. A *pedigree chart,* or ancestor chart, lists only the direct-line ancestors—parents, grandparents, great-grandparents, and so on—usually four or five generations to a page. A *family group record* enables you to list any one of those couples with their children.

Your software program will probably allow you to print blank forms. In PAF, select **File**, **Print Reports**, then the **Pedigree** or **Family Group** tab. The **Blank form** option appears under each of these tabs.

Forms can also be found on a number of sites on the Internet. Make sure you use a site where you can download or print out the forms at no charge. If you type "free genealogy forms" into Google or another search engine, you'll find several listings, including Family Tree Magazine. This site has a good set of forms, including a five-generation pedigree chart and a family group sheet. For an example of these commonly used forms, see pages 23 and 24.

You can print the blank forms to use as you wish. If your relatives are computer-literate, you can tell them where to find the forms on the Web, and they can complete the forms on-screen before printing and mailing to you. Or they can email a scanned image of the printed form as an attachment. (Not a bad idea if your relative lives on the other side of the country.)

Dig deeper. Once you have the basic information, you can probe for additional details for each person in your tree. It's probably unrealistic to try to get everything from the memory or knowledge of a living relative in one visit. If your relatives live fairly close by or you can get to them easily, focus on the form filling first, then go back later for the stories (see Chapter 15). Older relatives are often a gold mine for such information, and they will have stories and insights into the personalities of your forebears that you may not be able to find anywhere else.

Record the sources. If you are interviewing a relative, you should note on the back of each form who gave you the information, their relationship to you, and the date. And do this while you are taking notes—don't leave it until later. If you are talking to more than one relative and they are sharing information with you, such as both grandparents, note which one gives which information. It may seem tedious now, but we'll see how important this step can be after you enter the information on your computer (see Chapter 4).

Ask for documentation. If documents, such as birth certificates, are available, ask to see them. Verify the information. Make copies if possible.

Why Relatives Can't Always Be Trusted!

At this point, it's worth taking a moment to look at some of the major pitfalls that await the unprepared. How good is Grandma's memory, really? It's not always true that the reliability of information decreases in inverse proportion to the age of the person giving it. Some elderly people have fabulous memories. However, you can't simply accept information on face value if there is no backup documentation.

Without evidence, nothing should be taken as final until you have checked details from a more official source, such as birth or marriage certificates. Most families keep certificates and other valuable documents in a single place. Family bibles, old letters, wedding announcements, newspaper clippings, photographs, and school memorabilia can all be valuable for the clues and information they offer.

Whether they're kept in a wall safe behind a hanging picture in the living room or in Grandma's shoebox, sooner or later you will need to look for evidence to confirm what relatives are telling you. If you can't do that, you'll have to confirm what you can online or in other ways, as we'll see.

A Horror Story

I learned the hard way about the danger of accepting family sources without question. Back in the early 1970s, when I was starting out, I took a wrong turn that cost me twenty-eight years of dead ends. I had asked my mother before she died what she knew of her grandparents. She had replied confidently that her grandfather Louis Dix was French, born in Brittany. I never questioned it. The name seemed French enough to me, and I had no reason to doubt. Her elder sister confirmed the story. And so for the next couple of decades I learned a lot about how to do genealogy in France. Unfortunately, I could never find the birthplace of the elusive Louis, or any trace of him.

There comes a time when you simply have to admit defeat, when the evidence is just not there. At the point of giving up, I decided to give it one more try by going back to the beginning and taking it step by step, questioning everything. With the added experience I'd gained over the years, I soon found that Louis had never set foot in France in his life. He was from the fertile English farmlands and market gardens of Norfolk. Norfolk is not and never has been in France. It seems Louis—or Lewis as he appeared on other records—had moved north to work in the English coal mines when he was still a young man. His descendants—at least up to my mother—were all born in the industrial areas of County Durham.

I can only guess where the French myth came from. But I can imagine the children of the mining families of Durham, with the distinctive "Geordie" accent of north-east England, asking the stranger who "talked funny" where he came from. And I can imagine Louis, with his unfamiliar rural accent of the south, teasingly telling them he was from France. I'll probably never know the real reason, but that family myth combined with inexperience cost me twenty-eight years of lost time on that line.

Consequences of Wrong Steps

There is a sequel to this unhappy tale. By the time I discovered the error, I had already posted the Brittany, France, birthplace on an early version of the Internet. Although I acted quickly to correct the error, I wasn't quick enough. A few years later I received an email from someone tracing the same line. He had recorded that Louis was born in Brittany, France, and wondered if I had more information. He had, of course, found the early Internet site where I had in good faith posted that information. I was able to put him right, but who knows how many other Dix descendants there are out there, thinking they are one-sixteenth French?

The lesson is plain for all to see. Family stories can provide useful clues, but that's all they are without evidence. *Trust nothing and no one and draw no irrevocable conclusions until the information is corroborated by additional, independent and reliable sources.*

The approach outlined in this chapter is entirely consistent with the golden rule of genealogical research: Start with what you know, and branch out from there. Laying this vital foundation at the outset, and establishing a clear idea of time and place for your relatives, will give you much more confidence and lead to better results than launching too soon into surname lists, world trees, or other Internet databases.

Once you've interviewed family members and gathered supporting documentation, go back to your computer and add any additional names, together with extra details for people you have already entered, according to the instructions in this chapter.

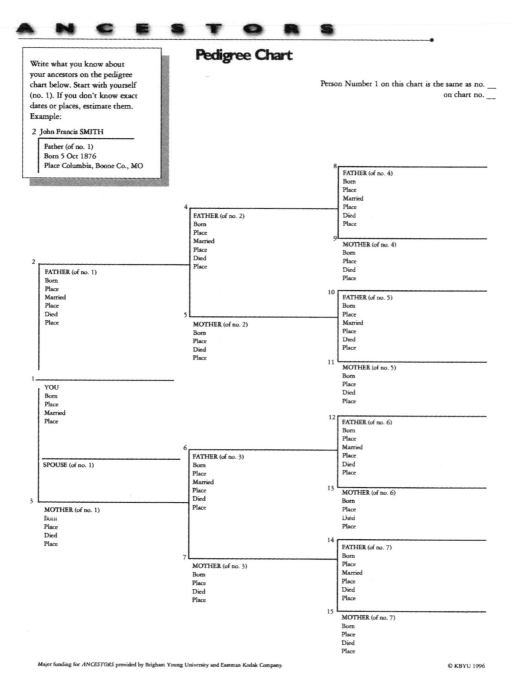

Pedigree or ancestor chart downloaded from a PBS television affiliate Web site. Several Web sites have forms like this that can help gather information from relatives. (Used courtesy of ANCESTORS/KBYU ©2001. All Rights Reserved.)

A N C E S T O R S

Family Group Record

Write name as:	Write date as:	Write places as:
Jeffrey Ryan MURRAY	23 Jan 1874	Las Vegas, Clark, NV or
		Baldridge, Dunfermline, Scotland

Husband's name		
Born	Place	
Mar.	Place	
Died	Place	
Father		Mother

Wife's name		
Born	Place	
Mar.	Place	
Died	Place	
Father		Mother

Children (In order of birth)

1 Sex	Name	Spouse
Born	Place	
Mar.	Place	
Died	Place	

2 Sex	Name	Spouse
Born	Place	
Mar.	Place	
Died	Place	

3 Sex	Name	Spouse
Born	Place	
Mar.	Place	
Died	Place	

4 Sex	Name	Spouse
Born	Place	
Mar.	Place	
Died	Place	

5 Sex	Name	Spouse
Born	Place	
Mar.	Place	
Died	Place	

6 Sex	Name	Spouse
Born	Place	
Mar.	Place	
Died	Place	

Other marriages

Sources

Major funding for *ANCESTORS* provided by Brigham Young University and Eastman Kodak Company.   © KBYU 1996

A Family Group Record expands details of couples on the pedigree chart to include their children, and their children's spouses. Additional pages are downloadable to enable more children to be added. (Used courtesy of ANCESTORS/KBYU © 2001. All Rights Reserved.)

4
SOURCES, NOTES, AND LOGS

Overview

In a few moments we'll begin adding source information to the names you've already entered on your family tree. But before we get to your keyboard and mouse, we need to pause long enough to drive the point home about how important source material is. From now on, whenever you enter a new name or a new piece of information to your tree, make sure you add a note showing where the information came from by filling in the source annotation immediately. Here's why.

Inevitably, as you increase the size and scope of your family tree, you will encounter other researchers whose lines cross yours. Then, you will face some choices. For instance, it may be that you have to decide whether a particular individual really is the parent to someone else on your tree. Are you going to accept the data you have found on the Internet without question? How will you make that judgment? Without any evidence or way to verify it, it would be foolish indeed to accept it as reliable.

This is where sources come in. If the data you are being offered is backed up by a reference to a specific page of a census, or the provider is citing a specific county death certificate which he says he has in his files, you are going to feel more confident, and you are less likely to find—years down the trail—that you have taken a wrong turn.

Here's another common scenario. Perhaps you have received an email from the owner of the other tree, who says his information came from "family knowledge." You decide to accept that information but you don't add anything by way of source annotation. After all, the information seems reliable enough and you don't really have time to type up all the source details. Six months later, after lots of other work on different lines, you come across the relative in question on a census record, but the date or place or other crucial information is different. Now you try to remember where your original information came from—it was someone on the Internet, but were they citing a birth certificate or a family Bible? You can't remember, and now you can't deal with the disparity.

Even when dealing with a handful of names, it's an exceptional person who can keep everything in his or her head. If you did keep a note of the first source, however, you can make an intelligent decision. Your new written census data is more solid than a vague reference to "family knowledge," so you would opt for the census information as the most reliable.

What Are the Best Sources?

While sources are critically important, it's obvious that not all sources are created equal. Just because something is written down in a family Bible doesn't mean it's correct. The best sources are records like **parish registers of births and marriages,** because professional people who were reasonably literate recorded those and often were eyewitnesses of them. Mistakes still crept in; but this type of record generally contains reliable information.

Census returns are good, too, though mistakes are more common than in the birth, marriage, and death registers. Census transcribers differed considerably in their abilities and conscientiousness, including handwriting. Some were downright sloppy. In most countries, the census taker relied on information given by the head of the family, although even that varied. Sometimes the family got it wrong, forgot an exact age, approximated a birthplace, and so on. So, for example, ages on census forms are frequently out by a year or two, especially as people got older. Some were rounded up or down. Spelling can vary markedly. And, by the way, some of the modern transcriptions of census and other records have introduced all kinds of errors.

Treat Transcribed Sources with Caution

If you are looking at scanned images of *original* records such as census pages, the Internet is as good as looking at the paper original, assuming the scan is a sharp one and easy to read. However, most databases you'll find on the Internet don't include scanned images of the original records. They are still much, much better than nothing, but just be aware that errors may have crept in to some of the entries. Any time you can use these sources just as signposts and still get at the original record, you should do so. Later, we'll explain how.

Some Web sites that charge for looking at their records have a two-tier system in which you pay a small amount to see a transcription of the data, and a rather larger amount to view the original record. Many people looking through such records

TIP: Sources, Best to Worst

Best: Parish registers of births (christenings), marriages, and deaths (burials). In many cases these are better than impersonal government records because the parish priest or minister knew the family and was an eyewitness to the event.

Next best: Government records—official birth and marriage certificates where the information was recorded close to the event. Also, other official sources such as census returns (original images where possible), Social Security indexes, records of military service, pension or probate records, and so on.

Good: Family information that was written down—family bibles with family history recorded there, old letters, photographs where the people are identified, and so on.

Helpful: Official death certificates. The problem with death records is that the informants were often unable to provide precise information and sometimes offered hearsay or dubious evidence. They can be helpful, but are not authoritative.

Useful leads: Living family members' recollections and memories.

Better than nothing: Family history information on the Web where the source is not identified, such as someone else's family tree or Web site, but where the site doesn't list sources in a way that they can be checked. Every effort should be made to verify such information from reliable sources.

simply rely on the transcripts or indexes that have been entered by volunteers on a keyboard because they save a few cents. Bad idea. Anyone who has spent time comparing a transcribed census or other record on the Internet with the originals knows the danger of not looking at the primary record.

A case in point is the official site of the 1901 British census. It costs a small amount to look at a transcription, and 50 percent more to look at the original record. Hence, many people just read the transcript. Don't fall victim to this false economy. Earlier, I said I didn't recommend spending money when it isn't necessary. This is one time where it is. Use the search engine to search through the data, but when you think you have found a match, view the scanned image of the *original* if the site offers it.

Sometimes the name or information you're looking for may not show up at all. Recently I received an email from a woman in Australia who had been hunting for an Oxton family on a census record, with no luck. Finally, she found it by accident under *Orton*. The transcriber had simply misread the name, though on the original record the name seemed clear enough to both of us. If you were entering this name on your records and noting the source information, you would make sure that this mistake is written down so you could find the record again if needed.

Make sure that you record sources as far as possible for every name and every separate piece of information. This is an essential habit to cultivate, so you may as well start forming it now. As you go through this book, it will become clearer how you can do that.

In order of reliability, think of a list of best-to-worst as indicated in the TIP box on page 27.

Entering Sources

Your next task is to enter source information for each person in your immediate family that you have entered on your tree. Normally you

> ### TIP: How to List Your Sources
>
> Think carefully when you are creating names or titles for your sources. Since source information is so central to good genealogical research, it's worth spending time to understand how to name and describe those sources in your genealogy software program.
>
> Most professional genealogists agree that source titles should list the place first, starting with country or state, then county, and then town or equivalent. This should be followed by record type, as in "England, Hertfordshire, Tewin parish register." Since your list will be ordered alphabetically, it makes life a little easier when you are accessing your source list because different sources for the same parish or town will appear together.
>
> When listing the record type, you can achieve more consistency by using the conventions listed in the Family History Library catalog on www.familysearch.org. Example: "Wisconsin, Brown County Vital Record."

would have done this at the time of entering each name. The Personal Ancestral File program that we downloaded at the beginning of the book will be our model for finding out how to create and record sources. Though the information requested differs in scope and detail, there are broad similarities in how all family history software programs handle sources. If you are using another program, use the on-screen Help or the manual if needed to make sure you understand the equivalent commands. (In Family Tree Maker, look for the little blue scroll icon next to each name). What all programs do is create a reference list of sources that you can use time and again to assign to a name, place, or event.

Step 1: Start With Your Own Name

Start with RIN-1. If you started literally from scratch and created a new file, RIN-1 is probably you. It doesn't matter for the purpose of this exercise, just follow these steps:

1. Double-click the RIN-1 name to open the Edit Individual window.

2. Double-click the **S** button to the right of the birth place information you have entered. The *S* stands for source. This will open a Select Source window to allow you to create a list of sources. Most programs offer a default list to begin with, but you can add your own and we're going to do so now.

3. Click the **New** button at the bottom of the window. The Edit Source window will open.

4. In the top box, under **Source Title**, type the name of the state, county, and town or parish, followed by the record type, e.g. "vital record."

5. In the **Author** box, type the name of the institutional representative that created the record. For example, "Register of Deeds, Brown County, Wisconsin, USA" or "Registrar, Registration District of Erpingham, Norfolk, England." If the record you are citing is a parish register, the author is the

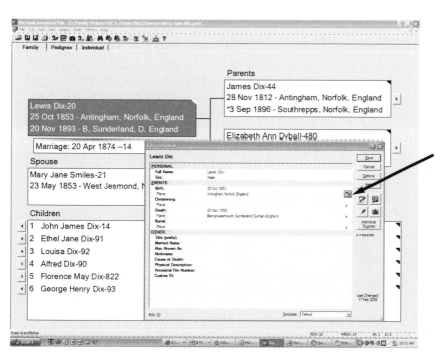

Entering sources in PAF. The "3" button triggers new screens to allow source details to be added (Personal Ancestral File, image copyright 1999, 2002 by Intellectual Reserve, Inc.).

minister who is named in the register as making the entry, complete with the name and location of his parish and the church denomination.

6. Click the **Repository** button. This is the institution where the *original* record is housed. This is worth considering for a moment. When you order a birth certificate, you actually receive a certified copy of the original registry entry, but the entry in the register, of course, stays where it is. The repository is therefore the place where someone else could go to see the original record.

7. Click the **Add** button and enter the information asked for. You might, for example, enter something like "Brown County Register of Deeds Office, Green Bay, Brown County, Wisconsin." Note that when you click on the repository button, it asks for an address.

8. Click **OK** to save.

9. Click **Select**, then **OK**.

TIP: Keep Your Source List Manageable

As you add sources for the various entries under each of your family members, your source list will expand. Your sources may be as simple as "Family knowledge" or as specific as "Wisconsin, Brown County, Census, 1900." Since you don't want your list to become so big that it's unmanageable, think before you add a new source.

If you have attached a nickname to an individual and the only source is Grandma, then "Family knowledge" is a good general category to create. You can add further details in the source box as needed. There is a balance between having a good list of sources and creating so many that the list becomes unwieldy. When entering a source, think of whether you are likely to use it again and, if so, make it generic enough that you can do so.

What you have just done is create the first item in a list of sources that will open on your screen every time you click one of those little *S* symbols—or the source icon if you are not using PAF. To return to the source, you simply click on the S. You can then just select whatever source on your list describes where you obtained the information. You can create as many sources as you like, and it's common to have several dozen in your list.

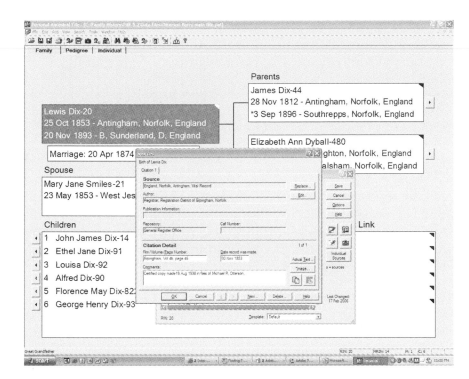

The PAF Sources screen shows the source plus citation information for the specific item. (Personal Ancestral File, image copyright 1999, 2002 by Intellectual Reserve, Inc. Used by permission.)

Help Features

All genealogy software programs have help screens that give more information about the various source fields. Not all give exactly the same advice, and some allow a wide latitude or variation in how you should record sources. However, stick to the approach given in the last couple of pages in relation to the source name, the author/institution that created the source, and the description of the repository. At first, entering source information properly can seem complicated, but after you have created your first few sources using a consistent method, it will become second nature.

If you select a source from the master list of sources offered by various software programs, edit it to be consistent with your others if needed.

Examples of Repositories

Some sources may be unique to your own files or collections, such as a family Bible. Original letters that have been written by grandparents or other family members may now be in your collection of papers or family records. In these cases, enter **your own name and address** as the repository.

If you download a census image from an Internet site, you have a digital copy, not the original record, which is still in some government record office. Because the digital image came from the Internet site, that is the repository—not your files.

What if the source is simply the recollection of someone in your family? You can create sources called Personal Communication or Personal Recollection, as long as you take one more step. You need to add what's called Citation Details.

What Are Citation Details?

After we entered the repository information and saved it as explained above, a new source was added to our source list. Obviously, there is a good chance you will want to cite this source some time again—for instance, if you obtain another vital record from the same locality. How, then, do you distinguish between the two different vital records?

When you select a particular source from your list a second time, a source window will open with the information you typed previously. You will not need to type it again. However, notice that the cursor has now moved to a new box called **Citation Detail** (see screen image, page 31). This gives you the option of identifying precise information about your document, such as the particular page of the census that you are using. This part of the source record will differentiate this particular piece of information from another piece in the same source. For instance, you might be referring to two completely different pages in two localities but in the same census. Or, you might be referring to different vital records from the same county or registration district.

It's important to record citation information so that the precise data can be verified by other researchers who might choose to check it. And finding this data again without citation information isn't always as simple as it might seem. You might refer to a particular name in a 1900 census and leave it at that, but someone else may find it difficult to locate again if they are using a different spelling or have some other date or place recorded differently. Citation information allows you to specify the precise location of key data within any record, whether it's a book, a microfilm, or some other source. So, for example, you can record the actual spot in the census of millions of names where your relative's name appears.

Suppose you were adding a citation for something under the heading "Personal Communication." It might be an email or a letter or even a conversation. In that case you would cite whom the letter is from, who it was addressed to, and the date. If it was a personal recollection in a conversation with a relative, you should similarly cite who said what, to whom, and when.

A moment's thought will show that the advantage in this is that your list of sources can be kept reasonable and manageable, even though it may still run to several dozen or even hundreds. Your broader classifications, like "Personal Communication," mean that you don't need to list every email from a family member as a separate citation. However, this only works if you *always* add citation details. Just adding "Personal Recollection" as a source without citations is inadequate and, actually, fairly pointless.

Other Helpful Buttons

By the way, there are a couple of additional features in the citation sections of some programs, including PAF, which are worth noting. You may have noticed an **Image** button or an **Actual Text** button. The **Image** button allows you to "point" to a scanned image, say a census record, which you have downloaded from the Internet, or a birth certificate you have scanned and saved to your hard drive. With a click of your mouse, you can enlarge the image to pretty much fill your screen. This is a great advantage because you have your sources at your fingertips at all times.

The **Actual Text** button is a place where you can record the precise text of, say an email, either in part or all of it. Emails are particularly problematic because they tend to have a short shelf life. They end up in trash folders or are lost when a person switches to another email provider. Copy and paste the key sentence or phrase into the **Actual Text** box and then record the name of the person who wrote the email, including their email address at the time, the date it was sent, and to whom. Once you have it saved in your genealogical program, your source information is as secure as your data itself.

Some of this source and citation information may seem tedious or demanding at first, but it's worth it. *Never think of adding a name or details to your family tree without adding the source information at the same time.* Develop good family history research habits at the outset and you'll build something for which your children, grandchildren, and future generations will praise you.

Step 2: Use Notes and Research Logs

Since the time the first version of PAF came on the scene in the 1980s, the Notes feature has been one of the most valuable—and perhaps one of the least used from what I've seen of casual researchers. Very few people seem to use the Notes to advantage. All genealogy programs have them—a facility that allows you to attach virtually unlimited notes or commentary to any individual in your tree.

Notes are not the same as sources. I've underscored the importance of noting sources for each piece of data. However, that may not always be sufficient. For example, you may be citing a particular census page, and showing the names on that page accurately. But how do I know that the steps you took to get to that census are the right ones? What if you took a wrong fork in the road and the census page actually relates to another family altogether, and you just don't know it?

This is where notes come in. *Make it a habit from the start to record exactly what steps you took to draw the conclusions you did.* Your notes should contain your reasoning, logic, and conclusions whenever it might be unclear why you made one decision over another one.

For example, you might be trying to determine whether a particular census family is on your tree, and you have to decide between two families of the same surname in the same locality. You weigh the evidence, and in the end it comes down to the

Research Logs in PAF and other programs

This is one time where PAF doesn't measure up to the other major genealogy software programs, possibly because new versions come out much less frequently than the other major software offerings. This is part of the price you pay for a free program. PAF 5.2 uses a notes selector process to keep track of research items, but the process is cumbersome and limited (use the Help menu, and select "To Do list," to find out how the program works).

The **Ancestral Quest** program, which closely resembles PAF in many other respects, does a much better job, allowing a research log for your entire tree or file. You can add and manage "To do" research reminders very easily from a number of places in the program.

In **Legacy 6.0 deluxe edition**, the research log is accessed from an icon on the menu bar, and offers a sophisticated range of choices for managing your tasks.

The Master Genealogist has a similar, wide range of choices for the research log, though, like much in this advanced program, it is less intuitive for beginners to use.

Family Tree Maker calls this feature a Research Journal. In FTM this feature is simple and intuitive, and easily understood from the Help menu. While lacking the advanced features of some other programs, it's perfectly sufficient for most users. For more on research logs, see page 35.

fact that the children have unusual names but ones that are common in their descendants' families. This, you decide, tips the scale in favor of accepting that family for the time being. You should record clearly in your notes the dilemma you faced and why you made your decision. Actually, you'll repeatedly find this helpful—even to yourself—when you are going back over records to check something or look for a clue.

There is no set formula or prescribed method for keeping notes. Some of my notes for individuals are very long. Others may just have a line or two. However, most programs will let you add unlimited text notes. My notes and research log for my troublesome non-French great-grandfather Lewis Dix are the longest in my entire family tree, with every logical step and deduction carefully recorded.

Research logs are related to notes, but are not the same. The better genealogy software programs include this enormously helpful feature. It is known in Family Tree Maker as a "research journal."

The log is a place where you record the specific research steps taken—that is, the sources consulted and the results or lack of results. So, you might record that on such-and-such a date you searched an online vital records database for a particular name and came up empty. Or you might write a letter to someone and it's ignored. You would still log the date of the letter, the contents, and, perhaps, "reply awaited." If you write to a relative and he or she has no answer to a question, record that fact carefully so you don't send another letter to the same person two years later. To be useful, the log must be specific. Logs will also tend to be briefer than your notes. If you are search-

TIP: Back Up Every Time You Exit

Most major genealogical programs save your working file automatically after each name or data change. When exiting, they prompt you to back up, or allow you to specify a preference to back up every so often. However, backup copies of your files to a removable disk or storage device are *not* automatic. If anything happens to your computer hard drive, months or years of hard work can go down the drain. It takes two or three seconds to back up to a removable medium, such as a zip disk, a CD, or one of the high-storage drives that connect to a USB port.

Earlier, when we set *Preferences* under the General tab for PAF, we chose to tell the computer to prompt us to back up every time we exited the program. However, prompting is one thing, doing it is another. If there are only two or three things you take away from this chapter, let one of them be the habit of backing up each time you complete a session on your computer.

ing a database, record the exact name you entered, including variations, the time period, and other search criteria.

You can also add action items or tasks as you are working on an individual—a reminder of something you still need to do, such as order a certificate or look up a census record. Unlike the notes that are attached to individual records, the research log can bring up your action items on a single person or a list for your entire tree. You can also prioritize your list.

As we'll see in later chapters, especially Chapter 17, this ability to prove research steps and sources is going to become increasingly important judging from the way Internet genealogy is developing.

You may also have noticed how few pieces of paper and how little clutter we have generated as we have worked through these first chapters. Most things can be done on screen. Your scanned photographs and certificates, your downloaded census images, your research notes, and a host of other information can now be built right into your genealogy program. As long as you are safely backing up—preferably in more than one place—finding your family tree in the age of computers doesn't have to be the messy, floor-strewn job that it was years ago.

5
FIRST STEPS
ON THE INTERNET

Quick Review

By now you should have completed the following:

- You have downloaded PAF (or have loaded another genealogy program).

- You have set up the program's preferences, entered your contact information, and played with it sufficiently to be reasonably familiar with its main features.

- You have entered your own name and the names of both parents, if known; the name of your spouse if you have one; the names of your children; and the names of your grandparents, if you know who they are. If you know the names and event details of any of the children of these couples—that is, your aunts and uncles, great aunts and great uncles—you've added them too.

- You have talked to living relatives to supplement what you already know personally, and you have added to your computerized tree as many birth dates and places, marriage dates and places, and death dates and places that you have been able to find for every one of these individuals.

- You have created sources for these names and events and added them to your software file accordingly.

- You have added notes for each individual and a research log, where appropriate, recording the dates you found the information, and the other comments that will remind you later of what you found and didn't find. This includes questions you asked relatives that they didn't know the answers to (or you'll end up covering the same ground twice, later on).

In other words, everything that you know or that your immediate relatives know about your family's key milestone events (names, births, deaths, marriages) is now on your computer. As you talk to relatives, you'll often encounter a great deal more information than this, and you should certainly record it in your notes, but we're not going to worry about the extra stuff for now unless it provides a vital clue about date or locality.

Step 1: Look at Your Road Map

Bring up the **Pedigree View** on your screen. When I go on a long drive through unfamiliar territory, I like to look at a map first. In PAF and most other software programs, the pedigree view is your road map. It sets out clearly a way of deciding where you need to go first.

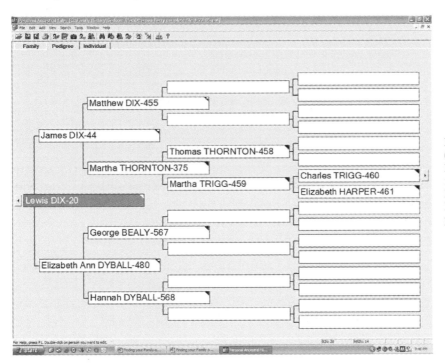

PAF pedigree view. (Personal Ancestral File, image copyright 1999, 2002 by Intellectual Reserve, Inc. Used by permission.)

The pedigree view is one of three basic views of your family information in just about all genealogical software. (The Master Genealogist calls this the Tree View.) These names are your direct ancestors—your parents, their parents, and their parents, and so on. Your default pedigree view will display four or five generations of your tree, though in this stage of your research many of the name boxes are likely to be blank.

There's a reason why we started in Chapter 3 with your own name, and then proceeded the way we did. Remember that the key principle in family research is to *start with what you know,* and branch out from there, step by step. Just leaping into the third or fourth generation back or searching the Internet for a great grandfather's name is no plan at all. At best, it's confusing. At worst, it will send you down the wrong road. I know that in repeating this I risk flogging the issue to death, but I've seen it happen too many times to let it pass. People stab in the dark for a familiar name and turn up dozens, hundreds, or even thousands of possibilities that just seem overwhelming. It's that feeling of bewilderment—of helplessly swimming in a sea of strange Web sites with confusing crosscurrents—that prompts many people to quit then and there. But you don't have to sail through uncharted waters.

Looking at your pedigree view provides you with a navigated path. For each pair of names (husband and wife), you now need to be as sure as you can be of the key event dates and places, and, of course, their names. As you anchor these names and dates and events, you will more easily find the children of each couple and build the picture of your various family groups.

Decide Which Line You Want to Begin with

As you look through your pedigree, decide which line you want to begin with. Are you most interested in your father's or your mother's line? And then what? Will you pursue their paternal or maternal lines? Often this is determined by how much you already know about each line. Sometimes people like to push back on their own surname first. The choice can also be influenced by the time frame or locality in which the person lived, since records might be more readily available for certain times and places. The choice is entirely up to you. I suggest that you select one line and work on it for a while. If it doesn't matter much to you, then choose the less common surnames of your grandparents, since research is often easier that way.

We are going to pick the low-hanging fruit first—in other words, we'll gather the information that's relatively easy to come by. If you encounter a difficulty, you can always switch to another main line and go back later to tackle the obstacle.

Step 2: Identify and List the Missing Information

This is a good time to start using the research log consistently if you aren't already doing so. Use the research log or equivalent in your genealogy software program to list the main items you are missing. First, look at the key events, dates, and places for each name on your pedigree display. (If your program is not displaying any more than just the names in the pedigree view, slide your cursor over a name and leave it there for a couple of seconds—the event details will then appear in a box). There will certainly be gaps in your pedigree—a missing birth or marriage place, or a blank where you should have the name of a spouse.

List the Outstanding Tasks and Prioritize Them

Be specific. Rather than: "Find birth date for so-and-so," write: "Check Arizona birth registers for so-and-so's birth. If not online, write to Apache County Bureau of Vital Records." People tend to work much better with lists that can be dealt with in bite-sized pieces. If your tasks are too broad or too general, they are more likely to sit untouched on your computer for months or years.

Make Reminders

List in the log a reminder to verify each name or date or event for which you have relied only on secondary sources, such as family memories or recollection. In addition to information that's entirely missing, you want to make sure that the information you have been given from secondary sources is verified by certificates, census records, or other primary sources if possible. With luck, because you have already talked to your closest living relatives, you already have some of these primary source certificates, or have been able to view or get copies of things like your parents' marriage certificate.

More Than a To-Do List

Start to think of the research log as more than a to-do list. Most software programs don't do a very good job of emphasizing the usefulness of research logs beyond a sophisticated to-do list. In fact, they are your past research trail as well as your future action list.

Because you can attach a research log to every individual, you have a method at your fingertips of recording clearly and concisely each step you take, and its success or otherwise. This kind of log is very much easier to access, filter, sort, and update than a long series of notes.

When you check the box alongside a log entry that says "Done" or "Completed," the entry isn't deleted—it stays in your file. Of course, you can filter your list so these completed items don't display when looking at your to-do list. But it's a big advantage to be able to go back and look at your completed steps, dead ends, and wrong turns, as well as breakthroughs.

If you are using Master Genealogist or a program that has a sophisticated log, read the instructions thoroughly. Then play with it until it becomes second nature.

Make it a central part of your activity, just as you would with entering source information. If your program doesn't have a decent research log, you'll have to fall back on the notes facility. If that becomes cumbersome, you might consider upgrading to a better program.

Step 3: Check the Social Security Death Index

We'll start with the assumption that you are researching in the United States. If you are researching in other countries, Chapters 10 through 14 will be helpful in this area.

An easy starting point to verify some of the vital pedigree information you have, or possibly to fill in blanks where you want names, is to check the Social Security Death Index (SSDI), which is searchable on the Internet free of charge.

While not a primary source in itself, the SSDI is the closest equivalent to a national death index for the United States. The SSDI contains the records of around 76 million Americans whose deaths have been reported to the Social Security Administration. That means the index includes many people born in the early to mid-1900s, which is about where family historians living today run out of information from their own or their parents' knowledge. The SSDI can quickly and relatively easily lead you to reliable information provided personally by the individual.

However, the SSDI does have limitations. It contains only the names of those people for whom a social security death claim was processed after 1962. People who died and for whom no claim was registered do not appear in the database.

Many genealogical Web sites provide a gateway to the Social Security Death Index. Simply typing "Social Security Death Index" into the Google search bar or another search engine will provide you with a list of Web links. Some of these are subscription services, but you don't have to pay for accessing the SSDI.

The ubiquitous genealogy Web site called Ancestry.com has the SSDI, of course, but the advantage of Ancestry.com's subscription service over a free search on FamilySearch.org is only in the currency of the database. Ancestry's data is somewhat more recent. But since the difference affects only those people who have died in the past couple of years, it's a reasonable decision to go with the free service unless you are already an Ancestry subscriber. Ancestry-owned RootsWeb also has the SSDI available free of charge. However, the free version at FamilySearch.org is easier to use, easier to interpret the output format, and has better name search algorithms.

So, I suggest you forget the other sites for the moment and log on to **www.familysearch.org.**

1. From the home page, click the **Search** tab at the top of the screen.
2. Click **US Social Security Death Index** from the menu on the left-hand side of the screen.
3. Enter the first and last name of your ancestor.
4. Click the **Search** button and see what you find.

If you are using the SSDI, and especially if you encounter something unexpected, it's worth clicking on the **Tips on How to Search the Social Security Death Index** link just above the search engine.

It's best to start by entering a minimal amount of information, and then add data in fields one by one if you need to narrow the search in case of a common name. This is a general truism when using search engines for genealogical data like this. Searching indexed information can be tricky, since the computer interprets what you enter, not what you mean. See the Tip box on search methods on page 44 for a clearer understanding of what can happen when searching.

If the name you are seeking is in the database, the search engine will provide you with:

- The person's birth and death date
- Their Social Security number and the place it was issued
- The zip code of their address and the locality at death

This may be all you need if you just wanted to verify a couple of dates. If you need more, it is only a starting point. You now have the information to complete and submit a request for a copy of the SS-5 form that was filled out when the person applied for a Social Security card. This completed form, when you receive it, should provide you with much more—the place of birth, names of parents, and other useful information. You cannot submit this request electronically. It must be on paper.

The Tips box on the next page points you to sites where you can see exactly how to submit that letter to request a copy of the SS-5 form under the Freedom of Information Act.

TIPS: Making SSDI Searches Easy . . .

1. The Web site **www.death-records.net/ssdi.htm** was created to provide genealogists with access to the Social Security Death Index from a single place. Among other things, it shows how to phrase a written application under the Freedom of Information Act for a copy of a Social Security card application.

2. The Social Security Administration also provides its own form for requesting a copy of a deceased person's Social Security application. You can find it online by logging onto **www.ssa.gov.** Click **Search** on the menu bar across the top of the page, and then type **SSA-711** in the Search box. That will take you to the link for the request form in PDF format.

Although the online search of the index is free and unrestricted, it will cost you $27 for a photocopy of the original application made by your ancestor if you decide to send for it. (You may want to read the next two chapters before you start writing checks to the Social Security Administration).

Record What You Find on the SSDI

Check the Social Security Death Index for each of the names on your pedigree chart that fit within its time frame. When you find information—even without submitting an SS-5 form—enter it in your software program and record the source. If your search of the SSDI comes up empty, or if you find multiple results and can't decide which ancestor is yours, make a note of that in your research log and notes as needed.

Now is also a good time to look up some of the names of the deceased children of the parents on your pedigree chart, since the SSDI easily allows you to confirm birth and death dates if you already have the names.

A Note about Security

We might pause to answer a quick question. In an age of identity theft and sophisticated white-collar crime, should we be concerned that the names of millions of deceased people with their Social Security numbers are freely available on the Internet?

The U.S. government, security agencies, and organizations like banks that might have the most to lose don't think so. By placing all obsolete numbers on the Internet,

TIPS: Knowing How to Search—A Practical Example

Let's use a real example to show you some of the unexpected results you can get when searching any kind of index. Try this example yourself to get a feel for using the SSDI database. Use the **www.RootsWeb.com** site and click on the **SSDI** link. Let's say I've learned from my living family that a relative by the name of Harry Raymond Smiles has died in recent years. He should be in the SSDI.

Looking at the search engine, I see that it's asking for first, middle, and last names (or the middle initial), and the Social Security number. I don't have the SS number. But do I enter Harry or Harold? To the right is a drop-down menu option that offers three choices: Exact, Soundex, and Metaphone.

Type in **Smiles** and **Harold,** and select the **Soundex** option before clicking the **Submit** button. The result is well over 100 names, from Samuelson to Semelka. If you take the trouble to look down the several pages of hits, you'll find none of them is our Harry Smiles. A similar, unsatisfactory result comes from selecting the Metaphone option. (See pages 137–38 for more on Soundex).

Change the dropdown menu to **Exact**. Click **Submit** again. This time, nothing at all is found. It tells me there are 181 Smiles (although this number could change any day), but no matching Harry.

Since I know his middle name was Raymond, let's try that. Still no result.

Now let's try *Harry* instead of *Harold,* and keep the *Exact* option. If I include *Raymond* as the middle name, I again come up empty.

Now let's try *Harry Smiles,* and *Exact,* but nothing else. This time I get two results, and from the fact that I know Harry died in New York recently, I can easily identify him from the other Harry born in Florida. Anyway, the search results showed one as Harry R. and the other as Harry F. so it's an easy choice.

Now I can send for Harry's Social Security card application if I wish.

Why the problem? The remote computer can only interpret what you type that matches its data, not what you mean. You may think you are being perfectly clear, but try a number of alternatives if you don't find what you want right away. If the name is uncommon, start with minimal information, such as a name. If the name is common, narrow the search by adding more specific information each time.

everyone can quickly check whether a Social Security number is obsolete and therefore being misused. Entering the number will quickly reveal the name of the dead person and their death date. That's a convenience for everyone from landlords to credit card companies, and it protects the community.

You've now used your first Internet database to begin building your family tree. We have barely scratched the surface. In the next three chapters, we'll look at online census records and how to use the Internet to find birth, marriage, and death records.

6
LOOKING FOR CENSUS RECORDS—PART 1

Overview

Checking the Social Security Death Index is like picking low-hanging fruit. It doesn't take much effort to get results. Once you know how to do it, you can use the same simple process time and again, provided your ancestors' deaths fall in the right time period. It's easy to work within a federal system that applies uniformly across all the United States.

Consistency is something that can be elusive when searching for ancestors in the United States. As we'll see in the chapter on searching for birth, marriage, and death certificates—vital records, as they're called—the huge number of counties throughout the various states began civil registration at different times and don't use a common standard when recording information. And they apply frustratingly different rules in making that information available to the public, with relatively little official effort to place data online. That can make for a hit-and-miss experience when trying to find a birth, marriage, or death certificate.

Fortunately, there's another, powerful nationwide source available that usually makes a better starting point. This chapter will show you which census records are available online and how to use them.

The United States Census

Many governments count their people every ten years. There's good reason for doing so, including the need to understand complex social trends, predicting the tax base, and determining the need for social services. The United States has been organizing ten-year census counts since 1790, making it the first country in modern times to call for a regular census. Fortunately for Americans searching for ancestors in old census records, the U.S. government tended to ask quite a lot. The records that resulted are a treasure trove for family historians. They are much richer in the things they yield than census records in other nations, and they show much more than can be found on a single birth, marriage, or death certificate.

What Censuses Show

Depending on the years your ancestor lived and which census forms you're examining, you might find not only the location of your ancestor's family, including the names of parents and children, but also:

- their age or birth year
- the number of years married and number of children
- when they came to the United States and from which country
- the state or country of their parents' birth
- their current employment
- whether they owned or rented their home—and even the net worth of their property in dollars

What you can gain from these records is a wonderful snapshot in time—a picture of a whole family in their working and living environment. You can also see their neighbors—including other relatives that might have lived nearby. You will know whether they were literate, whether they spoke English, and even be able to make a good guess as to whether they had a foreign accent. By checking successive census records, you may see them moving about the country and changing jobs. You can watch their children grow and marry and have children of their own.

Privacy Limitations

Privacy restrictions mean that the latest census you can see is the one taken a little over seventy years ago from the present date. That means a span of census records every decade from 1790 to 1930 (with the exception of the 1890 census, which was destroyed by fire except for a few fragments).

Which Census Records Can You Find on the Internet?

In addition to the U.S. federal census, some states and counties undertook their own local censuses at different times. There are also special population surveys, such as slave schedules or those with a military focus.

The subject of Internet census records is so large that we'll need to devote two chapters to it. In this chapter we'll look at where you can find federal census records on single sites. The best-known sites require a subscription, but there are other sites that deliver the same U.S. federal censuses at substantially reduced or even zero cost.

The next chapter will examine the increasing amount of census data being put online by volunteers, including some state censuses, all of which can be accessed at no charge. Census data for countries other than the United States will be examined in subsequent chapters.

For our first tour of U.S. census data on the Internet, we'll use a practical example as we look at the information in this order:

1. **Transcribed census data,** taken from the original records and now online in an easily readable form. This is the next best thing to digital images of the original pages. Transcriptions provide typed, searchable text of each household that can quickly be found by entering a few key words in a search engine on-site. The 1880 U.S. census (and the 1881 British and Canadian censuses) is an example of a transcribed census that can be accessed for little or no cost.

2. **Digital images of original census pages**. These are the best census records available, because you are looking at the record as it was originally compiled, without having to worry whether some modern transcriber interpreted the handwriting correctly. Large commercial organizations and government bodies have already put a substantial number of censuses on the Web, and more are coming. Most have been indexed to allow for easier searching. The quality control in the transcription process varies, so a simple search occasionally fails to find the desired individual or family. However, we'll look at some search methods that reduce these problems. Of course, commercial or government sites charge for access to census records. Some charge a nominal amount for a single view, while others want to sell you a monthly or annual subscription which can be quite expensive.

Let's get started with our search:

1. Log on to www.familysearch.org. Most companies, governments, or institutions charge for letting you look at their services. One exception is The Church of Jesus Christ of Latter-day Saints, which has put literally millions of names from census records on its Web site at www.familysearch.org. Just

why Mormons do this—and the benefits to genealogists—is so significant that it deserves special attention in Chapter 17. The site offers very much more than census data—we've already used it to look at the Social Security Death Index—but, for now, let's take a look at what this site offers in the way of free census records.

You don't need to register on FamilySearch.org in order to use it. Registration will let you access some other features such as collaboration, but we don't need to think about that yet.

2. After logging on to the home page, click the **Search** tab at the top of the screen.

3. From the menu on the left, select **Census**.

4. From the dropdown box, select the census you wish to search. You can access the **1880 United States Census,** the **1881 Canadian Census,** and the **1881 British Census** free from this site.

5. Key in the name you are searching for. Start with less information and add details to narrow the search for more common names.

6. Click the **Search** button.

A Practical Example

In the last chapter, in one of the Tips boxes, we looked on the Social Security Death Index for a Harry Smiles, who died in New York. (If you skipped reading the Tips box on page 44, "Knowing How to Search—A Practical Example," it would be a good idea to go back and read that now so you have a foundation before proceeding.)

Let's say that when we found Harry, we were able to send for his Social Security card application. When it arrived, it gave us the names of both of Harry's parents, including the maiden name of his mother.

We then repeated the process and found Harry's father, Homer, on the Social Security Index. He was easy to find, because an "exact search" came up with only one Homer Smiles in the whole of the U.S., and his Social Security number was issued in Leeds, Jefferson County, Alabama. That tallied with son Harry's Alabama birthplace and the right time frame, so we could be confident that we were on track.

The next step was to fill out another SS-5 application and send for Homer's Social Security application. When it arrived, we found that the parents of Homer were Henry Smiles and Sarah Prophet, so we were back another generation. Because

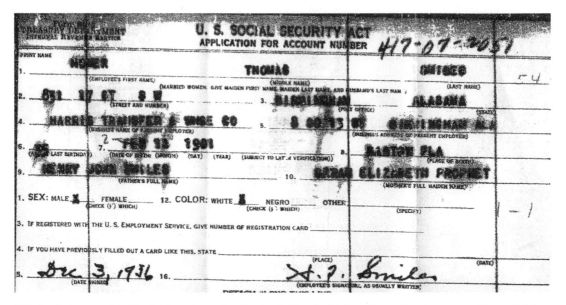

This is what a completed Social Security application looks like. Social Security applications are readily available under the Freedom of Information Act.

both of these people died before Social Security numbers came into being, the SSDI was of no further use to us for this couple.

The image on this page shows us what a completed Social Security application looks like. The quality isn't good in this case, but it's readable. The good news, however, is that because we've now discovered that Homer was born in 1901, it's a safe bet that his parents, Henry Smiles and Sarah Prophet, were born before 1880. That means they were living when the 1880 census was taken and, with any luck, we should be able to find them listed.

From the census menu on the FamilySearch.org site, let's enter the data we know for Henry Smiles and Sarah Prophet.

I recommend that you work through these examples from your mouse or keyboard even though the names mean nothing to you personally. It helps to become familiar with the look and feel of the search facilities you will use shortly to hunt for your own ancestors.

This is absolutely the best way to learn quickly.

The 1880 census was the first U.S. census to be put online on any Internet site, and the year was picked partly because it falls right at the time when family knowledge begins to run out, and such things as the SSDI database are no longer applicable.

A search for Henry using various combinations comes up with nothing recognizable. For the moment, we don't know why. Perhaps he went by another first name, or the spelling of the surname was changed substantially and we can't recognize it from the index. Maybe the transcribers of the index missed him or made a mistake that makes the name unrecognizable to the search engine. Or, maybe he was born somewhere outside the United States.

Leaving aside that dead end for the moment, we'll search for the name *Sarah Prophet*. Because the name *Prophet* is fairly unusual, we'll enter only her name in the census search. We will, however, check the box next to **Use Exact Spelling** at the bottom left of the screen.

After clicking the **Search** button, we see the results—a list of six Sarah Prophet names. But which one is ours, if any of them? Here, a little common-sense detective work is needed. Even before clicking on each name in turn, we can learn from the screen something of each individual and her family. Alongside the year of birth (the angled brackets indicate approximation) we can see that three were born in South Carolina, and one each in Louisiana, Rhode Island, and Mississippi. One of the South Carolina Sarahs had moved to Illinois when the census was taken.

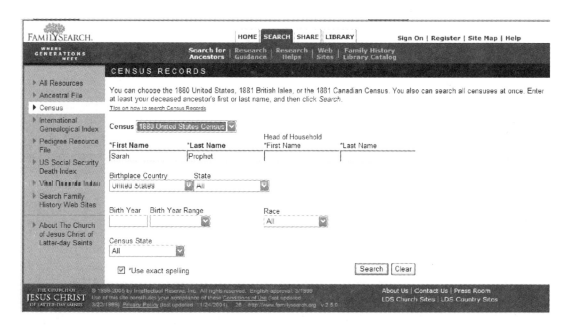

Census search for Sarah Prophet on FamilySearch.org. (FamilySearch.org, image copyright 1999, 2005 by Intellectual Reserve, Inc. Used by permission.)

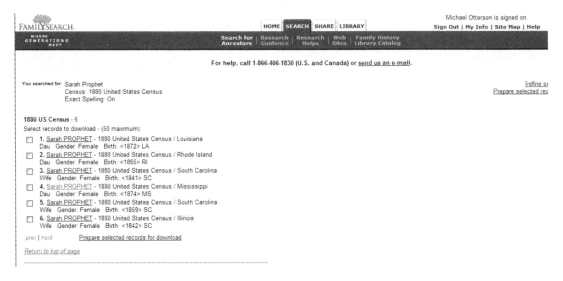

Results of census search on FamilySearch.org. (FamilySearch.org, image copyright 1999, 2005 by Intellectual Reserve, Inc. Used by permission.)

We know our Sarah gave birth to a son in 1901; she was probably between 20 and 45 years old at the time, making her birth year sometime between 1856 and 1881. We can allow for a little wiggle room on either side. Only four of the six show birth years in this period, so we can eliminate the two South Carolinian Sarah Prophets who would have been 59 and 60 years old in 1901—too old to be bearing children.

By clicking on the four remaining Sarah names, we find that three of them were Black. The U.S. census gives racial type. Although not out of the question, it's unlikely that this would have been a mixed racial marriage in this time period, and we have no evidence that it was. That leaves only the Sarah Prophet from Mississippi. It isn't conclusive by any means—there could be another Sarah who wasn't recorded on the census or was missed in the search for some other reason. We certainly want to check alternative spellings of the name (Proffitt is more common). But it looks promising. What we need now is to find out if we can link this particular Sarah Prophet to a husband named Henry Smiles. But first, take a moment to see what information is available just with the click of the mouse. From the screen that details "our" Sarah's individual record, click the **Household** link near the top right of the screen. This is the information for the whole household in which Sarah lived. If this were your family name, now would be the time to record and save the information in our notes and research log. Notice that Sarah is just six years old and going to school.

Now it's time to explore elsewhere for Sarah when she's at marrying age.

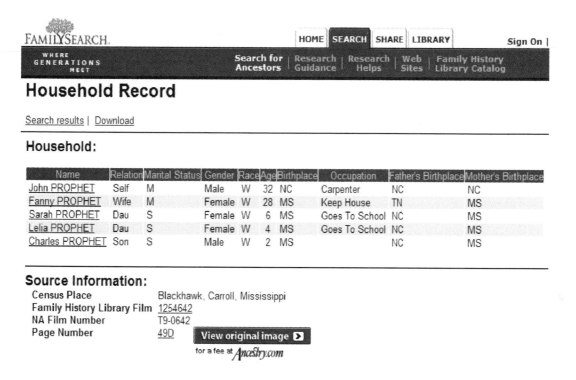

This is the Household view on FamilySearch for the 1880 U.S. census, where members of an entire family can be seen together. Sara Prophet is a six-year-old in this snapshot. Source information is given below the list of people in the household. (FamilySearch.org, image copyright 1999, 2005 by Intellectual Reserve, Inc. Used by permission.)

Search Digital Images of Census Pages

Every United States federal census that has been preserved between 1790 and 1930 is now available on two or three large subscription sites—and in its original form. There are also extensive collections of British censuses. These sites are the mother lode of census repositories, where everything is in one place with a consistent look and feel, and searchable with powerful search utilities. The records are scanned images, just like photographs. Because they are not transcriptions, when you find a census record you know you don't have to worry about mistakes made by a modern transcriber.

Another advantage of seeing the original census record on screen is that there may be additional, sometimes vital information on the original that was not included in the transcription.

To Spend or Not to Spend

Sooner or later you will face the inevitable choice as to whether you want to use a subscription service for its wealth of data and ease of use. Everything is relative. For someone with hundreds or even thousands of names on a family tree and many opportunities to confirm sources and explore new lines, $200 for access to the U.S. census collection, together with lots of other databases for a year, is not bad when you consider it costs $27 to send for a single Social Security application. But for many people starting out on their family tree quest and uncertain whether they will stick at it, it's not unusual to see them balk at laying out hundreds of dollars. Retired people on fixed incomes are in the same situation. Subscription costs, after all, are in addition to the price of certificates, Social Security application forms, and other costs that the genealogist is faced with.

Fortunately, there are some great options, and if it's U.S. census records you're after you can now access them free of charge in most states, and for a lot less than an Ancestry.com subscription in the others. Here are some of your options:

Free trials. The most obvious option is to take advantage of the free trial offer on regular subscription sites. Ultimately, this is a temporary solution, of course, but one worth considering because you'll get to sample the many other databases apart from censuses. The Tip box on page 55 shows some cost comparisons of the most popular site at Ancestry.com. If you are going to try a free subscription for a couple of weeks, then make sure you accumulate a healthy list of things to check *before* you start your subscription so you can take full advantage of your free trial. Then you can better evaluate whether you want to keep the subscription.

One caution with some large subscription services: When you take up a trial offer, you must give your credit card number. The subscription renews automatically unless you cancel it, and you cannot cancel online—you have to make a phone call.

HeritageQuest Online. HeritageQuest Online is your key to free or less expensive census access in the United States. Its parent company, ProQuest, services libraries and institutions but not private individuals. It was once necessary to physically make a visit to a library that subscribed to ProQuest databases in order to access the collection. Not any more. Dozens of libraries in some forty states now allow their patrons online access free of charge. In a few states, there is still a charge for remote access from home to these holdings through a historical or genealogical library gateway, and yearly fees range from around $30 to $40 on average ($60 for New York). This is still a lot less than an annual Ancestry.com subscription, and you pick up all the added benefits of being a member of one of those societies.

TIP: What a Subscription Will Cost You

For now, Ancestry.com has by far the largest collection of online data in a single place. Although some of the data can be accessed free of charge elsewhere (e.g. US censuses—see below), the increasing size of the Ancestry collection makes it an option for researchers who intend to stick at tracing their family trees for the long haul and want the convenience of lots of key data on a single site.

At the time of writing, Ancestry's various packages can be summarized (with figures rounded to the nearest dollar) as:

US deluxe membership if you pay monthly: About $30 a month.

US deluxe membership if you pay once a year: About $13 a month.

That buys you everything in the US collection. If you want to add the world collection, such as UK censuses and other records, and whatever else comes online internationally:

World deluxe membership if you pay monthly: About $40 a month.

World deluxe membership if you pay yearly: about $29 a month.

For the latest fee structure and options, go to:

www.ancestry.com/subscribe/signup.aspx?Sourceld=&Targetld#chart

Among HeritageQuest Online's holdings are the set of U.S. federal censuses (1790 to 1930, less the 1890 census), valuable databases like the Freedman's Bank records (a treasure for African-Americans) and Revolutionary War pension applications, as well as more than 25,000 fully searchable family history and historical books. If one of those books mentions the name of your ancestor, you can probably search the book text online.

The launching point to see which libraries subscribe to HeritageQuest Online databases is the Web site at **www.eogen.com/HeritageQuestOnline**. This page contains a detailed, state-by-state list of the libraries that offer that facility.

Family History Centers. In the unlikely event that none of these options meets your needs, you have another choice. Although less convenient than working from your own home, check out the more than 5,000 Family History Centers operated by The Church of Jesus Christ of Latter-day Saints throughout the world. These centers are almost everywhere. For instance, the list shows 32 in the state of Alabama alone, 49 in the state of New York, about 70 in France, and more than 40 in New Zealand. Most are now connected to the Internet, including Ancestry.com. A worldwide network of customer support with toll free numbers in 120 countries is being established to help visitors. This is remarkable, considering that patrons pay nothing to use the centers, including Internet access. You can very easily search for the family history center nearest you, and find the hours of operation and phone number, by logging on to **www.familysearch.org/eng/library/fhc/frameset_fhc.asp.**

When you've found the closest one, phone and confirm if they have free access to Ancestry.com's Web site. These centers are usually open several hours a week, including evenings and weekends, and are staffed by volunteers who will show you how to use the equipment. The experience and expertise of the volunteers varies considerably, but there is usually someone there who is savvy enough to help you get started.

Although searching online is much faster than looking at films in a reader, you can also check out the various microfilms and microfiche collections, including census records, while you're in the Family History Center. If the center doesn't have the film, they will order it for you at nominal cost. They will keep a loaned film in the library for a month or so while you work on it.

Finding Census Information—A Practical Example

Now let's take a practical look at using these online census sources to continue our quest. We last left Sarah Prophet as a six-year-old girl on the 1880 free census on www.familysearch.org, living in Blackhawk Precinct, Carroll County, Mississippi, with her father, mother, younger brother, and sister. But we were not at all certain that this particular Sarah Prophet is the one who later married Henry Smiles.

As before, I suggest that wherever possible you follow this example online using the same names and steps. That is the best way to become familiar with the approach. You will use many of these principles and concepts when tracing your own family.

Let's see what we can find on the scanned images of earlier and later censuses using the HeritageQuest Online data. We're going to build our understanding of this family, piece by piece, until we have a clear picture.

If Sarah was only six in 1880, we ought to look first in the 1900 census, when she is likely to be married. Follow along with these steps to carry out our search:

1. Log on to HeritageQuest Online via your library or genealogical society gateway.

2. Click the **Search Census** button on the on-screen menu.

3. If Sarah was married by 1900, she won't appear under her maiden name. So let's first look under the known name of her husband, Henry Smiles. Select the **Advanced Search** tab to start looking for Henry.

4. Enter a minimal amount of data—the given name and surname, the census year, a ten-year age range, and sex.

5. Click the **Search** button.

The result is just one match—a twenty-seven-year-old man living in Florida. To see if he's the husband of a Sarah, we can click on his surname to be taken to the original census image.

Immediately we can see the likelihood that we have the right family. Here's what we find on the census form:

- The husband and wife, Henry and Sarah, have moved to Florida.

- Sarah's birthplace is shown as Mississippi.

- From the 1880 data we already know that her father was born in North Carolina and her mother in Mississippi. On the 1900 record, we find exactly the same information.

Our confidence level has increased substantially that the 1880 Sarah Prophet and the 1900 Sarah Smiles are the same person.

If they are, we can confirm Sarah's parents and sibling details from the 1880 census that we looked at earlier.

There is a two-year discrepancy in age between the censuses of 1880 and 1900. If Sarah was 6 in 1880, she should be 26 in 1900, but the record shows 24. Is that significant? Not really. The census taker wrote down what he was told. Sometimes people exaggerated or minimized their age for their own reasons. (One amusing study has shown that women in the English census were prone to understate their age early in their lives and overstate it in later life). Sometimes people just forgot. It was an era in which birthdays and event dates were less significant than they are today and not always officially recorded. A two-year difference in a census twenty years apart is acceptable.

The HeritageQuest Online service is available online through public libraries and is one of the best options for armchair family historians in the US. (Image copyright 1999–2006: ProQuest Information and Learning Company. Used by permission.)

Now we can begin to build on our knowledge of the family. From the 1900 census we learn:

- Henry had a second initial, J.

- He was born in England, to English parents, in November 1873.

- He immigrated to the United States in 1893.

- In 1900, we see that the couple is childless—they have been married only five months (shown as 5/12 in the column).

- His occupation is a crane man.

- The couple is living in a rented house in Polk County, Florida.

- Sarah's middle initial is E.

- Her birth date was June 1875, in Mississippi.

- Her father was born in North Carolina, her mother in Mississippi.

- Both of them can read, write, and speak English.

Because we have enough to identify this couple easily on a later census, the next step on the Internet is to look at those of 1910, 1920, and 1930. But first, we will want to enter all that we've found in our software program, including adding the *source* to each new name and event, and updating our research log and notes so we can keep track of our steps. I suggest that you not wait until the end of your research

Above: 1900 Census page including Henry J. and Sarah E. Smiles, Polk County, Florida, in 1900. (Image copyright 2005 MyFamily.com, Inc., and reproduced from Ancestry.com. Used by permission.)

Below: The same Smiles entry, enlarged.

session to do this—make notes and record sources as you go. We can also include in our research log what we plan to do next.

As we continue our search, the 1910 census is what we look at next, but we find the family only after entering "H" in the search engine because Henry doesn't yield a result. (Incidentally, this is one example of the difference in effectiveness of search engines and the way databases are indexed—the Ancestry.com search engine would have found the initialed Henry even if we'd entered his full name).

Here in 1910 we find the family of husband, wife, and three children living in Birmingham, Alabama. We note Henry's age as forty, which puts his birth at 1870, three years earlier than previously recorded. We will need further evidence before deciding which birth date is right, but we make a record of that finding in our notes. We also see that he describes himself as an engineer. Sarah is shown as having four children, only three of which are living. Details of the three children are included in the household—Homer, Eliner, and Howard. Homer, only eight in this census, is one of the people whose death we found on the Social Security Death Indexes when we were first trying to find something about the family. If we needed any further confirmation that we have the right family, this is it. We record the new findings in our PAF or genealogy software program, using the same spelling that we found in the census.

In the 1920 census we encounter something unexpected. Sarah, only thirty-nine years old, is a widow, living with her three children in a rented home in Birmingham, Jefferson County, Alabama. Her second child's name is spelled *Elinor* in this census.

We're now beginning to get a picture of this family as they moved around parts of the United States. Widowed in her thirties, with three children, and before the coming of Social Security benefits, Sarah certainly must have had a number of struggles. Her eighteen-year-old son, Homer, is working as a shipping clerk for a railroad, and, according to the census, she has taken in a boarder. How and where husband Henry died is still to be found.

By the 1930 census the picture has changed considerably. Youngest son, Howard, has now married, and is living with his wife, Barbara, and their three year-old son, Eugene, in Milledgeville, Baldwin County, Georgia. Howard's widowed mother, Sarah, is living with them.

This is what family history is all about. From entries on old government forms—some of them little better than scratchings—we can put together a fairly accurate picture of a whole family's life and plot it against what was happening in the United States at the time. What became of Sarah as she lived with her son's family may have to wait until the publication of the 1940 census. How did she fare during the Great

State Georgia County Baldwin Township or other division of county GM 320

Incorporated place Milledgeville city (Part of) Ward of city ___ Block No. ___

Unincorporated place ___ Institution ___

DEPARTMENT OF COMMERCE FIFTEENTH CENSUS OF POPULATION

NAME	RELATION	HOME DATA				PERSONAL DESCRIPTION					EDUCATION		PLACE OF BIRTH		
			Value			Sex	Color	Age	Marital	Age at marriage			PERSON	FATHER	MOTHER
SINTON, LISA	Wife H					F	Ng	22	M	20	No	yes	Georgia	Georgia	Georgia
HAWKINS, FANNIE	Head H	O	4500		No	F	W	82	Wd		No	yes	Georgia	No. Carolina	Virginia
—, BERNARD	Son				Y	M	W	54	S		No	yes	Georgia	Georgia	Georgia
—, DUDLEY	Son				Y	M	W	50	S		No	yes	Georgia	Georgia	Georgia
—, MARY	Daughter				Y	F	W	40	S		No	yes	Georgia	Georgia	Georgia
BLACKWELL, WALKER	Head	O	3,500	R	No	M	W	38	M		No	yes	Georgia	Georgia	Georgia
—, RUBY	Wife H				Y	F	W	41	M		No	yes	Georgia	Georgia	Georgia
WARD, BENJAMIN	Head				No	M	W	87	M	26	No	yes	Georgia	Georgia	Georgia
—, MATILDA	Wife H				Y	F	W	74	M	20	No	yes	Georgia	Georgia	Georgia
—, SARAH M	Daughter				Y	F	W	47	S		yes	yes	Georgia	Georgia	Georgia
—, CANNON	Grand-Son				Y	M	W	23	S		yes	yes	Georgia	Georgia	Georgia
SMILES, SARAH E	Mother	R	20	R	No	F	W	48	Wd	19	No	yes	Mississippi	No. Carolina	Mississippi
—, HOWARD	Head				Y	M	W	24	M	20	No	yes	Alabama	England	Mississippi
—, BARBARA	Wife H				Y	F	W	23	M	19	No	yes	Alabama	Germany	Unknown
—, EUGENE	Son				Y	M	W	3	S		No		Alabama	Alabama	Alabama
BRITT, ALEXANDER	Head	R	20	R	No	M	W	32	M	24	No	yes	Georgia	Georgia	Georgia
—, GEORGIA	Wife H				Y	F	W	30	M	22	No	yes	Georgia	Georgia	Georgia

1930 census extract for the Sarah Smiles family. U.S. census forms yield a huge amount of information in comparison with those of other countries. (Image copyright 2005 MyFamily.com, Inc., and reproduced from Ancestry.com. Used by permission.)

Depression, which was about to descend on America following the 1929 Wall Street crash? What happened to her other two children? As we'll see later, there are other ways of discovering clues and answering these questions.

And what of Henry, the husband who died an early death? By the time we get to the last chapter of this book, we will have found the ship that he arrived on and traced his origins across the Atlantic back to a tiny northern English village. There, we will find his ancestors back to the 1700s and a lot more.

7
LOOKING FOR CENSUS RECORDS—PART 2

Overview

So far we've looked at the major online sources where some or all of the US federal census data, and some overseas censuses, can be found in one place. The advantage of these sites is convenience; the disadvantage, depending on where you live and what is available through your local libraries, can be the cost.

Before leaving U.S. census records, we should take a look at another significant source: The multitude of volunteer-based Web sites at the county level where information can usually be obtained free—if you can find it. Because this is where the Internet can become confusing, this chapter will help you walk through the opportunities without becoming hopelessly lost.

A Note on Volunteer Sites

Praise for putting local census information online is due mostly to the thousands of volunteers whose passion for family history leads them to spend hours of their own time interpreting impossible handwriting and transcribing it for use by anyone on the Internet. The commitment of these dedicated people is quite extraordinary. Virtually all of them are committed to the concept of providing freely available information for everyone. While they appreciate the fact that subscription sites need to generate the money to undertake massive acquisition and indexing projects, they believe that there should be an alternative. As a result, more and more data—vital records, census records, tombstone transcripts, and a host more—are being added daily to the Internet.

These volunteers take advantage of the fact that many individual states have conducted their own censuses in the years between the federal enumerations. These state censuses can fill in gaps or provide information that might be elusive or entirely missing when using the federal records. That applies particularly to the censuses in years on either side of the 1890 records, most of which were destroyed by fire. We'll look at some of those sites right away.

Census-online.com

Because the hundreds of Web sites hosting local census data are so varied in appearance and content, you not only have to track down the data to the locality where it was recorded, but also figure out exactly what you are looking at when you get there.

Occasionally, you'll come across a Web site that combines the skills of a competent Web designer with the experience of an avid genealogist. One such place is **Census-online.com**. I've listed this first because this beautifully designed site

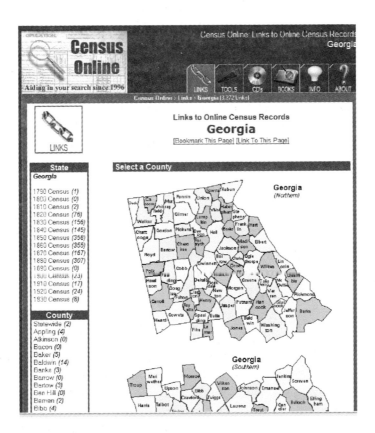

Census-online.com avoids the clutter and confusion of many volunteer web sites and has a standard format for each state, making it simple to use. (Image, copyright Census Online, home page: www.census-online.com.)

is extremely simple to use, doesn't clutter its screens with a mass of confusing data, and is a terrific signpost for census data in the United States, Canada, and the UK. The site itself doesn't contain the census data, but it will point you quickly to it.

Simply log on to **www.census-online.com,** click **Links to Online Census Records** at the top of the home page, then click the link for the country (United States, Canada, or British Isles) you wish to search. You can see at a glance on this same page the number of individual databases attached to each state—from a handful to literally thousands. Simply selecting the state you want will provide a map of counties. Click on the county and you'll be presented with an easy-to-read list of census databases. At this point it's a matter of luck whether the records for the county in which your ancestor lived have been digitized. You can browse through these lists, opening the records to view and search for your ancestors' names. In many cases there is no search engine with these sites, so you will have to use your browser's built-in search facility, such as the **Find on this Page** utility under the **Edit** menu in Microsoft Internet Explorer.

Remember that once you get to these individual collections of census data, you are outside of Census-online.com and into whatever Web site you have selected, so you'll have to deal with the huge differences of approach on each site, as we've mentioned. Actually, many of the links found within Census-online.com will take you to sites that are part of the USGenWeb volunteer census project.

USGenWeb Census Project

Thousands of volunteers have joined forces all over the world to transcribe genealogical data and make it available to everyone. In the United States, many of them work under the banner of **USGenWeb.** The name USGenWeb is associated with providing free Internet sites for genealogical research in every county and every state of the United States. The operative word is *free*.

In recent years, administrative differences and complex policy questions have led to different organizations using the USGenWeb terminology and designations on their Web sites. These issues are beyond the scope of this book and, I suspect, the interest of the average reader. I mention it so that when browsing through census and other data online you will understand why there appear to be three different organizations associated with USGenWeb, yet with similar objectives. The bottom line is that volunteers continue to produce masses of data, and it continues to be added to the Internet daily.

To get a feel for how these sites look, log on to **www.usgenweb.com.** This is

USGenWeb Project national website at www.usgenweb.com. Copyright Linda Haas Davenport, National Coordinator, 2006.

the first of the three organizations associated with USGenWeb that we'll deal with here. On the left side of the screen are links to all the state Web sites. From there, you will find gateways to individual counties and various types of records, including some census records. These sites are not dedicated to census records.

Rootsweb.com

At the second associated site—**www.rootsweb.com/~census**—you'll find total consistency in look and feel as you move from state to state because you are staying within the same site looking for census data instead of being sent to individual counties. Recent improvements to the site have made it much more intuitive to use and very easy to find any completed transcriptions.

Take a moment to log on to the site right now. Notice the **Census Online Inventory** on the right side of the screen. You can click on the link for the state you're interested in. Let's take a look at Virginia for the purposes of this example. You will see a list of the counties in that state. Clicking on a county will bring up whatever entries have been transcribed and put online. This varies a great deal depending on how much progress the volunteers have made. The data is uniformly displayed in text format, which can be searched using your browser's Find function.

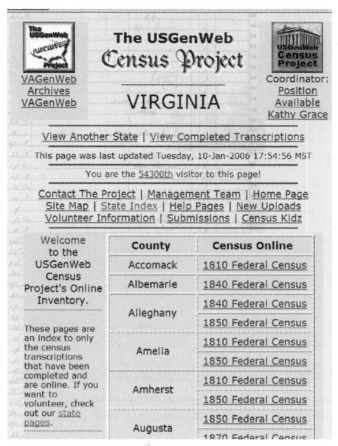

The USGenWeb Census Project coordinates the work of volunteer transcribers, but it's also a growing source of online census information. The site is accessed at www.rootsweb.com/~census. This example shows the Virginia inventory page for transcribed census data. (Image copyright 1997–2005, Maggie Stewart-Zimmerman & Kelly Jensen-Mullins for The USGenWeb Census Project. Used by permission).

USGenNet

Now let's look at the third site using the name USGenWeb. Log on to **www.us-census.org** and select **On-Line Census Inventory.** This site is hosted by USGenNet. It has a nice, easy feel to it and is quite intuitive to use. Most of the menu on the opening page is self-explanatory, and a couple of clicks will take you to available census data. The site has an effective search engine that can search every transcription on the site at once, not just a single state or county—a huge plus if you aren't certain where your ancestor came from.

Notice that in the Scanned Images column there are two kinds of View buttons. The one with a white background indicates a link to scanned image files. The blue

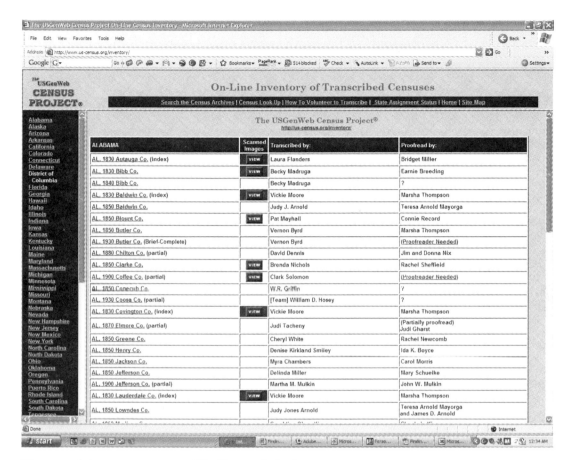

Site accessed at www.us-census.org. (Used by permission.)

buttons against the blue background indicate links to indexes of scanned images. Any database with an index will make your search job much easier.

On many volunteer sites, there is an option to ask volunteers to undertake a census name look-up for you by posting a message on the message board. The genealogical community tends to be very accommodating, but the rule is that you don't ask too much too often, and in return they don't charge for their services. A note of thanks from you afterwards is sufficient. By the way, *never* ask Web masters or project coordinators to do your research. They are busy enough already.

Each of these three USGenWeb sites uses a different approach, and there is some commonality of data. For instance, different sets of volunteers may have transcribed the data for the same counties. In other cases, some sites have data posted and others are still looking for transcription volunteers. To keep things simple, I suggest looking first on **www.rootsweb.com/~census** and **www.us-census.org.** They are both easy to navigate and just deal with census data. If you don't find what you're looking for, move on to **www.usgenweb.com,** where the individual county sites offer more than census data—sometimes much more. This advantage is offset by the fact that every site is different.

Look at Original Images

As we've seen, most of the pages on the volunteer sites contain census data that has been transcribed. Sometimes you can see the original images without having to pay a subscription to view them. A few of the county links on certain sites will take you to .tiff or .gif files that display as images on your screen. They may be of frustratingly low resolution, however.

Whenever possible, try to get the original record even if you are fairly satisfied with the transcribed information you have found. Often, there are extra snippets of information on the original record; but even if that isn't the case, the original record will deliver you peace of mind if nothing else. If you are working with a federal census on any of these sites, consider cheaper methods of verifying the data by accessing the original census image once you have located your ancestor's family. There are several options for doing so:

- Visit a Family History Center, if there is one near you, and view the images on computer. If the center lacks that facility, order the microfilm for the cost of shipping.

- Contact one of several commercial companies that provide census photocopies. Some are on CD, and are quite expensive. **SK Publications** at **www.skcensus.com** is economical if you know the page number of the census and you're pretty sure that the name you've found through your online research is your family. It costs only $4 a page for a high-resolution photocopy of the page. If you don't know the page number, the price soars to $25. You can handle everything on line by email and credit card.

- Contact a state or county historical society, many of which can be found online and have state census records on microfilm. Check their look-up policies on their Web sites.

Use Search Engines

A quick way to turn up Web sites that might otherwise be missed is to type the locality you are interested in, together with the word *census,* into a search engine designed especially for genealogy searches.

GenealogyPortal.com is such a site, and has a combination of search engines that can concentrate on localities or particular types of records. It also has a tendency to find a lot of links that are outdated.

Standard search engines, such as **Google,** have become so sophisticated that they can now yield very satisfactory results. Try entering the name of the state or country you wish to search, plus the county name, and the word *census.*

Signposting Sites

Linkpendium.com is a relative newcomer to the Internet, but its designers are not. They are the founders of RootsWeb and are planning big things for the site. Linkpendium.com is a powerful signpost site that points users to online databases. You can search by locality, which brings up a wide variety of places and types of records online, or by surname. At the time of writing, Linkpendium.com is U.S.-oriented.

What makes Linkpendium worth a visit is its organization and ease of use. When you first log on to the home page, you see a long list of U.S. states. Clicking on any state will link to a page with statewide resources at the top. Every county appears with a number of links or databases alongside the name. This makes everything very user-friendly. Clicking on a county name brings to the screen every kind of online database associated with that county, listed by topic in alphabetical order.

Check the census entries. Many of them have quite different data than you will find in the regular ten-year censuses by the federal government.

An especially useful feature is the **$** sign located alongside databases that charge for access. You can therefore use this site much more efficiently if you want to avoid searches that constantly run into fees.

The site is found at **www.linkpendium.com/genealogy/USA.**

GenealogyLinks.net, unlike Linkpendium.com, pushes international online databases as well as those in the U.S. Again, it is cleanly organized and you can see immediately from the home page what's available. As you begin to drill down into

TIP: Where to Find Blank Census Forms

Because it can be very difficult to read the small print in the columns for various censuses, it's good to know that you can easily view or even download the equivalent blank census forms. Ancestry.com provides this service at no charge, even if you aren't a paid subscriber. To find the forms, go to **www.ancestry.com/trees/charts/census.aspx** and select the one you need. The same facility is available for the seven British censuses now found online, from 1841 to 1901. The equivalent page for England and Wales is **www.ancestry.com/charts/ukcensus.aspx.**

Another helpful feature on Ancestry.com's site is found below the search box for a specific census. Here you'll find an explanation of exactly when the census was taken (the actual day) and other useful information specific to that census.

the site, you'll see the emphasis on delivering online data and not just general learning resources. Start at **www.genealogylinks.net.**

Although we're focusing on censuses in this chapter, a particular strength of this site is what it offers in terms of marriage databases—not only for the U.S., but also substantial collections from Europe that can be searched free. Unlike Linkpendium, GenealogyLinks does not put an icon alongside fee-based offerings, though these offerings are not so frequent that they become irritating. We'll discuss more on GenealogyLinks.net's marriage collections in the next chapter on vital records.

Cyndislist.com. One of the most frequented genealogy sites on the Internet, Cyndislist.com has for years been regarded as the mother of all signposting sites—a jumping off point when looking for particular topics or databases. It is a truly colossal list—more than a quarter of a million links to various genealogy sites of every description, and constantly growing.

If this is your first visit to this site, go straight to the **"No Frills Index"** (the menu is in the left margin) and read slowly through the list to get a sense of the breadth and depth of what is now available. Resist clicking on every category that interests you or you'll never get to the end of the list and you'll simply feel overwhelmed. There will be plenty of time for that later when you're looking for specific topics.

When you've read through the "No Frills" Index, look at the expanded lists in the left-hand menu, starting with **Topical Index** then the **Main Index**. There is also a menu link to the same information arranged alphabetically.

The "No Frills" category index on www.cyndislist.com. (Reproduced by permission of Cyndi Howells.)

With some understanding of what this site offers, you can now look for census information under the heading **Topical Index.** Remember that everything in the census list is not a lead to online data resources. Many of the listed links will take you to background information to the censuses or helps for searching or understanding the records. However, you can see that the sub-categories are logically arranged so you can see the specific list of international census data and indexes online. These include links to the free census projects undertaken by volunteers.

Summary

Whether or not you will find what you are looking for on a U.S. census record transcribed by a volunteer is, for the near future, going to be very much a matter of luck. That doesn't mean you shouldn't check out these sites periodically, because the rate of data transcription—as well as the total online collection—is increasing all the time.

Once you've done all you can with online census information, evaluating and exploring all the options in this and the previous chapter, you're ready to look at other kinds of records. That's where we'll turn our attention now.

8
BIRTH, MARRIAGE, AND DEATH RECORDS

Overview

If genealogists regard census records as a prized source of family information, vital records are not far behind. While they don't give the picture of a whole family that can be found on a census, they provide more precise detail about an individual's key life events. "Vital records" is the term generally applied to the official records of birth, marriage, and death, sometimes irreverently referred to as "hatch, match, and dispatch." Because they are recorded close to the event itself, vital records are the most reliable of all genealogical data and among the most important tools for building your family tree.

In the United States, you will find few original vital records online if you are looking for scanned, digital images like the census pages we saw earlier. What you will discover on the Internet for the U.S. falls broadly into three categories:

1. Information about where records can be found, whether online or at the state, county, or town level. Sometimes you will have to resort to old-fashioned snail mail to apply for a certificate copy, although you can often order from a Web site or by fax or email.

2. Indexes of names, indicating that certain records—hopefully the ones you want—are in a designated place.

3. Records from which some or all of the data has been transcribed and put online, either by official action of the registration or custodial authority or by volunteers.

In the United States, the biggest barrier you will encounter is the lack of centralized control of civil registrations. In the U.S., unlike some other countries, this is not a national government responsibility. In fact, it's more likely to be found at the county than the state level, so you will have to dig around county administrative Web sites or sometimes those of courthouses or city libraries to find what you are looking for. Of course, you may often not know where to look, and will need to rely on census records or other indicators, such as family stories, for clues. Nevertheless, some order can be brought to your searches and considerable information can be unearthed without ever leaving your home. On the plus side, more and more vital records are coming online, as we'll soon see.

What Do Vital Records Show?

Vital records are important not just because they were recorded at the time of the event, but because of the many clues they contain. For instance, a typical birth certificate lists at least the date and place of birth, and probably the residential address and the names of both parents—including the mother's maiden name. It's then easy to extrapolate a rough time period when the parents themselves were likely to have been born and married. This, in turn, provides a starting point for building a picture of the next generation back.

Because the civil registration authorities in the United States are at the county or local level, there is considerable variation in the information that is recorded in various vital records. Similarly, different nations have adopted varying conventions in what they think is important to put on a certificate of birth, marriage, or death.

What's the most you can expect? In addition to everything mentioned, some American birth certificates show the names and sex of children previously born to the same parents, and their ages, and the occupation of the father. Marriage certificates may show the names of the couple, their residences and ages, whether they have been previously married, the names of parents on both sides, occupations, witnesses' names, and the name of the church and denomination. Or, they may not. You just have to hope that when you track down that certificate, it has more than bare-bones information.

Privacy Issues

Inevitably, there will be privacy matters to contend with. Even if you find where an event is registered, it may be the policy of the local county not to give you a certificate unless you fall within their definition of a close relative. This is more often the case with birth certificates, especially quite recent ones. Many local and national governments take their stewardship of vital records so seriously that they make it very difficult for people to get access to them for research purposes. With the relatively recent rise in the problem of identity theft and concerns about privacy, it's understandable that government agencies holding birth, marriage, and death records aren't anxious to let just anyone get a copy of information that may be misused.

Yet, it makes little sense for local authorities not to lessen these restrictions with the passage of time. When dealing with the life events of people long since dead, all a civil registration authority has to do is stamp their photocopy of the birth, marriage, or death registration with something that says "Not Valid for Identity Purposes." Some do exactly that. Others want you to provide a photo ID—literally—or refuse to provide you with anything unless you're next of kin.

When Did Mandatory Registration Begin?

Whereas the United States was the first nation to begin regular censuses, most states were much slower in requiring civil registration. In comparison with Europe, the United States is still a young country. It was well into the 1900s before civil registration became mandatory throughout the country. Fortunately, some U.S. counties began the process much earlier than that. State registration almost always began later than county registration (we'll be looking for both types of record). In the 1800s, many people ignored registration altogether, even when it was an option; and finding a recorded birth, marriage, or death in the 1800s is very much hit-and-miss.

In Britain—the place to which so many Americans trace some of their roots—vital records kept by the government started with civil registration in England and Wales in 1837. Before that, local parish churches did the job way back to the 1500s, though less effectively. Government registration books are kept in a central repository in the UK and in many county facilities as well.

A certified copy of an English or Welsh registration of birth, marriage, or death can be provided to anyone submitting a written application with a small fee. Views of the pages containing the alphabetical indexes of vital records are readily available online at little cost. Scotland's government registration started a little later. The British have also remained pretty consistent in what they include on their certificates for the past 170 years or so. For more detail of vital and other records outside the United States, see Chapters 11 through 14.

Does It Matter Where We Start—Vital Records or Census?

Strictly speaking, there is no absolute rule as to whether you begin by searching for vital records before or after you have looked for census information. Individual circumstances often dictate that route. Still, it's usually easier for researchers in the

United States to use the censuses first to pinpoint the location of the family. The censuses and the Social Security Death Index are federally mandated records, and as such you can get a picture of the whole country and where your families lived at key times. Armed with that information, it's much easier to look for the vital records in the right place.

Now let's get back on to the Internet and use some real-life examples of how to track down some of these births, marriages, and deaths.

Step 1: Get a Glimpse of What's Being Added Online

We can get a quick overview of the increasing number of vital records online by visiting two sites. ProGenealogists is a professional group of researchers based in Salt Lake City who do research for a fee. This page on their Web site is particularly instructive: **www.progenealogists.com/genealogysleuthb.htm.** Take a look at the length of the lists of resources in various categories. The Vital Records list dwarfs any of the others.

Looking down the Vital Records list, you'll see that many of the databases have a **$** next to them. Just about all of these subscription databases are on the Ancestry.com site. Ancestry is really setting the pace for acquisition of these vital records, and the list is growing at a rapid rate. If you don't have an Ancestry.com membership or can't afford one, remember that these databases can be accessed free at Ancestry.com through the many Family History Centers mentioned earlier. The ProGenealogists site, by the way, is updated constantly, so it's an excellent site to bookmark and check regularly.

The other Web site in our overview is **www.searchsystems.net.** This site advertises itself as "by far the best resource of business information, corporate filings, offenders, inmates, criminal and civil court filings, vital records, property records, unclaimed property, [and] professional licenses" on the Internet.

Log on to the home page. More than 35,000 public record databases are available. For some of them, such as criminal records and bankruptcies, you pay a fee for a search, but there is no registration and no monthly or annual fee. However, we're interested in vital records, so right underneath where it says **By Category,** click on **Births.** Notice in this very long list of online birth records that almost all of them are free to search online. The databases by no means give you complete coverage of counties since the start of civil registration. My purpose in drawing attention to these two sites is to help you appreciate how rapidly vital records are coming online. In most states and counties of the United States, there is an effort to improve public access to records for people tracing their family trees.

Step 2: Check State and County Sources

First, we'll show you how to do a quick check of which records are held officially in each U.S. state and county—and the span of years they cover. **Vitalrec.com** is a useful starting point for finding out where to locate birth, marriage, and death certificates. The site is a front-end for an online ordering service and an Ancestry.com sponsored site, but finding the initial information you need costs nothing.

What this site provides for you, basically, is a nicely organized overview as long as you know exactly where to look on the page. By clicking on a specific state and following the links, you can see when birth, marriage, or death registration began in any particular locality, whether records are available, and the years they cover. If you know where your ancestor was from, an Ancestry.com companion service—VitalChek—allows you to order the certificate online. However, it's not usually difficult to find links to the state government offices, county courthouses, or other repositories where you can order online, or by phone, fax, or mail—and usually for a lot less.

A Practical Example

Let's go through a practical example and find a death certificate for someone I know died in the early 1900s. Late in 2005, while testing a new genealogy software program, I came across a Robert Otterson, who was born in England but was listed on the 1900 U.S. census. Since I'm very familiar with most of the English Ottersons, I examined it closely and identified him as Robert Pearson Otterson, with his wife, Catherine. Until that time I had assumed that he and his wife had lived their lives in England, though I had never discovered where they died. I knew of only one son, whose marriage or death records I could not locate.

I now quickly discovered from the U.S. census data that Robert left England in 1882. According to the same census, his wife joined him in the United States three years later and the family made a home at 534 Third Street in Green Bay, Wisconsin. The most intriguing reference in the census, however, was to the fact that Catherine Otterson had given birth to two children, neither of them living by 1900.

Even though this was a branch for me and not a root, it struck me that there was something poignant about a couple immigrating to the United States, losing both their children, and eventually dying childless in a foreign land. I wanted to find out if that was true, and I was curious about what happened to their son, Edward, who I knew was born in England.

Follow with me the steps we needed to take to track down Edward's death, because you'll be using the same step-by-step process many times for your own ancestors. Since I couldn't find the death in the English records during the period between Edward's birth and the time the family moved to the States, it seemed a safe bet that it occurred after the family arrived in Wisconsin. He must have been somewhere between three and eighteen years old. I knew I would need a vital record to find out—in this case, a death certificate. Let's see how to get it:

1. Log on to **www.vitalrec.com.**

2. On the home page, click the arrow in the **Select a State or Territory** drop-down box and select **Wisconsin.** Or click the **Wisconsin** link from the state list further down the screen.

3. Every state has approximately the same screen layout. Click the **Wisconsin Vital Records Office** link, found at the top left of the screen, the first title

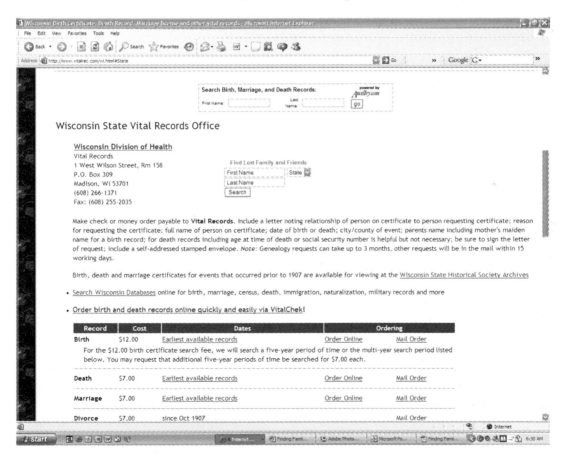

Vitalrec.com is an excellent way to find out quicky what vital records are available and where. Explanations for each state are laid out in identical format. Start at www.vitalrec.com. (Copyright VitalRec.com.)

in the list. (This link and the one immediately below it are key places on every state page, so it's as well to remember them and not be diverted by other seemingly relevant-sounding links.)

4. Beneath the dark green bar, a little down the screen, you can see the types of information available. The cost of the certificates—$7 for a marriage or death certificate or $12 for a birth certificate—is well within the range applied across the country. (Be aware that not every state is as friendly as this—the New Mexico page, for instance, advises that the records are restricted to family relatives). Click the **Earliest available records** link in the Dates column of either the Birth, Death, or Marriage rows.

Clicking one of those links will lead us to a table showing the earliest records available, county by county, throughout Wisconsin. Not every state will be this specific. Carefully read what's on the screen, looking for information on what periods the records cover and how to order. Avoid **Order online** invitations under "Related Links" or you will get back in the loop of subscription offers—unless, of course, you want to opt for the convenience, and cost isn't an issue.

On the Wisconsin page, we learn from the accompanying text that registration of events became mandatory in that state in 1907. Before that, registration was voluntary and only about half the people complied. But the good news from the table is that death records for Brown County go back as far as 1834, and the birth and marriage records even earlier.

Step 3: Order the Certificate If Found

Now that we know records exist, we have to get to the Brown County site to see how to access these records. To do this:

1. After completing step 4, as detailed on page 77, Use your **Back** button or scroll up to the Vitalrec.com page for Wisconsin, and this time select: **County Vital Records Offices,** the second-to-top item from the left-hand menu.

2. The resulting page will show you a list of Wisconsin counties. Click **Brown** from the list at the top of the screen. (Do *not* get drawn into the *List of Searchable Databases* below this unless you want more subscription offers.)

3. Now you're on the Brown County page (but still in the Vitalrec.com Web site). Avoid clicking on *Related Links,* and instead click **Brown County Register of Deeds** at the top of the page. This will take you out of the Vitalrec.com site altogether and into the county site.

WISCONSIN DEATH CERTIFICATE APPLICATION

Send completed form, self-addressed envelope and appropriate fee to:

BROWN COUNTY REGISTER OF DEEDS
305 E. WALNUT ST, ROOM 260
P.O. BOX 23600
GREEN BAY WI 54305-3600

Make check or money order payable to: BROWN COUNTY REGISTER OF DEEDS
(No out-of-state personal checks or checks #500 or less accepted)

PENALTIES: Any person who willfully and knowingly makes false application for a death certificate is guilty of a Class I felony [a fine of not more than
$10,000 or imprisonment of not more than 3 years and 6 months or both per Wisconsin State Statute 69.24(1)].

DEATH INFORMATION		
FULL NAME OF DECEDENT (First, Middle, LAST)		DECEDENT'S DATE OF DEATH
PLACE OF DEATH	CITY, VILLAGE, TOWNSHIP	COUNTY
NAME OF DECEDENT'S SPOUSE	DECEDENT'S AGE / BIRTHDATE	NAMES OF DECEDEN'T PARENTS

APPLICANT INFORMATION

THE FOLLOWING INFORMATION IS ABOUT THE PERSON COMPLETING THIS APPLICATION

YOUR Name (Please Print)   YOUR Daytime Telephone Number ( )

YOUR Street Address   Apt. No.   MAIL TO Address (if different)   Apt. No.

City / State / Zip   City / State / Zip

RELATIONSHIP TO PERSON NAMED ON THE CERTIFICATE

According to Wisconsin State Statute, a CERTIFIED copy of a death certificate is only available to a person with a "Direct and Tangible Interest." If you do not meet the criteria for boxes A – D, please refer to instructions on the back.

Check one box, which indicates YOUR RELATIONSHIP to the PERSON NAMED (decedent) on the death certificate.

CERTIFIED COPY

☐ A. I am a **member of the immediate family** of the PERSON NAMED on the death certificate. (Only those listed below qualify as immediate family.)
CHECK ONE: ☐ Spouse   ☐ Child   ☐ Parent   ☐ Brother   ☐ Sister   ☐ Grandparent

☐ B. I am the **legal custodian or guardian** of the PERSON NAMED on the death certificate.

☐ C. I am a **representative who is authorized**, in writing by any of the aforementioned (A through B). The written authorization must accompany this application.
Specify whom you represent. _____

☐ D. I can demonstrate that the information from the death certificate is necessary for the **determination or protection of a personal or property right** for myself/my client/my agency (includes funeral director, informant and medical certifier named on the record).
Specify interest. _____

NON-CERTIFIED COPY

☐ E. I am a **direct descendent** of the PERSON NAMED on the death certificate (blood grandchild, great grandchild, etc.). (I may receive a non-certified copy of both the "Fact of Death" certificate and the "Extended Fact of Death" certificate.)

☐ F. Other: Non-certified copy only. Copy will not be valid for legal purposes. (Refer to instructions on the back.)

FEES

☐ First copy   **DEATH OCCURRED 2003 or later**   ☐ Extended Fact of Death or ☐ Fact of Death $ 7.00   7.00

☐ First copy   **PRE-2003 DEATH**   ☐ Extended Fact of Death or ☐ Fact of Death

☐ Each additional copy of the same certificate, issued at the same time as the first copy.

☐ Fact of Death Certificate (without cause of death and disposition) _____ X $ 3.00 _____
(can be used for banking and most other financial transactions)

☐ Extended Fact of Death Certificate (with cause of death and disposition) _____ X $ 3.00 _____
(can be used for insurance benefit claims)   No. of Copies

NOTE: FIRST COPY FEE INCLUDES RECORD SEARCH AND IS NOT REFUNDABLE IF RECORD IS NOT FOUND. TOTAL _____

Typical vital record application form. This one is for Brown County, State of Wisconsin. The application will be for a non-certified copy unless the relationship between the applicant and the deceased is a close family one.

TIPS: Clicking the Order Online Links

If cost isn't an issue, you can click one of these links and follow the on-screen instructions. The search window will show you the records that are available after state registration began. It will not take into account any county records before those dates.

Whether you place an order is a matter of choice. However, the cost may end up being several times what you would pay for the certificate if you found and ordered it yourself. When I was ordering the certificate for Edward Otterson from Brown County, I ran a duplicate order for the purpose of this chapter through the VitalChek link, right up to the point of hitting the submit button. The cost for a $7 certificate including delivery: $47.50.

4. From there it's very easy to navigate to where you need to be because the screen is devoid of clutter. Click **Order Records** from the menu to the left.

5. Click the link labeled **Death.** You will be routed to a PDF version of the application. (You can see a sample of it on page 78.)

6. Print the application and submit it with the $7 fee.

If you followed these steps, less than a week later a death certificate would arrive for Edward Otterson. From the certificate, you would learn that Edward died of heart failure at only eighteen years old.

Of course, details offered by the state and county pages vary. Vitalrec's state pages do not all have active links to county offices because such services don't always exist. Many county pages don't conveniently list the earliest available records, either, and some may not have much to offer at all. Application processes also vary substantially, as we have seen. Still, the route we've just followed can be duplicated in its essentials for any state in the U.S., assuming that the records are available. When using Vitalrec.com, the key is to remember the pathway to follow—the top two menu choices on the top left of each state page.

Step 4: Expand the Search to Other Internet Sites

There are obvious difficulties created by the inconsistency of civil registration from state to state and county to county, and by the fact that you may not know where to begin looking. But there are other ways to slay this particular dragon. The Web sites discussed in the remainder of this chapter can help. They are:

1. International Genealogical Index (IGI)

2. USGenWeb

3. Ancestry.com

4. Genealogy.com

5. A number of signposting sites

6. Google, and other Internet search engines

7. National Center for Health Statistics

FamilySearch.org and the IGI

The International Genealogical Index (known as the IGI) on **www.family search.org** is an enormously helpful database, consisting of hundreds of millions of birth, marriage, and death dates and places for deceased people from many nations. It is one of the most helpful tools on the Internet, and it's free and easily accessible.

So why haven't we mentioned it until now? Paradoxically, while some of the IGI's data is often legitimately criticized by genealogists as suspect, much of it is among the most reliable information you'll find online. You just need to know how to differentiate.

The IGI—helpful though it is—isn't a substitute for original records and doesn't pretend to be. My purpose has been to take you through a step-by-step process which minimizes the likelihood of mistakes and spending time on false trails. First we encouraged you to gather information from family and extended family, and then to confirm everything you can by accessing Social Security and census records. Next came vital records.

All of these sources are relatively high on the reliability scale. It's far better to proceed from a solid foundation, with confidence in your sources drawn from primary records, before branching out to secondary sources. To begin with the IGI—or by randomly searching surname lists too soon—is a risky business unless you know how to recognize the most reliable and least reliable data. It may lead to some short-term gains, but it can also lead to a lot of work on branches that don't even belong in your family tree because you haven't nailed down enough key relationships to be certain of your path. I can't count the times I have heard people say that

---

TIP: Big Changes Planned for FamilySearch.org

While the manuscript for this book was in preparation, The Church of Jesus Christ of Latter-day Saints was well advanced in a massive overhaul of FamilySearch.org. According to attendees at a 2005 genealogical conference in Salt Lake City, Utah, and several press reports, the next phase of this Web site will include some major innovations. It's likely that the IGI as it has been known will disappear, along with other databases on the same site, such as the Ancestral File. In its place will be something even more usable and useful. When the new site is launched (it will be the same Web address), just follow the logical equivalent in screen prompts to access the online databases. Whatever it's called, the new site will include all the data from the earlier databases.

their family tree is "all done" because they have found a mass of information on a Web site and have just accepted it without corroboration or sources. This is a very bad idea.

Using the IGI

We'll return to FamilySearch.org many times in succeeding chapters. Our purpose now is to look just at the IGI. To do this:

1. Enter **www.familysearch.org** in the address bar of your browser.

2. Select the **Search** tab from the menu across the top of the page.

3. This leads to an option to search a series of databases individually or all together. Select **International Genealogical Index** from the menu at the left of the screen.

4. Remember Homer Smiles? He was one of the stepping stones we used in Chapter 6 to trace our way to Mississippi-born Sarah Prophet and her English husband. In the on-screen search engine, type in **Homer** as the first name and **Smiles** as the last name.

5. From the dropdown menu under Region, select **North America.** Leave all the other fields blank, including the check-box for Use Exact Spelling.

6. Click the **Search** button.

The search finds three Homer Smails and one Homer Smiles, and we can see at a glance that the Homer born in Polk County, Florida, is our man. Clicking on his name brings up Homer's birth and death date and the names of his parents.

Clicking the **Family** link on the right side of the screen, alongside the parents' names, shows the parents—Henry John Smiles and Sarah Elizabeth Prophet—with two sons, Homer and Howard, along with their birth and death dates.

Obviously, this is valuable information, but the key to using the IGI effectively is to understand what it is, and to examine the sources.

Message and Source Information

At the bottom of the individual record screen for Homer Thomas Smiles is a heading titled **Source Information.** In this case, we read "No source information is available," and just above this, under the **Messages** heading, is the entry: "Record

How a Single Marriage Record Proved Vital

In Chapter 1, I made brief reference to Jim Wiltsher, a British immigrant to New Zealand who, at sixty years of age, had decided to start researching his English ancestry. Jim wrote to me wondering about connections with my lines. Though we never found any direct connection between our two family trees, we did find enough to take some of Jim's lines back to the 1800s.

Since he had not been sure of his grandfather's name, but understood him to have been "George, the son of George," that was our starting point to searching the online British census records from the area where he grew up, but we came up empty of anything that seemed a match.

We needed that confirmed "anchor" in the pedigree chart, so the next step was to turn to *vital records*. We sent for the grandfather's marriage certificate. The indexes were accessed on line, and the certificate was ordered by credit card over the Internet from the British Public Records Office. Three weeks later, after receiving it by mail, Jim sent a scanned image of the copied marriage certificate to my email address.

We now had the grandfather's age, and therefore his year of birth. We also had the name of the grandfather's father from the marriage certificate—which, despite family recollection, turned out to be Charles Herbert, not George. With that last key piece of knowledge, it was only a matter of minutes to locate these families in every ten-year census from 1851 to 1901, a period of fifty years, and then to fill in the missing pieces to this life sketch from other online sources. Further, the place where the great grandfather and his own father were born turned out to be the ancient village of Tewin in the county of Hertfordshire. It was built by a band of pagan Saxons who called themselves the Sons of Tew (after their god) in 459 AD; but the villagers converted to Christianity around 604 AD. Parts of the village church dates back to those ancient times. By the end of a single evening we found Jim's second great grandfather's family (he was born in 1790) and more than 100 Wiltsher christenings in the village over a 100-year period.

Of course, written records don't extend back beyond a few centuries in most cases, and Jim won't ever be able to go back to antiquity. But he has found his likely ancestral home, and the place oozes with ancient history, from Saxon, Danish, and Norman invasions to the peaceful, beautiful countryside it is today. And the key to unlocking this was a single marriage certificate that simply gave the correct name of the groom's father.

submitted after 1991 by a member of the LDS Church. No additional information is available."

All this information is significant, because it gives us a hint to the possible reliability of the data. The IGI—and presumably its intended successor—draws data primarily from two sources. The first is primarily from Latter-day Saints all over the world, who submit their family information directly to the Church. (Chapter 17 explains why Mormons have a passion for family history.)

The second source of IGI data is from what the Church calls **extracted records**. Since 1894, when the Genealogical Society of Utah was established to help Church members trace their lineage, the Mormons have been trying to preserve the world's genealogical records. In the 1930s, with the advent of microfilm, they began sending cameramen into dozens of countries, meeting and negotiating with other churches, civil registration authorities, national governments, and others to secure preservation of the records. Typically, the Mormons undertake this work at no cost to the original archive, and leave a copy of the microfilm with the archivist. Meanwhile, the original films are safely stored in a massive underground vault, 700 feet deep beneath the Rocky Mountains. More recently, digital cameras have taken over from microfilm.

The collection of records is made available to everyone through the main Family History Library in downtown Salt Lake City, Utah—the largest of its kind in the world. As we have seen, copies of the films can be deposited or loaned among more than 5,000 branch libraries all over the world, known as Family History Centers.

Back, now, to the information on the search results screen for Homer Smiles. As we can see, this information was submitted by a Church member, and we have no knowledge as to whether this person was a skilled genealogist or an amateur who made frequent mistakes. We can't accept the information without finding other, corroborative sources. What we are seeing on screen should be a starting point, not an end point, for a search for a vital record or census. It's also an indication that someone else is probably researching this line (see Chapter 9).

Now let's enter another name, and again I encourage you to follow this sequence with the book next to your computer keyboard and enter the data exactly as given here. The steps we are about to take are extremely important for knowing how to get the most out of this site—one of the largest.

Let's use the example of Jim Wiltsher. As we saw on page 83, Jim's family has now been traced to the ancient Saxon village of Tewin in Hertfordshire, England. Using a combination of British census and vital record indexes on the Internet, we have traced Jim's line through his great grandfather, Charles Herbert Wiltsher, to Charles' parents, Richard and Maria. We have also narrowed the birth of Charles to the third quarter of the year 1836, in Tewin. A birth certificate will be needed to obtain an exact birth date for Charles and the maiden name of his mother, Maria.

So, what can we find on the IGI? Let's follow these steps again.

1. Enter the name Charles Wiltsher into the search engine in the IGI.

2. Specify only the **Region** British Isles, the country of England, and the county of Hertford, from the **Region, Country,** and **County** dropdown boxes.

3. Click the **Search** button.

4. You'll be confronted with a results list of ten Charles Wiltshers of various spellings. It takes only a few seconds to single out the fourth on the list, a Charles Wilshire christened in Tewin in 1836. Click on his name.

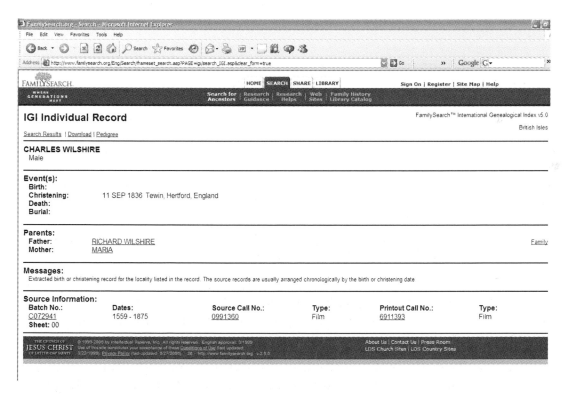

The IGI individual record screen. Manipulating the links at the bottom of the screen, such as batch and source information, allows highly tailored searches. (Image copyright 1999, 2005 by Intellectual Reserve, Inc. Used by permission.)

Sure enough, this entry shows parents of the newly christened Charles as Richard and Maria. The christening date is 11 September 1836. A christening date is almost as good as a birth date in earlier years—in fact, the birth date centuries ago was often not recorded by clergymen because it was the baptism or christening with which they were professionally involved. Burial dates often substituted for death dates for the same reason.

This time, the **Messages** and **Source** information at the bottom of the screen read differently. The Message says that the data is from an "extracted birth or christening record for the locality listed in the record." *Extracted* means that this data has been extracted or transcribed directly from the vital record film by volunteers or people employed by the LDS Church. That means much more quality control than someone who just submitted a name without sources, as described earlier. This christening reference is, in effect, a vital record.

We can even see what the source of that extracted record was. In this case, clicking **Source Call No.** takes us to the main Family History Library Catalog, where film number 0991360 is shown to be "Parish registers, 1559–1926, Church of England, Parish Church of Tewin (Hertfordshire)."

We're not finished yet. This film could be of great interest to us if generations of Wiltshers lived and died there. Click the **Parish Registers** part of the title. The screen shows us a number of details about the registers, which we can add to the sources and/or notes in our software program for this item.

Among these details are not only the films, with dates as far back as 1559, but notification that all of these names can be accessed online because this is an extracted record.

Customizing the Search

Back on Charles Wilshire's IGI Individual Record screen, click on the number underneath **Batch No.** This action takes you back to the search engine, but now the batch number has been entered automatically in the appropriate box. Hitting the **Search** button at this point will bring up an alphabetical list by surname of every christening record in Tewin back to the 1500s.

You can narrow the search even further by simply adding surname details. If we enter Wilshire (any spelling) in the surname box, the list reduces to thirty-nine names of christenings. In effect, you have moved from doing a surname search of the entire database of millions of names to searching all people of the same surname within a single parish over several centuries.

We can click on every one of those names to see the details. It's quite a simple matter to look at christenings in a list like this for children that have the parents' names in common. By putting the christening dates in chronological order, we can often build a picture of an entire family in this way. For example, clicking on **Rebecca Wiltshire,** number four on the list of thirty-nine, shows us that Rebecca Wiltshire, who was christened in Tewin in 1823, had parents whose names—Richard and Maria—are the same as those of Charles' parents. It seems likely that Charles and Rebecca are brother and sister.

Continuing down the list, we add Mary Ann (christened 1819), Emma (1832), William (1826), Thomas (1821), and Elizabeth (1815) to the same family. Interestingly, of these seven children, our previous census and vital records searches yielded only three. These dates are earlier than any we could obtain from birth certificates, which weren't kept until 1837.

We can now apply exactly the same process to find Richard and Maria's marriage, which turns up in the IGI exactly where it should be—in 1814, about a year before the birth of the first child. Maria's maiden name is revealed as Hill, and the marriage was at Tewin Parish Church of England, where the later christenings took place.

This is a great illustration of the tremendous power of the online databases on FamilySearch.org. It's simplistic to dismiss the IGI just because some of the data is

Searching by batch number is an effective way of selecting a narrow range of names from a single parish. (Image copyright 1999, 2005 by Intellectual Reserve, Inc. Used by permission.)

submitted from sources other than vital records. As we've seen, it's easy to differentiate if you know how. We found all of this information without ever once leaving our keyboard. The data can be selectively downloaded from www.family-search.org in a GED-COM file, from which it can be imported into your software program. By the way, when it downloads, you will have to deal with a problem in how

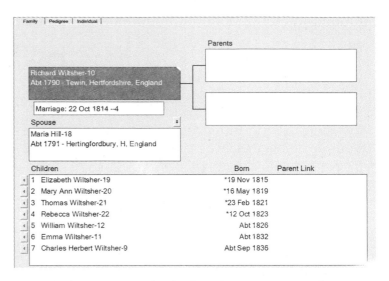

The Richard and Maria Wiltsher family, as they appear in PAF, after downloading the data from the IGI. (FamilySearch.org, image copyright 1999, 2005 by Intellectual Reserve, Inc. Used by permission.)

the software handles sources. The source will be entered automatically, but you'll need to go into your software program and edit it in accordance with the guidance we gave in Chapter 4. This flaw in the way source information is downloaded from the IGI is well recognized by professionals but won't be fixed because bigger and better things are on the way for this site. Just remember that the source for a vital record must begin with a place and end with a record type. The source is not the IGI itself, no matter what your downloaded GEDCOM file might say.

Because the IGI contains hundreds of millions of names from dozens of countries, it should be clear what a valuable resource it is. However, the information should never be used in isolation if you intend to branch out from any of these names. Even extracted records are secondary sources, and they should be checked for 100 percent accuracy by obtaining a copy of the microfilm through the Family History Center nearest to you and examining the original record from which the online data was extracted. As we've said, this often yields extra information.

Now that you have been introduced to this database, begin entering in the search engine the names of your own ancestors from your family tree to see if they are listed. Typically, The Church of Jesus Christ of Latter-day Saints has a self-imposed 100-year privacy rule, and won't display extracted data with dates more recent than that. Information submitted by Church members about their own family members does not fall within this restriction, however, and the dates and places may be more recent.

USGenWeb

We first referred to the USGenWeb project in Chapter 7 when tracking down census records. This is the umbrella name for much of the volunteer effort going on in the United States to transcribe official records of various types and place them, free to all, on the Internet.

RootsWeb provides the Internet space for the USGenWeb Archives Project, which is useful when looking for vital records. Vitalrec.com took you to official county resources, and the IGI is most useful for its extracted records. The types of vital records found in the USGenWeb network are different again, since they are mostly the work of volunteer transcribers. Let's take a look at the site:

1. Log on to the home page at **www.rootsweb.com/~usgenweb.** This network of sites is easy to navigate. While every state and county site is different, there is a lot of consistency in how the resources are listed and how they are saved in text format.

2. The home page shows an alphabetical list of U.S. states. Click on any state under the **Table of Contents** column to produce a list of counties. Each county link leads to a list of resources. These files have all been contributed by volunteers, and include a huge variety of information. Some 640,000 volunteer transcription projects have been logged to date.

The USGenWeb Archives Project is growing in importance as more and more data is contributed by volunteers. (Image copyright USGenWeb Archives Project. Used by permission.)

The value of the USGenWeb archives will continue to improve steadily over time. Parts of the USGenWeb Archives Project are already extraordinarily advanced. An estimated one-third of all the headstones in the U.S., for example, have been transcribed—a remarkable achievement.

Vital records in these archives are found at the county level. In addition, the resources from a county may include obituaries, cemetery lists, church records before civil registration began, census records between the federal censuses, and much more. While new material is being added daily, you can't often expect to find a continuous stream of data covering decades at a time. You are most likely to be successful if you are looking for dates before 1925. Much of the time, volunteers contribute the material based on their own research interests. It's another case of looking at a jigsaw puzzle with most of the pieces missing. Here and there you can see parts of a clear picture, but the information is patchy, and finding your ancestors' names ultimately comes down to luck.

One big advantage of this site is that there is a "national search engine" that can do a single-state search or search the entire United States GenWeb archives. Given the difficulties referred to earlier—the lack of a central government repository for all U.S. records because registration is a county responsibility—the advantages of this search facility are obvious.

Ancestry.com

As mentioned earlier in this chapter, Ancestry.com's online databases for subscribers include a large and growing number of important vital record collections, ranging from Alabama marriages before 1825 to parish records in Yorkshire, England.

Ancestry.com's aggressive acquisitions policy is one of the family historian's best allies. Much of the progress made in recent years in online family history has been made possible because of Ancestry.com's growth as a company, and much, much more is to come.

One very helpful feature throughout the Ancestry.com site is the detailed explanation that accompanies every database, just below the search engine. These are very clear and very well written, so you know exactly what kind of data you're looking at. The descriptions are written with the assumption that the researcher is not an expert, so beginners can easily assess the relevance and significance of the database.

Genealogy.com

Ancestry.com's sister company, Genealogy.com, tends to have more educational information for beginners, though it also has substantial data collections. This Web site points you to state and county vital record sources. And there is an excellent

Ancestry.com
Discover Your Family Story

Welcome, **Mike_Otterson**   Log Out Upgrade My Account Help

Home | My Ancestry | **Search** | Family Trees | Ancestry Community | Learning Center | Store

Albemarle County, Virginia Births, 1886-89

Ranked Search Exact Search

Enter as much info as you can – even a **guess** can help. See search tips

First Name

Last Name

Keyword(s)

Search

RELATED PRODUCTS

State & Country Maps
Get a fascinating look at the past. *Large-scale maps*

Learn More ▶

Description:
Nestled in the Appalachian Mountains of central Virginia, Albemarle County boasted a population of nearly 30,000 residents in the mid-1880s. This database is a collection of birth records from the county between 1886 and 1889. Taken from existing county documents held by the state, it provides valuable information regarding nearly 2200 children. Researchers will find the child's name, race, sex, birth date, and parents' names. Page numbers refer to the original county document from which these records were taken. For researchers of central Virginian ancestors, this database can be a valuable source of information.

Source Information:
Fridley, Beth. *Albemarle County, Virginia, Birth Records, 1886-1889.* [database on-line] Orem, UT: Ancestry, Inc., 1999.

Ancestry UK | Ancestry CA | Corporate Info | Affiliate Program | PRIVACY STATEMENT | Contact Us
Copyright © 1998-2006, MyFamily.com Inc. – Terms and Conditions

Above: A typical search facility on Ancestry.com. Each database is accompanied by a helpful explanation of its origins and purpose. (Image copyright 2005 MyFamily.com, Inc., and reproduced from Ancestry.com. Used by permission.)

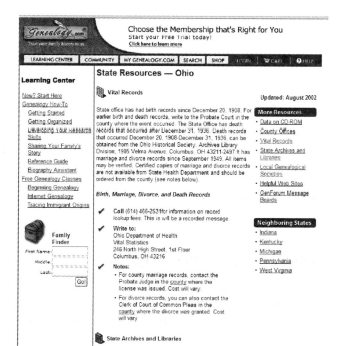

Left: Sample screen image of a State Resource page. This is an excellent quick-reference point for knowing what you are likely to find and not find in state and county records. (Image copyright 2005 MyFamily.com, Inc., and reproduced from Genealogy.com. Used by permission.)

summary for every state's offerings of records, including what is available, for what period and where.

Your starting point is **www.genealogy.com/00000174.html**. The fees for access to the data on the site itself are comparable with Ancestry.com. It's also possible to get access to a limited number of databases for a few dollars a month, so look at the online resources and determine if the scale of charges in those databases seems relevant to you.

Signposting Sites for Vital Records

We mentioned three specific signposting sites in the last chapter on census records—Genealogylinks, Linkpendium, and Cyndi's List. All are good for vital records. Of these three, the best one for marriage records is **Genealogylinks.net.** This is the menu for marriage databases at the time of writing:

- Large Marriage Databases
- UK & England Marriages
- Ireland Marriages
- Scotland Marriages
- Wales Marriages
- United States Marriages
- Europe Marriages
- Canada Marriages
- Australia Marriages
- New Zealand Marriages

Some of these categories represent huge collections of names. For instance, the large marriage database includes links to:

- The RootsWeb marriage database of 600,000 marriages. The convenience here is that you can do a global search across every state from one search engine.
- The Western States Historical Marriage Index, housed at Brigham Young

University's Idaho campus, contains some 400,000 marriage records, with more being added continually.

- FreeBMD—a very important site for England and Wales (examined in detail in Chapter 11).

A helpful page on **Cyndislist.com** is "Related Categories" for primary sources. Strictly speaking, "vital records" refers to birth, marriage, and death records. When they are unavailable, a number of other records can serve as substitutes, and some of them are almost as reliable.

Log on to Cyndi's List and find the page on Primary Sources at **www.cyndislist.com/primary.htm.** On the right side of the page is a list of links to resources for biographies, cemetery and funeral home records, land records, marriage data, military records, newspapers, obituaries, ship passenger lists, wills, and other data. Refer to the Appendix for further information on U.S. military records (including Civil War), and for pointers to specialist areas of research such as African-American, Native American, and Jewish.

Google and Other Search Engines

Genealogists have a tremendous asset in the form of today's sophisticated search engines on the Internet. Instead of having to type in the precise name of an organization, you can just specify the topic. For instance, you can't be expected to know that vital records in Vermont are divided between two departments depending on the year of the event—the Vermont Department of Health and the Division of Public Records of the Department of Buildings and General Services.

When using Google, it doesn't matter. In the search engine on **www.google.com**, just type in "Vermont Vital Records" and click the **Search** button. A long list comes up on the screen, but right at the top is "Vermont Department of Health Vital Statistics and Vital Records." Clicking on that link leads you to a full explanation of what records are available, and where, plus links to the Public Records Office.

Although you can't order online in this case without going through a commercial service, you can still find out where to phone or write. Vermont, incidentally, is one state that started registration early. Statewide civil registration began in 1857, and many records are available from much earlier.

Try the same approach for the states in which you're interested, incorporating "Vital Records" in your search criteria. You will almost always get a useful Web link within the first half-dozen listed if you enter information that is precise enough in the search box of your favorite search engine. Include the county name as well as the state name. For example, "Brown County Wisconsin Vital Records" leads within a couple of clicks to a number of useful links.

In addition to Google and other popular search engines, it's worth mentioning that more innovative ways of searching the Web are now emerging. Because they have significant implications for genealogists, we'll look at them more closely when we get to future developments in Chapter 17.

Local Historical and Genealogical Societies

Local historical and genealogical societies specialize in gathering important historical data, and many have significant collections unavailable elsewhere. Use a search engine like Google to enter the name of the state or county, together with "Historical Society" or "Genealogy Society," or search on Cyndi's List.

Once you settle on a locality where your family has lived for generations, membership in a local genealogical society is worth considering. The "locals" always know more about regional sources, what projects are underway, and the nuances of local place names and history. You also have the advantage of talking to people who are serious about their family history, and will assume you are too. Such people are always willing to encourage those whose expertise ranges from beginner to intermediate. Many have online message boards and mailing lists, so you don't necessarily need to leave your home to become involved.

National Center for Health Statistics

The National Center for Health Statistics, which exists under the Centers for Disease Control and Prevention, maintains a handy Web site that lists the vital records available in every state as well as the District of Columbia, New York City, American Samoa, the Canal Zone, Guam, Northern Mariana Islands, Puerto Rico, and the U.S. Virgin Islands. There is also a link for information about events on the "high seas."

Go to **www.cdc.gov/nchs** and from the home page scroll down to the heading **Top 10 Links.** Click **Help Obtaining Birth, Death, Marriage or Divorce Certificates.** This leads to an alphabetical list of states. You will still have to follow the links to the county level, and once again you may be forced back to other means of getting down to the precise area you want. Nevertheless, you can use this site as a quick reference to see when the official records began, how much certificates cost, and where to write.

I have included this site for another reason. If your Internet access is charged by the hour and you think you might use this reference frequently, it might be worth downloading the entire file of state and county information from the site, which you can do in PDF format.

The file size is 529 kb. Pay attention also to the Application Guidelines at the bottom of the alphabetical states list, under **How to Use This Web Page.** This tells you precisely what you should include in an application letter, and can save you time.

More Than Online Records

By now you should have a pretty good idea of the extent and variety of what is already

The Centers for Disease Control website is a good quick reference to what vital records are available in each U.S. state and territory. (Image used by permission of Centers for Disease Control and Prevention.)

available on the Internet, and what the future promises. But accessing data directly online, while increasingly rewarding, is only a part of the story. The other great benefit brought by the Internet is the ability of researchers to coordinate and collaborate, which is where we'll turn next.

9
TEAM WORK
ON THE INTERNET

Overview

If there were a prize for the single greatest advantage that the Internet has brought to family history research, the ability to team up with others, share information, and cooperate on research would be a strong contender. This is an area where you can make tremendous gains if you do it right. By one estimate, more than 95 percent of people who post all sixteen names of their second great grandparents on the RootsWeb Surname List alone—that's just four generations beyond yourself— find a living relative researching part of the same family tree.

The Internet has allowed people to connect with each other as never before, and it didn't take genealogists very long to recognize its power. Whereas it once might have taken years to accumulate a few dozen names on a tree, many people who have been working for only a few months have accumulated hundreds or even thousands of names from other enthusiasts, along with photographs and stories of some of the people those names represent. A few years ago I obtained a digital image of my second great grandmother—from a painting made in the mid-1800s—from just such a connection. I had no idea previously that the painting even existed.

The concept of cooperation over the Internet is very simple. It all starts by posting part or all of your research interests on various genealogy Web sites, together with your contact information, usually an email address. Other people do the same, and, if either of you notices a name that appears to be in common, you get together to share information and possibly cooperate on future steps. Cooperation or team work can take several forms, and I'm going to be specific about how certain terms are used in the rest of this book. They are not necessarily universal, but they are used by some professional genealogists and the distinctions are significant.

- **Coordination.** This is when two or more people are researching the same family tree, and they work together to avoid duplication and wasted effort.

Perhaps one person researches a father's line while the other one tackles the mother, or they work on different siblings in the same family. While they keep their activities distinct, they constantly share their findings with each other.

- **Collaboration.** There are times when it's helpful for two or more people to focus on one particular name—perhaps an end-of-line or a particularly thorny problem. People collaborate by working on different avenues of research on a name or a place, thus dividing the work and constantly comparing notes.

There are many other forms of team work on the Internet in addition to sharing details of your own family tree. It can be simply a shared discussion on a Web site that has nothing to do with your family at all—say, a discussion of how to find on an old map a particular place that has been obliterated by the growth of a nearby city, or the definition of a long obsolete profession. All of these activities, and many variations, have found their place in the genealogical online community.

Yet the same Internet that has delivered these advantages, and that has been such a boon to genealogists, has also been the biggest source of false data and the cause of countless wrong turns.

Much of what some online enthusiasts have acquired is solidly researched, with verifiable sources. But sadly, there is so much that isn't. I receive emails almost every day from people asking whether such-and-such a person on my family tree is related to the same name on theirs. I know immediately that we have a problem when they offer no time frame, no location, and no evidence that the two names are associated. They have just seen a name on a list, and have fired off a hopeful email. Some Web sites are actually structured to do just that—to look for the same names with similar time frames and locations that produce "hot matches" that are fired off by email to subscribers.

I've also connected with many people on my own initiative when I've seen a likely relationship. Sometimes that leads to a downloaded GEDCOM file, only to find that in a list of a few hundred names there isn't a single source listed. An inquiring email back to the sender sometimes results in a, "Sorry, I got it from the Internet and this is all I have." In such circumstances, there may be nothing to do but to begin the laborious process of checking every name and date, one by one.

The truth is, there is an avalanche of bad data cascading over the Internet, and it's critically important to be able to separate the wheat from the chaff. One of the primary purposes of this book is to help people make precisely that distinction. Working with others on the Internet can be a fast track and bring real benefits, but fast tracks can also lead to crashes. This chapter will provide you with some of the advantages of sharing efforts with others, and how to avoid the pitfalls. First, let's discuss why we share information with others.

Finding Stories: Making the Past Come Alive

The following story is a simple result of people contributing different pieces of the same picture, combined with Internet research. Let's take a look at the story and how it was put together.

It was well after dark on the night of May 4, 1941, and three-year-old Frederick Andrew was fast asleep but still in his clothes. His parents were older than usual for those of a three-year-old without brothers or sisters—Freddie's father was thirty-nine, his mother thirty. They had been married less than five years.

Their home in the Everton area of Liverpool's inner city was identical to its neighbors. Like most others in large English industrial centers, it had been built of its dark red brick before the turn of the century, and the Andrews rented it from the city's stock of nearly identical terraced houses. A few miles from the working-class neighborhood and its soot-stained chimneys lay the sprawling Liverpool Dockland, which for the past three nights had been the target of the greatest German air raid on this large port city since the war began.

The mournful wailing of the air raid sirens sounded again, as they had on each of the past three nights. Except for those families who were determined to defy government orders and brave it out in their homes, everyone grabbed their children and headed for the nearest street air raid shelter. Minutes later, the distant thud of ground anti-aircraft guns signaled the approach of the Junker 88s and Dornier bombers of the Luftwaffe. Soon the sky would be illuminated with parachute flares and, far above them, the explosive shells of ground fire.

For some, the decision whether to seek the safety of an air raid

Liverpool and neighboring Birkenhead, straddling the River Mersey and photographed from a German aircraft. (Image copyright Liverpool City Council. Used by permission.)

shelter or to stick it out at home was a nightly struggle. Even in an air raid, the odds of a direct hit on a particular house were favorable to the occupant. The Andrew family, like many others tired of constant disruption and sleeping in their clothes, eventually learned to forego the shelter and take refuge under the stairs in their own home.

But the ferocity of the past few nights' bombing had signaled something different. Nothing like this had been seen before in Liverpool, and families were ordered to evacuate and head for the nearest street air raid shelter. Built to accommodate fifty, each would be more packed than usual on this night. Dark and cold with poor ventilation, the shelter's 14-inch-thick brick walls and 1-foot-thick reinforced concrete roof nevertheless offered protection from the force of bomb blasts and flying debris. That is, unless there was a direct and very unlucky hit.

On the night of May 4, in the rain of incendiary bombs and mines that were dropped over Liverpool, hundreds would die. The eight-day blitz—the last intense campaign of the war on this strategically vital port—claimed 1,741 lives.

When the dawn light revealed the extent of the devastation, the Andrew home at 50 Carmel Street was still intact. But a bomb had fallen directly on the nearby air raid shelter in St. Domingo Road. Among the dead were the family of three-year-old Frederick and his parents. All three of them were buried a few days later—like hundreds of others—in a neighboring suburb because the local cemetery couldn't accommodate the number of dead.

This story is true in all its essentials. It draws from government records of civilian deaths in World War II and from vital records. It includes research on museum and historical Web sites, from accounts of the blitz to details of the construction of air raid shelters found online. Yet it could not have the poignancy it has without the account of someone who knew of the family's preference to shelter under the stairs and why they didn't on that particular night. Added to that was the contribution of the minister of the church where the family was buried. That personal detail—which makes the story

Still-strung electric tram cables seem the only things left untouched after an intensive "blitz" on Liverpool, May 1941. The shells of bombed-out buildings form a new skyline. (Image copyright National Museums, Liverpool, World Museum Liverpool. Used by permission.)

what it is—came to me by email, more than fifty years after the event and many years after it had first been told and written down in a notebook. In other words, it is a story that could be told only with the collective contribution of several people.

Accounts like these are the stuff of family history. They become fixed points in an endless timeline—glimpses of other lives as real as our own, yet from a strangely different world. They allow us to see not only the family as a unit, but to savor the context in which the family lived. Even if we can't find photographs of the family itself, the Internet allows us to find pictures that create unmistakable images of that time (see Chapter 15).

How to Share and Collaborate

Most often, you will be looking first for people who can provide names and dates and places of people on your family lines. With luck, they will be able to open the door to more of the personal history as well.

The first step is to get your own family tree—or specific parts of it—onto the major Internet sites where other family tree enthusiasts are looking.

Step 1: Upload Your Tree to the Major Web sites

You are now about to submit your work to giant, internationally used Web sites where other people will see it and contact you. You will also be looking on those same sites for names, dates, and places that are familiar to you because they're on your own family tree.

You will come across a number of apparent connections and possibly different interpretations of the data. Only by having some of your names, dates, and places solidly anchored in fact can you be sure of the path you will take. Accuracy, therefore, is paramount.

Be cautious as you upload your files. What follows are directions for uploading to several of the most well-known collaborative sites.

The Pedigree Resource File

When you log on to **www.familysearch.org** and click the **Search** tab near the top of the page, you'll have the option to select **Pedigree Resource File** from the left side of the screen.

The Pedigree Resource File is a lineage-linked database, which means if you find an ancestor in the database there's a very good chance you will be able to click on the names of that person's parents, then their parents, and so on. This database is therefore different than the IGI on the same site, even though some of the names are common to both. The IGI is based on an individual record for each person, not on pedigrees.

The Pedigree Resource File is a database of well over 100 million names contributed by people like you, and it's growing all the time. You'll want to upload your information here first.

Registering with FamilySearch

Because the essence of sharing and collaboration involves giving your name and address and contact information, you will have to register with FamilySearch.org to share your data with the Pedigree Resource File. Does that mean that you'll be getting a knock on the door from Mormon missionaries? Absolutely not. The Church is strict about its use of genealogical data, and the site itself carries a warning that submitter information is provided to help only in the coordination of personal family history research. Users are told that use of this information for any other purpose, including marketing, advertising, or commercial solicitation, is strictly prohibited. The Church holds itself to that standard.

Sharing GEDCOM Files

See the Tip box on page 103 if you need help in creating a GEDCOM file.

Once you've registered at **www.familysearch.org,** click the **Share** tab near the top of the screen. The explanatory screen will provide two advantages of sending a GEDCOM file to the Pedigree Resource File: (1) safe preservation and (2) sharing.

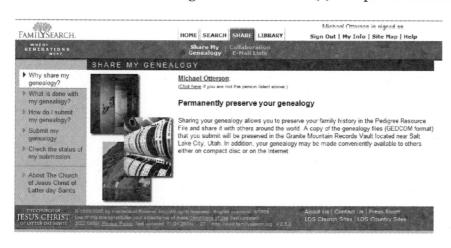

Preserving your family history in probably the safest place on earth—the mountain vaults of Utah. (FamilySearch.org, image copyright 1999, 2005 by Intellectual Reserve, Inc. Used by permission.)

There is probably no safer place on earth to protect your family history than in the Granite Mountain Vault near Salt Lake City. It was built specifically to do everything that other storage facilities do not do. Deep inside the granite mountain, the vaults are not only safe from fire and flood but are also built to withstand a nuclear blast.

After clicking on the **Share** tab and reading the explanatory screen, look at the menu of options. Select **Submit my genealogy** and read the disclaimer information carefully–especially the parts about including living people. After accepting the terms, follow the simple screen instructions for submitting your GEDCOM file.

Once you submit your GEDCOM file, it will be checked for format errors before being placed in the vault. If there are errors you'll receive an email and a chance to fix the problem and resubmit. The data you have submitted will be added to the constantly growing collection of CDs that are available free at a Family History Center or for purchase to use in your home. The full Pedigree Resource File isn't yet available online—that is, all of the notes and sources—but the key data is.

As you prepare your GEDCOM for uploading, make sure you remove any notes that might mention a living person, and set your GEDCOM to designate any living people with the label "Living" rather than including their names and event details.

You can easily check what the data looks like online by following these easy steps:

1. Click the **Search** tab at the top of the FamilySearch.org home page.
2. Select **Pedigree Resource File** from the menu at the left of the screen.
3. Type in the name of one of your ancestors and see the list of name offerings that results.
4. Click on any name to see how the data is displayed.

You can also experiment by just typing in the first name "Fred" and the surname "Johnson" but leaving everything else blank. You'll get Johannesen and Johnstone without having to specify surname variations. Click on any of the results and you'll see lots of vital record-type information. The names of spouses or parents are also links to more details of those people. Notice that the screen gives you the name and address of the person who submitted the information—at least it was the address when the data was submitted. It will also show you the number of the CD on which the information appears, and whether the data includes sources and notes.

TIP: Creating GEDCOM Files

Internet genealogy isn't effective without understanding how to create and exchange GEDCOM files. All dedicated genealogy software programs allow the creation of these files.

In all the major software programs, the standard way to create GEDCOMs is to click on **File, Export**, and then follow the on-screen instructions. You can create a GEDCOM of your entire file, or select categories of people such as ancestors, descendants, or members of a single family—even individuals.

You may be offered several options, depending on your software program. If you know you are sharing data with an individual using the same program, you can opt for the GEDCOM file format offered by that program—PAF, Family Tree Maker, Ancestral Quest, etc. If you are unsure which to choose, there is usually an "Other" option. In that case, select 5.5. You may then see options for character sets, but unless your data contains non-Roman alphabet characters, just select the first option on the list.

Be especially careful to look at the options for what to include in the file. As standard practice, exclude information for living people. Your program will assume a person is living if born within the past 100 years or so, unless there is a death date, but you will have to tell your program to exclude such people. *Include* sources, but *exclude* notes, which are more likely to contain sensitive information.

Once you have specified the kind of data to include, your software program will do the rest, creating and saving your GEDCOM file to a place on your computer that you specify. You can then attach it to any email, copy it to another disk or a CD as you would with any other file.

Keep a copy for reference of any GEDCOMs you send to others.

Importing a GEDCOM file is simple. Go to **File, Import**, and follow on-screen instructions. Examine such files carefully, including source information, *before* adding the data to your own family tree. Your software will explain how to merge files, but be very careful. It's generally best to merge data one family at a time until you become proficient at it. Merging is one of the trickiest software operations you will undertake, so read your software instructions carefully and always backup your main file before attempting a merge. That way, if anything does go wrong, you can scrap the changes.

Uploading files to RootsWeb

Next, we'll do something similar with RootsWeb. RootsWeb exists primarily to bring people together, so most of its services are tailored to that end. It is huge and free to use.

RootsWeb is owned by Ancestry.com, which provides the space and the funding for the RootsWeb site. RootsWeb's **WorldConnect** and Ancestry's **OneWorldTree** now share information, so entering data into Ancestry's database automatically gets it onto WorldConnect as well. They display differently, however, and they do not contain identical information. To get started:

1. Log on to the RootsWeb home page at **www.rootsweb.com.**

2. Scroll to the **Search Engines and Databases** heading.

3. Click the link for **WorldConnect Project.** Your first job will be to submit your family tree—or as much as you are satisfied with—to WorldConnect. The Project provides a set of tools that will allow you to upload and display your family tree in just a few minutes.

4. At the top right of the screen, you will see the heading **Submit Your Family Tree to WorldConnect.** Click the **Start Here** link underneath that heading.

5. This will take you to a User Setup/Edit screen. Enter the User Code of your choice and a Password. The User Code is just like a user name. It will be displayed on the screen where people see your tree. The password will never be visible. Keep careful note of the code and password because you will need them any time you want to make changes to your tree.

6. Click the Standard button, and you will be taken to a screen that allows you to create a new GEDCOM account.

7. Enter your name, your email address, and click **Setup.**

8. Fill out the form on the screen. Most of the form is self-explanatory, but a couple of suggestions are in order: (1) When entering the title of your tree, try to make it somewhat descriptive. Rather than just making the title the surname, add a location and even a time period, for instance. Something like, "Hamilton, from Bristol England to London, Ontario, 1750–2000" would be appropriate. You should make yours as descriptive as possible for others who are searching. (2) You may also want to add or elaborate on such information in the page heading or footer, items number 6 and 7 on the form.

9. After each line item on the form is correctly filled in, click the **Upload/Update** button to send your family tree to the site.

Once your file is uploaded, you can view it through the WorldConnect Global Search, as can anyone else on the Internet.

Note the two different screen views, on this page and the next. The first is a standard pedigree view in WorldConnect, using Lewis Dix as the root person. The other is a screenshot of the same person in a pedigree view in OneWorldTree on Ancestry.com. The data is the same, but Ancestry has a more sophisticated display and a range of on-screen tools.

You are now set to share your own information and to search other family trees. Use the search facilities in WorldConnect to explore. If you find a name that could be a possible match to someone on your family tree, check carefully that the dates and places correspond closely or exactly to yours. If you see something that looks like a clear match, then write to the submitter of the information and ask for more details. On WorldConnect, you can see the submitter's email address. Some other genealogy sites act as go-betweens so that correspondents can remain anonymous until they know they are related and may want to exchange email addresses later.

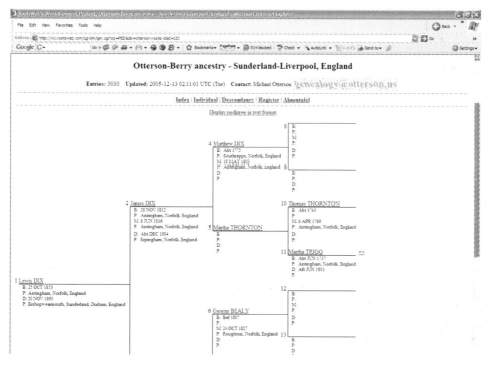

WorldConnect pedigree view on RootsWeb. (Image copyright 2005 MyFamily.com, Inc. Used by permission.)

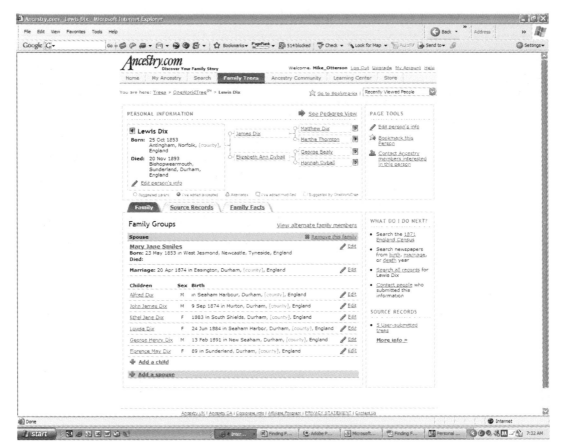

This image contains the same data as in the WorldConnect screen view on page 105, but displayed in Ancestry's OneWorldTree. (Image copyright 2005 MyFamily.com, Inc., and reproduced from Ancestry.com. Used by permission.)

Using Ancestry.com

Ancestry.com's method of connecting people who are researching the same lines on OneWorldTree is a little more proactive.

Once you've found a name you're interested in on a OneWorldTree family tree, you can connect with others by clicking one of two links on the right side of the screen image: **Contact Ancestry members interested in this person** or **Contact people who submitted this information.** Clicking on those links will bring up a list of everyone who has searched for this or similar names or who is researching this line, and you can browse the list for possible matches. The matches are ranked by relevance.

MyTrees.com

One subscription site that offers access for a reasonable fee is **MyTrees.com,** run by a company called Kindred Konnections. The company allows you to access their databases for as little as $5 for a limited period. If you submit your family tree for general viewing they will extend that access period to a month or more, depending on how many names you deliver. Their object, obviously, is to make the database as large and therefore as useful as possible. You can easily sign up again after your $5 term expires. The site allows you to do this automatically or to set the default to cancel your subscription after your term ends.

As with other sites, you have the facility to post your information, in such a way that other users will be likely to contact you if they identify common ancestors. In this case, you can upload a GEDCOM file of your entire tree, and ask the site's search facility to examine your names against every other name submitted by others users. After a short time— it may be a few hours depending on the size of your tree—you will be presented with a list of possible matches.

> ### TIP: Researching in the UK
>
> If your family tree extends into Britain, try GenesReunited.com as an additional place to list your surnames. This is a site frequented by lots of beginners, but it has the ability to generate an extraordinary amount of response.
>
> For a more detailed description of the benefits of this site and how to use it, see Chapter 13.

All the cautions I've mentioned previously still apply. Don't think of your computer or any other computer as *smart*. It is only making its best guess based on apparent similarities. You still have to apply intelligent judgment as to whether your ancestor is the same person as someone else's, case by case.

What to Do with GEDCOM Files You Download

Because the essence of collaboration is sharing, and the basis of sharing genealogical information is the GEDCOM file, you need to plan what to do with GEDCOM files that you download.

All the software programs we mentioned at the outset have clear instructions for importing or exporting (downloading or uploading) GEDCOM files, so there is no need to repeat them here. That doesn't mean you shouldn't take precautions. The worst thing you can do is download a GEDCOM file and merge it with your own family tree without satisfying yourself that the data is reliable. This is especially the case with large trees that will take a long time to check.

The best course if you are downloading something that looks promising is to rename the file with a separate, descriptive name, including the name of the person sending it to you. You can then keep it in an Import/Export folder where you can look at the data carefully at your leisure. Start with the names that also appear on your own family tree, and then create a GEDCOM of selected names from the file that you received that you can prune and graft onto your tree.

You can usually determine quite quickly whether the information is reliable. First, are any sources or notes included? If not, email the sender and ask for them to be sent. If that fails—or even if it doesn't—check the quality of the data by doing some spot checks against available census records. Watch for the tell-tale signs of careless work:

- children not arranged in date order
- towns mentioned without counties or countries
- marriage dates without places that can easily be determined

Even the language used in email exchanges will give you a reasonable idea of whether you are working with someone with experience or not. Finally, import into your own tree only those names for which you feel reasonably satisfied. Include in the source information (e.g. in the comments section) the name and contact details of the person who sent it.

This approach also works both ways. When you upload a GEDCOM, make sure it contains everything you would want to receive in terms of its quality.

Privacy Issues

One decision that you now have to make is related to the privacy of the people on your tree. WorldConnect and OneWorldTree can either restrict information or completely remove all names on your tree if the person might still be living. When you select the **Clean** option, the program will take out any of the information you specify in the additional options. For example, you should replace all the living people's names with the word *Living,* and remove everything else related to that person, including notes and sources. A user examining your data will at least know that a family had a certain number of children, and that they are still alive.

If you select **Remove**, these individuals will be removed completely and no trace will remain. The restrictions you specify in the other options will then apply to every name remaining in your tree. (See also "Genealogical Standards and Guidelines" at the end of this chapter).

The FamilySearch.org site follows the same general guidelines and requests removal of information about living people before a GEDCOM file is submitted. You

TIP: Be Cautious When Viewing Computer-generated Trees

The data you enter into WorldConnect will automatically transfer to Ancestry.com's family trees database. It's especially important for beginners to understand the unexpected results that can appear in some of these databases, and to know exactly what you are looking at.

There is a world of difference between joining an email list and having an intelligent conversation with a real person, and allowing a computer to make judgments or "best guesses" through a set of algorithms as to who might be related to whom on your tree.

For example, on one recent occasion when I was browsing Ancestry's family trees database I noticed the name of one of my familiar ancestors who died in 1846. I clicked on the pedigree view and found that the computer was suggesting his father and earlier ancestors. The only problem was that the "father" was born in the 1300s!

Such anomalies are common because the computer seeks out the most likely match from all the data it has available. The on-screen text tells you that this is the "vote" or choice of the "Ancestry community." Actually, it's the computer's choice from what many in the Ancestry community have submitted independently.

This obviously is very dangerous if the person browsing the data is led to believe that what they are seeing in the pedigree is the most likely choice just because there are more "votes" for it. In the case just cited, I was able to go in and enter more specific data. But if the anomaly had been less obvious, a casual researcher could have simply assumed that plausible looking data was correct. I repeat what I have said over and over: Never, ever accept what you see on screen until you have corroborated it from primary or secondary sources. Ancestry recognizes this, of course, and your original tree always remains intact while the "community tree" offers suggestions.

As computers and genealogy software become more sophisticated, there will be more efforts to create "best guess" family tree scenarios from available data. There is nothing wrong with the intent, but we should all carefully understand the limitations. The screen is giving us options, not facts. (See also Chapter 17).

should also do this when simply exchanging GEDCOM files with any other person, whether through a major Web site or not. Use the option in your software program when creating the file to designate living people as "living." Obviously you can make an exception if a living person gives you permission to do so.

Should You Include Notes and Sources in Uploads?

There is a difference between notes and sources. When you upload a GEDCOM, include the sources and your research log if you have the option. If the data is circulated, then hopefully the sources and research log will be too, and the net effect will be to increase the quality of data on the Web.

Notes are another matter. You may use notes in a variety of ways, but they probably contain references to living individuals—maybe even candid comments about how helpful or unhelpful a relative might have been. There may be sensitive references to a family myth or legend that you don't mind having in your own notes but would hesitate to share with just anyone on the Internet. Do not include notes and sources if you use them to record sensitive information.

My personal preference is to choose the option to label a living person as "Living," to include source information if the online software allows it, but to remove notes from everyone in the tree. I then make it clear elsewhere in the setup page that I encourage people to email me by adding a page footer that says, "Email for extensive notes and additional sources." In the "Message for Living" box I enter: "Please email for information." My email address is listed at the point of entry to my tree information.

I do this because I want to correspond with people who may be related, even distantly. I like to know who is interested in my lines. If they are interested enough to want my data, they've probably got information on collateral lines that I might be interested in.

TIP: Don't Worry about Sharing Your Email Address

Does publicly sharing your email address prompt unwanted junk mail from other sources? No. You will notice on the RootsWeb screen display for your family information that the email address is displayed graphically. You can't just click on it to create an email. RootsWeb and other sites do this to prevent spiders from finding your email address as they scour the Web. These automated devices can not recognize your email address from the way it's displayed.

If you change your email address, remember to update all the sites where you have posted your interests.

Setting the options in the way I've described encourages serious researchers to contact me and allows for meaningful coordination on both sides.

The only leverage I have to encourage them to contact me is to promise additional information. Serious family historians always respond. Beginners often do not, because they haven't yet learned how crucial sources and notes are.

Allowing Others to Download Your GEDCOMS from the Web

You can also specify whether or not people can download your family tree in a GEDCOM file to their own computer, from the Web where you've posted it, without reference to you. Again, this is a matter of personal preference. As we've seen, some people download what they find on the Internet and accept without question everything that's there, never worrying about the absence of notes and sources. Or they create another GEDCOM without sources and then email the information to various relatives. The number of people who now have that unsourced family tree can grow exponentially. One recent professional estimate put the number of Internet users who are pursuing genealogical information at one in twelve. That means an incalculable number of people could be pushing false information.

So, again, by declining the unrestricted download option I hope to encourage serious researchers who see something of interest to email me at the address I have posted. I can then decide when I receive that email whether I want to send a GEDCOM file, how much of my tree to send, and whether to include all, some, or none of the notes. I would always include sources in such an exchange. The point is that I can retain those options and can make a judgment according to circumstances.

Step 2: Register on Surname Lists, Mailing Lists, and Message Boards

Once you've added your family tree to the major sites so other people know what you're looking for and how to find you, you need to look at the next category of possibilities for sharing on the Internet.

This covers such things as surname lists, mailing lists, and message boards, of which there is a wide variety. Strictly speaking, mailing lists and message boards aren't the same thing. The **message board** is a place you visit to check if messages have been posted, like a bulletin board in an office or workplace. You post a message and leave it there indefinitely, in the hope someone with information will see it. You can easily start your own message board focused on names or places of interest to you. A message board is best suited to specific inquiries on such things as end-of-line research—somewhere you have become stuck and where someone, months or even years from now, might see it when searching on the same name.

Think of a **mailing list,** on the other hand, as a place to have a continuous back-and-forth conversation with a group of people about a specific topic or line of research. Typically, such conversations begin for a while and then shift to another topic that someone else on the list has raised.

Conceptually, since all of them are aimed at sharing information and opening up possibilities for collaboration, we'll deal with all of them in the same section of this chapter. You might try entering your name and contact information on a variety of these lists.

RootsWeb Surname List

RootsWeb's surname list is one of the most productive sites on the Internet for generating the names of people with whom you can share research. Since there are around a million surnames on this list, it's pretty likely yours is there, too. Along with each name are associated dates and locations, so if you see the surname you are researching, together with a locality where you know your ancestor lived and within a similar timeframe, you may be in luck.

You can examine each posting to get the email address of the person who shared it, and then email them directly. One nice thing about the RSL is that contact information is updated annually. If a person fails to respond to a reminder notice from RootsWeb, their information is dropped from the site. This means you don't waste a lot of time emailing people with obsolete addresses.

To quickly learn how to add your own surnames:

1. Log on to RootsWeb at **www.rootsweb.com.**

2. Click the link to **RootsWeb Surname List/RSL,** under the Search Engines and Databases heading.

3. Click **What is the RSL?** Here you'll get a detailed explanation of the RootsWeb Surname List and how to add any surnames to it.

4. Hit your browser's **Back button** to return to the previous menu, then click **Add** or **Edit your surnames** and follow the on-screen instructions. The method for entering names, places and time periods is very precise, but the instructions are clear so read them carefully. If you don't get the format right, the Web site won't accept your names.

Obviously, the more unusual the surnames on your family tree, the easier it will be to find a match if there is one on the list. You can enter 100 surnames at a time, but it's unlikely at this stage you'll have anywhere near that many. Instead, choose the more unusual names for the main lines on your tree and enter them one by one.

If you've followed the instructions carefully, your entry for each surname will look something like that shown below. If you have submitted more than one surname, you can click on your own name tag and see them listed in a table.

Surname	From	To	Migration	Comment	Submitter
Garwood	1790	now	Weybread,SFK,ENG> MDX,ENG>DUR,ENG		Otterson

The surname you have entered will be in the first column on the left, and the beginning and ending periods in which you are interested appear in the next two. The word *now* in the To column means you are searching for descendants down to the present day. The Migration column is where people most commonly make mistakes. Here, you should type in the location for the earliest name from this branch of your family tree. You can enter just a country; or a town, county, and country; but don't enter any spaces between the names. The required abbreviations are precise, and may be selected using the on-screen link. A space is provided for comments when entering your surname data. Your name tag appears automatically in the last column.

Your names will stay on the list for a year, after which time you'll receive an email to verify your contact information. If you respond, your information will be posted for another year. There is no charge to use the RSL.

Other RootsWeb Mailing Lists

If you return once again to the home page of RootsWeb and look under the **Mailing Lists** heading, you'll find a link titled **Index (Browse All Lists).**

Here you can locate other lists on the RootsWeb site, including:

- **Place lists** centered on particular localities. A huge choice of countries is offered. Try clicking on the link to any state or country. Select **Browse the Archives** from the bottom of the screen to get a feel for the kind of email traffic on the site.

- **Lists that consist of correspondence on miscellaneous topics**, often about specific databases or progress on making certain materials available online.

Joining a mailing list on RootsWeb is called **subscribing**—and it's free. After you have added your name and contact information to any of these lists, you will start receiving a separate email every time someone posts something to the list. If you feel you are receiving too many emails, you can subscribe to a **digest version** of the list, which means that several postings made to the list will be consolidated and sent to you as a single large message. Look for the on-screen instructions for these steps, and also for steps to unsubscribe if you decide you no longer want to receive emails. You can browse or search the archives of these mailing lists any time without subscribing.

To create your own list:

1.   Log on to the RootsWeb home page at **www.rootsweb.com.**

2.   Scroll down the screen to the heading titled **Mailing Lists** and click the **Requests for Mailing Lists (new or adopted)** link. The instructions for becoming the administrator for your own list are quite simple.

Feel free to browse the various mailing lists on the RootsWeb site while you are on this topic. One interesting location is a Gen-Newbie list—a list for beginning genealogists only, where you can ask beginner-type questions without feeling like you are the only one that doesn't "get it." RootsWeb and other mailing lists are really quite good for getting the feel of a locality. It's a good idea to watch the email correspondence for a while to get the hang of the protocol and what people are asking before you join in.

GenForum

GenForum is the part of Genealogy.com's Web site that allows people to post their surname and other interests and share information from the general to the specific. The quickest way to the Genealogy.com message boards is to bypass the home page and the commercial offers and go straight to **www.genforum.com.**

Personally, I find the Genealogy.com interface one of the easiest to use. It is clean, simple, and intuitive. It costs nothing to browse the message boards and post messages, even though this is a subscription site.

TIP: What to Post and Not to Post

When posting emails, keep them reasonably short—short enough for someone to read quickly as they are scanning down a list.

When adding your description, title, or topic, include the surname, locality, and time frame if you can get it to fit. It makes browsing a list much easier. No one wants to look through masses of text in dozens of postings to see what they are about.

And don't disclose personal information—yours or anyone else's—in your postings.

It's probably easiest to start by looking at the surnames, so pick the first letter of one of the more unusual surnames in your pedigree. After clicking on the letter, see if the surname is in the list. There's a very good chance, since the lists are extensive.

Click on the surname and see the postings that have been made by people researching that name. If the list of postings is too long, you can shorten it by clicking one of the tabs above the list that will display only the more recent messages. A better way is to specify what you're searching for in the search box under **Search This Forum.** This search engine will find any text string in the forum postings. Post a message on this site to get a feel for how it works.

Ancestry.com

It doesn't cost anything to register with Ancestry.com if you are just posting your name and research interests. Log onto **www.ancestry.com** and click the **Ancestry Community** link in the horizontal menu bar across the top of the screen.

Follow the on-screen instructions to create your own **public profile**. This involves creating a user name (Ancestry suggests you use a name tag rather than your real name), together with your research interests. Begin with just three or four names and localities that are of interest to you. You can add more as you become familiar with the setup and gauge the amount of email traffic generated.

When someone contacts you it will be anonymously, through Ancestry. You can click on their user name to reveal their profile. Depending on how much they decided to enter when they created their own profile, you may learn the locality where they live, their relative experience in family history research, and a list of their research interests. When you are satisfied that the person on the other end of the correspondence is a genuine researcher (almost all of them are), you can exchange private email addresses and GEDCOM files if there is a lot of information to share.

To search and create message boards on Ancestry.com:

1. Click the **Ancestry Community** link from the menu at the top of the site's homepage. This is the same place where you created your public profile.

2. In the Message Boards window you will see a search facility. To get the feel of the Message Board setup, enter one of your more unusual surnames in the **Names or Keywords** box, and leave the **Posted within** dropdown window at **Any time.**

3. Click the **Find** button. You will see on the screen a table of results. A number at the top shows you how many matches your search found. You can browse through as many of these as you want or have time for, looking for anything familiar that might be a connection with your ancestor.

If you have too many results, then narrow your search by typing in a full name rather than just a surname. If

Benefiting from Collaboration

Often, mailing list exchanges make connections and lead to contacts that you could not possibly have found otherwise. Remember Henry Smiles and Sarah Prophet, the couple we followed through the late 1800s and first quarter of the 1900s, several chapters back? It proved fairly easy to find Sarah's mother, Francis (Fanny) Carter in the 1880 census. But I suspended work on that line at that point and turned to other more pressing research.

Just over two years later, when this particular line was furthest from my mind, I received an email from Teresa Bransby. Teresa was descended from Sarah's aunt and had seen my posting on RootsWeb. Teresa's email to me contained a marriage date from a family Bible that I could never have accessed otherwise, plus details of the Carter family descendants through every census from 1850 to 1900. Added to that were cemetery records that Teresa had transcribed from a cemetery book for Carroll County, Mississippi. Everything came complete with source citations and notes.

A descendant of Henry Smiles, unknown to Teresa and living in Alabama, later filled in much of the Smiles family's life experience in the 1900s from stories that had been passed down orally.

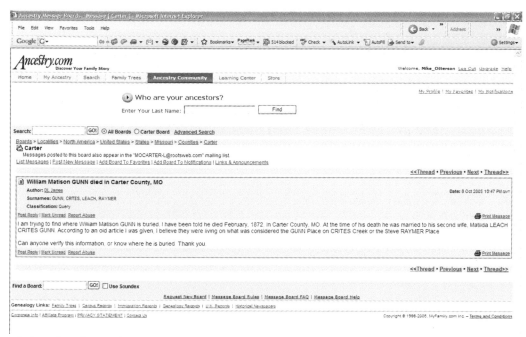

Typical posting of research interests on Ancestry.com. (Image copyright 2005 MyFamily.com, Inc., and reproduced from Ancestry.com. Used by permission.)

the name is a common one, you could enter in a name plus locality. Generally, start with a wide search and narrow it bit by bit, rather than start with a too-narrow search first.

Select Mailing Lists from Cyndi's List

Cyndi's List is the gateway to a huge number of mailing lists from which you can select just the few in which you may be interested.

1. Start on the home page at **www.cyndislist.com**.

2. Type **mailing lists** into the search engine. You can browse from there through mailing lists for many countries, individual localities, surnames, or special interest areas, such as cemetery records or ships' passenger lists.

Examine Your Software Program

Many genealogy software programs contain a menu item that links to collaboration sites or common databases on the Internet. For instance, Family Tree Maker's

Internet menu option links to Genealogy.com's World Family Tree, a subscription resource.

In many cases, these links are to sites we have already discussed.

Ancestral Quest's collaboration feature in their software program is quite sophisticated, and a little different. Their course is to set up a common Web site for different researchers in a group (often from the same family). People can add or edit information to the family tree, but it is password protected and there are sophisticated provisions that guard against dubious material.

TIP: Posting a Good Query

You can increase the likelihood of getting responses to your postings by observance of a few simple rules:

- Be selective about where you post. Don't just copy and paste the same message on dozens of message boards. Make sure you're on the right forum.

- Remember name, date, and location, and be as specific as you can. Leave any of these out, and the value of your posting reduces dramatically. Include name, date, and place in your subject line.

- Don't ramble. Imagine other readers looking over your shoulder. Short and to the point is the rule.

- Whatever you post is public for everyone. Keep that in mind when posting a query. Don't include personal details of anyone living, and be discreet about sensitive information even for the deceased.

- If you are interested in an individual, mention him or her by name, not just the surname of the family.

- Don't ask simple questions like where to find a gazetteer or where your nearest family history center is, when you can find that out easily by yourself online.

- Stick to one subject per posting, or people won't make it to your second one.

For more information about writing good queries, go to **www.cyndislist.com/queries.htm#howto.**

One advantage is that you always have the latest backup on the Internet, so even if your house burns down and your entire computer files are lost, the years of research aren't! The disadvantage is that all contributors have to be using Ancestral Quest.

Guidelines and Protocols

An appropriate way to end this chapter on collaboration is with the official guidelines and standards of the National Genealogical Society of the United States, since they provide an excellent framework for collaboration on the Internet. Find more by logging onto their Web site at **www.ngsgenealogy.org.**

Genealogical Standards and Guidelines: Standards for Sharing Information with Others

Conscious of the fact that sharing information or data with others, whether through speech, documents, or electronic media, is essential to family history research and that it needs continuing support and encouragement, responsible family historians consistently—

- Respect the restrictions on sharing information that arise from the rights of another as an author, originator or compiler; as a living private person; or as a party to a mutual agreement.

- Observe meticulously the legal rights of copyright owners, copying or distributing any part of their works only with their permission, or to the limited extent specifically allowed under the law's "fair use" exceptions.

- Identify the sources for all ideas, information and data from others, and the form in which they were received, recognizing that the unattributed use of another's intellectual work is plagiarism.

- Respect the authorship rights of senders of letters, electronic mail, and data files, forwarding or disseminating them further only with the sender's permission.

continued ➔

Standards for Sharing Information with Others (cont.)

- Inform people who provide information about their families as to the ways it may be used, observing any conditions they impose and respecting any reservations they may express regarding the use of particular items.

- Require some evidence of consent before assuming that living people are agreeable to further sharing of information about themselves.

- Convey personal identifying information about living people—like age, home address, occupation, or activities—only in ways that those concerned have expressly agreed to.

- Recognize that legal rights of privacy may limit the extent to which information from publicly available sources may be further used, disseminated, or published.

- Communicate no information to others that is known to be false, or without making reasonable efforts to determine its truth, particularly information that may be derogatory.

- Are sensitive to the hurt that revelations of criminal, immoral, bizarre, or irresponsible behavior may bring to family members.

10
SHIP PASSENGER LISTS
AND NATURALIZATION

Overview

No other country in the world has been populated by as many immigrants as the United States in so short a time. Other than some 4.5 million Native American Indians, the entire population derives from ancestors who came to the United States as voluntary or involuntary immigrants.

American history is also relatively recent. In 400 years of immigration, only the past 230 years or so was during a period when the United States was an independent nation. The great waves of immigrants did not begin until the latter part of the nineteenth century. That's not much in terms of world history. Consequently, most Americans don't spend very long researching their ancestors before they find themselves looking overseas. Family traditions and stories abound, whether based on documented fact or myth, so many families have a rough idea where to start.

The first indication of where your ancestors came from may well be from family stories or tradition. The first concrete evidence may be from a census record if the immigration was in the past century and a half. But beyond those obvious indicators, what else you can find may depend on what you can dig up from ship passenger lists or naturalization records. In this chapter, we'll discuss where best to look online.

Where Do Americans Come from?

Genealogists often talk about the largest ethnic groups in the United States. Some estimates claim that 70 percent of Americans have roots in the British Isles—that is, Britain and Ireland. But according to the 2000 census, about 36.4 million Americans reported British ancestry and little more than 10 percent of the country claimed Irish.

A German embassy press release from Washington, D.C. exulted after the 2000 census was analyzed that 43 million Americans list German as their primary cultural heritage—more than any other national group if you don't count the British and Irish as one.

The huge migrations from Europe in the 1800s and early 1900s—including Italians, Russians, Poles, Greeks, and just about every other nationality—have long since given way to a massive inflow from Latin America, Africa, the Middle East, and Asia. And, of course, substantial numbers of African-Americans in the United States face a particularly difficult task in tracing their roots. About 15 percent of the country now identifies itself as African-American, and about the same number as Hispanic.

Four immigrants and their belongings, dockside, 1912. (Library of Congress, Selected Images of Ellis Island and Immigration, 1880–1920.)

Which Ship?

Finding the ship on which your ancestor arrived in the United States isn't always easy. But neither is it always a critical step to finding them on the other side of the Atlantic or elsewhere in the world. If you know the national origin of your ancestor from, say, a U.S. census record, then a shipping record from the mid-to-late 1800s may not offer much more than you already know. On the other hand, a single clue from a ship's register can make all the difference between fruitful research in the "old country" or a dead end at the dock side. Apart from all that, there is something indescribably satisfying about knowing exactly when an ancestor arrived in the New World and seeing that name on a ship's passenger list.

For practical purposes, most Americans won't find ancestors on ships' lists before 1820 for the simple reason that they were not usually kept. As the dates become more recent, we begin seeing lists compiled for various government entities, and the detail in such lists also increases with time. For the first half of the twentieth century, the amount of information is considerable.

Immigrants on deck of Atlantic liner S.S. Patricia, 1906. (Library of Congress, Selected Images of Ellis Island and Immigration, 1880–1920.)

If your ancestors arrived between 1907 and the middle of the century, you will find much more than the name of the ship and the date and port of embarkation and disembarkation. You may also find listed the last residence in the home country plus the name and address of the closest living relative there. You might also find a physical description, the precise date of birth (not just the country, but the city or town), and the planned destination in the US and even the name of relatives already in America.

Step 1: Check the Biggest, Easiest Online Lists First

Since the focus of this book is on using the Internet to find information, we'll look first at the online databases that deliver the most names and are most easily accessed. New York was the port of entry for so many immigrants that it's the logical place to start. Many other online records are available for a variety of ports, as we'll see shortly. But it should be understood that a vast number of names of American immigrants are still on microfilms that haven't yet been digitized, so a trip to a library or Family History Center to look at the films may be productive.

To help familiarize ourselves with what's online, let's look at a real example and go through the process step-by-step. This will take only a few minutes and you can then substitute any of the names of your own ancestors with the benefit of knowing what might be possible.

Ellis Island, New York, Database

We left Henry Smiles back in Chapter 6, where we found him in the 1900 U.S. census, a twenty-seven-year-old, recently married and living with his wife, Sarah Prophet, in Florida. The census told us that he was English-born, that his parents were English, and that he immigrated to the United States in 1893. We were not certain of his age, because the censuses of 1900 and 1910 gave us different birth years— 1870 and 1873.

This, however, is plenty to go on. And we're in luck, because the easiest way to check European immigrant passenger lists in this period is the Ellis Island database. Ellis Island was the point of entry in New York for 22 million immigrants to America between 1892 and 1924, and their names have been transcribed by volunteers.

1. Go to **www.ellisisland.org.**

2. To get a feel for how this free site works, type in Henry in the **First Name** box and Smiles in the **Last Name** box.

3. Since we have two conflicting dates for his birth (1870 and 1873), type in 1871 in the **Approximate Year of Birth** box, and select "+ or- 3 yr" from the dropdown menu next to it.

4. Click on **Start Search.**

Only one passenger matches the search, and it looks like a good match, because the middle initial is J, which we already know from the censuses.

We can go further. Click on the name of Henry J. Smiles, and the site presents additional details, including the last place of residence—a vital piece of information. In this case, we see that Henry J. Smiles came from a place called Alnwick in England, and that he was twenty-three years of age, a passenger on the ship Britannic, which sailed from Liverpool.

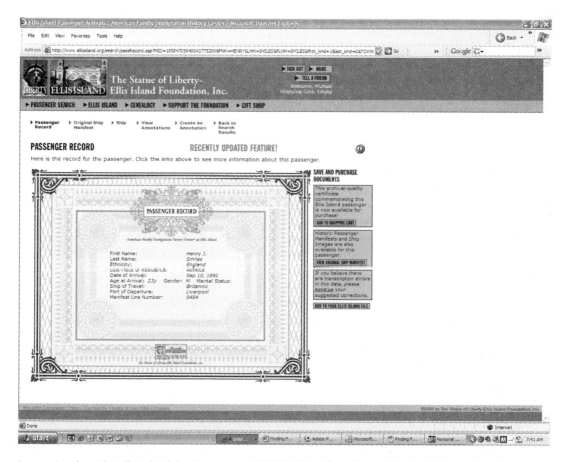

Screen view from the Ellis Island database at www.ellisisland.org. (Used by permission of the Statue of Liberty-Ellis Island Foundation, Inc.)

All of this information has been transcribed from an original document, so what we are looking at is not a primary record. However, hit the back button and this time click on **Ship Manifest.** The result is a digital image of the actual passenger manifest, handwritten and beautifully preserved. We now have a primary record of Henry as a passenger, even though the birth information he gave is not technically primary information. You can even click on **Ship Image** to see what the Britannic looked like. In the manifest view, we also find additional information, including the fact that he intended to travel on to Chicago, and that he carried only one piece of baggage.

Now instead of just a name we have a probable picture of an adventurous twenty-three-year-old single man, setting out alone on his great journey like so many millions of others did, without much to his name but probably with a good deal of optimism and ambition.

I like the Ellis Island database not only because of its obviously immense value, but because of the way in which the site itself is presented. Information like this should be free to everyone. It's a part of our national heritage and we shouldn't have to pay to see it. However, if you would like a framed copy of the ship manifest entry for your ancestor, or a framed picture of the ship, you can pay for it and order it online.

Castle Garden, New York

What if your ancestor arrived at some other time outside the three decades spanned by the Ellis Island online database?

Before Ellis Island became the main U.S. immigration center in 1892, immigrants coming through New York landed at Castle Garden, on what was known from earliest times of Dutch settlement as The Battery. This site is found at **www.castlegarden.org.**

You have free access on this site to another 10 million immigrants from 1830 through 1892, and work is progressing on the transcription of another 2 million back to 1820. More than 70 million Americans can trace their ancestors to this early immigration period, according to the Castle Garden Web site.

While you can't get as much information about individual passengers from this site as from the Ellis Island database, it is still a great asset to online researchers.

The screen image on the next page shows how the data from the Castle Garden site is displayed. This example is a distant relative of mine. The same search shows that Catherine was traveling with her three-year-old son, Edward. Her husband,

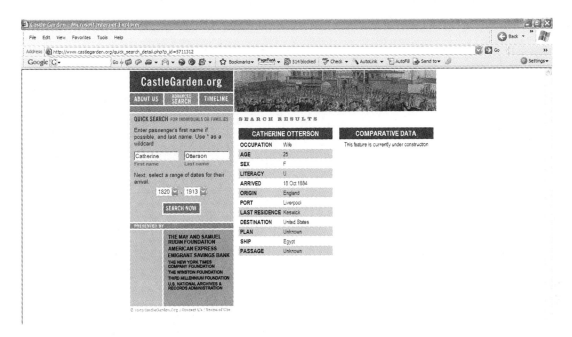

Screen view from the Castle Garden Web site at www.castlegarden.org. (Used by permission.)

however, is not on the same ship. He came two years earlier, possibly through a different port. It was common for the husband to come first, find a job, and a place to settle, and then send for his wife and children.

Of course, we aren't dependent on these two databases, as we'll now see as we widen our search to other time periods and to other ports.

Step 2: Widen Your Search to Other Periods, Ports

There can be no hard-and-fast rules about where to concentrate your search of passenger lists because so much depends on the specific information you already have about your ancestor. If you know the port of entry and the time period, the search will be easier. If not, you may have to work systematically through the databases. Here's what you'll find at each.

Ancestry.com

There is an impressive list of immigration records, including ships' passenger lists at Ancestry.com, but you need deluxe membership to access the details. You can buy U.S. deluxe membership for about $30 per month if you aren't ready for an annual subscription.

From the **www.ancestry.com** home page, click on **US Immigration Collection,** near the bottom of the page. The main options are:

- **New York passenger lists, 1850–1892.** This database is a complete index of passengers arriving mostly between 1850 and 1892—the most important period covered by Castle Garden. The difference between the Ancestry site and Castle Garden site is that on Ancestry you can link from the indexed names to the actual image of the original ship manifest. As an example, the image below is the original record that corresponds with the same data in the screen image from the previous page. This is enlargeable on screen and also rendered in an easy-to-read transcribed version. You can also browse these lists by year, then by month, and then by selecting the ship's name.

- **Passenger and Immigration List Index, 1500s-1900s**. Today's carefully regulated international travel and immigration controls make it hard to imagine how open the U.S. borders were before 1820. Before the mass migrations of the mid-to-late 1800s and early 1900s, the ships were not passenger vessels at all, but primarily trading ships with a handful of passengers taking what extra space was available. Lists of passengers' names were usually not even kept, so the chances of pinpointing an ancestor on a shipping list before 1820 are remote.

The Passenger and Immigration Lists database is not a passenger list at all in the usual sense, but a valuable compilation from a vast number of other sources of some 4.5 million names of people who arrived in U.S. and Canadian ports from the 1500s through the 1900s. Usually, each name is accompanied by the year of arrival or the year when the person's name first appeared in the public record (such as a census record), the port of entry, and the person's age. The source document for the

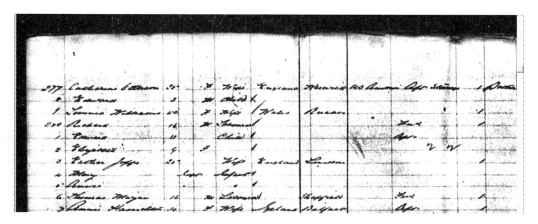

Image copyright 2005 MyFamily.com, Inc., and reproduced from Ancestry.com. Used by permission.

TIP: Port of Departure May Not Be What It Seems

When looking at the port of departure on passenger lists, remember that this is not necessarily an indication of the passenger's country of origin. For instance, ships leaving Liverpool, England, often stopped at Queenstown, Ireland, to pick up extra passengers for America. Many ships from Europe stopped at multiple ports before the trans-Atlantic voyage. The port of departure on the passenger list may be the last port the ship left before reaching the U.S., or it might have been the first port in the journey.

Similarly, if the last residence is listed, treat it cautiously. Passengers might have stayed with relatives near the port of departure for a time before leaving. The last residence is a clue, not a definite evidence of a long-term stay.

information is cited, along with a description of the source so you can find it. This database is being updated every year with substantial numbers of immigrants.

- **New York, 1820–1850 Passenger and Immigration Lists.** These lists span a thirty-year period and contain more than 1.5 million names. The lists result from Congressional action to reduce overcrowding of passenger ships by requiring ship captains to keep a list and present it to customs officers on arrival in port. The transcriptions are taken from National Archives microfilms.

- **New Orleans, 1820–1850 Passenger and Immigration Lists.** This is the equivalent list for New Orleans, containing 273,000 names of individuals who entered the U.S. through this southern gateway.

- **Other ports.** A list of miscellaneous passenger lists, ship arrivals, and immigrant records of various kinds and from various ports and time periods is included in Ancestry's offerings.

GeneSearch

Joe Beine is a professional genealogist living in Denver, Colorado. His Web site at **www.genesearch.com** lists a huge amount of helpful information about available online passenger lists in the United States, including periods later than we have already covered. The site lists just about every port in the United States that has published its passenger arrival lists—including the crossings at the land borders of Canada and Mexico. To access the arrival lists:

1. Go to the **www.genesearch.com** home page.

2. Scroll down to the bottom of the screen, to the **Passenger Lists and Immigration Records** heading.

3. Click **US Ports of Arrival & Their Available Immigration Records 1820–1957.**

4. There are two links near the top of this page: **Finding Passenger Lists 1820–1940s (arrivals at US Ports)** and **Finding Passenger Lists Before 1820.** I recommend that you click on both of these links and read whatever corresponds to your area of interest. The information is extensive. Be aware that some of the material described consists of indexes of names on microfilm, while other links take you to actual passenger lists, including some digital images of original manifests.

In the indexes, you will find reference numbers to thousands of microfilms. The NARA numbers refer to the National Archives. The FHL number belongs to the Family History Library in Salt Lake City, Utah. If you can't find the actual names you are searching for online, you can use these numbers to order a film sent to the Family History Center nearest to where you live, for no more than the cost of shipping the film (see Chapter 6, page 56).

Progenealogists.com

Many other Web sites offer lists of passengers and naturalizations, and it's worth working through them. A good list of immigration Web sites is located at **www.progenealogists.com/genealogysleuthb.htm** under Naturalization and Passenger Lists.

Stephen Morse

Check also the Stephen Morse tools for improving searches of immigrant records. Morse has done a great deal to make it easier to track immigrant ancestors. For instance, you can click multiple country boxes to pull up only those names from certain countries—useful if you have anything other than a rare name and want to browse the database. His set of tools is available for free at **www.stevemorse.org.** His site also has links and guides to more immigration resources, and there are additional tools other than improved search engines. Take a look at this site, and then bookmark it.

Cyndi's List

This is a particularly useful site for finding immigrant lists for specific countries, and not just for immigrants into the United States. Immigrant records from Britain to Australia, for instance, as well as many other migrations, are found here. In the home page search engine on **www.cyndislist.com,** type in "passenger lists" and then scan the resulting lists for those areas in which you are interested. As usual, this site will launch you into a huge number of possibilities.

FamilySearch.org

FamilySearch.org does not have online ship passenger lists, but its collection of microfilms on the topic is formidable. The films are accessible (unless you live in a remote area), through one of the thousands of Family History Centers. If finding your ancestor on a ship's passenger list becomes a key step for you in your quest to build your family tree, and you can't find the name online, then a visit to a Family History Center is recommended.

It's easy to see which immigration records have been microfilmed:

1. Log on to the Family History Library Catalog online at **www.familysearch.org.**

2. Click the **Library** tab at the top of the home page.

3. Select **Family History Library Catalog.**

4. Click **Place Search.**

5. Type in the name of the port that interests you—for instance, Boston, and select the port city from the next screen.

6. This will bring up an extensive category list of genealogical resources. Select the link that includes **Emigration and Immigration** in its name. Sometimes there will also be a link to **Emigration and Immigration— Indexes.** You will now be able to see the library's collection of immigration resources specific to the locality in which you are interested. One problem you'll face, however, is that most of the films are arranged by date of ship arrival, not by the names of passengers. Until these films are digitized and indexed, it can take a lot of time to search for your ancestors that way.

7. Once you are viewing the screen information for a specific title—for instance, "Passenger lists of vessels arriving at Boston, 1820–1891; with index, 1848–1891, 1820–1891"—the key to finding the number of the microfilm you want to view at a Family History Center is in the button at the top right of

the screen that says **View Film Notes.** Clicking on that button displays information about the specific roll of microfilm, including the film number that you will need to place your order.

The system works well for most ports, but the lists for some, such as Boston or New York, can run to many pages. At the foot of each such long list is another button, **Next Film Notes,** which will take you through the pages. Be aware that the New York lists run to 7,000 rolls of microfilm!

If I were looking for an Otterson immigrant ancestor who came through the port of Boston, I would click through the screens until I came to the one shown on page 133. The indexes show that Part 208 would cover those surnames, so I would order film number 205863 for delivery to the Family History Center nearest to me.

To be candid, such searches are not always this easy. Not all titles have film notes, and the lists—as in any large library—can be confusing if you are not used to them. Browsing and clicking on possible leads is time consuming, but is sometimes the best way to become familiar with a site that you think you will revisit.

Genealogy.com

If you are interested in a subscription to Genealogy.com, the site has the following indexed databases for immigrant passengers. You can access them for a monthly subscription of about $15. If you are confident that one of your ancestors falls within these time periods and places, that could be a relatively inexpensive way of finding key information. As always, however, there are no guarantees.

- Baltimore, 1820–1952
- Boston 1848–91, 1902–20
- New Orleans 1853–1952
- New York City, 1820–46, 1897–1943
- Philadelphia 1800–1948
- Minor ports, 1820–74 and 1890–1924

RootsWeb

Log on to **http://lists.rootsweb.com/index/other/Immigration** to see the immigration lists on RootsWeb. You do not have to subscribe to a mailing list to search the archives for any correspondence that might be of interest to you. Type

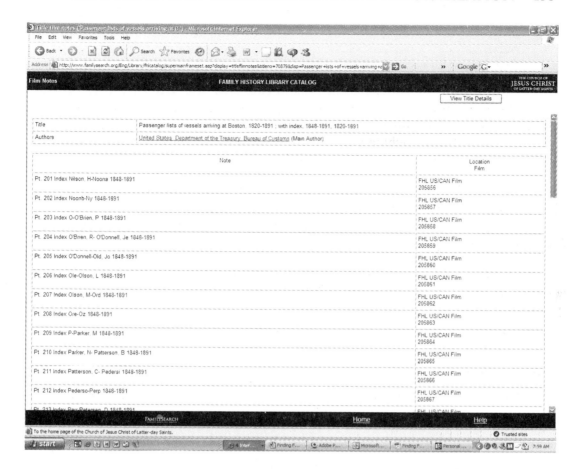

Library Catalog on FamilySearch.org–sample of immigrant passenger lists. (FamilySearch.org, image copyright 1999, 2005 by Intellectual Reserve, Inc. Used by permission.)

in the name of your ancestor to see if anyone in the archives has previously addressed the topic.

If not, you can subscribe for free and throw out a question for discussion. There are many people only too willing to offer guidance if you have hit a brick wall.

The page referred to here also covers other records, such as Australian and South African immigration.

See also the earlier reference to Message Boards, on page 111.

Immigrant Ships Transcribers Guild

One site that is worth a visit is produced by several hundred volunteers who belong to the Immigrant Ships Transcribers Guild. The Guild's purpose is to transcribe immigrant ship passenger lists, and its members do so at their own expense and in their own time to provide the data free on the Internet.

Log on at **http://immigrantships.net** and click the **Passenger Lists** link at the top of the screen.

The site is extremely easy to use, and is equipped with a site-wide search engine. You can browse literally thousands of ships' lists for specific voyages or use the search engine for a global search. The data covers a variety of immigrant routes—not just Europe to North America.

Another link on the home page is labeled **Compass,** and it is an excellent signpost system to other valuable immigrant information.

Step 3: Search for Naturalization Records

Naturalization records are the documents that were created when an immigrant applied for naturalization or citizenship in his new country of residence. Depending on the time period, these records can provide much more than a ship's passenger list, including names of family members and key dates and places.

Naturalization in the United States was not a single-step process. Among the online lists you will examine will be declarations of intent, which were normally filed with a local courthouse. Because the naturalization process required residency qualifications, as well as the lodging of a petition and the granting of a certificate, the process took several years. Before the 1900s, citizenship was automatic in some cases—for instance, the minor children of a new citizen, or a woman who married a U.S. citizen were automatically granted citizenship.

The key date and event for U.S. researchers is the passage of the Basic Naturalization Act of 1906, which standardized the previously haphazard method of gathering information and greatly added to the amount of information now available to researchers.

Where to Start

A good starting point for naturalization records in the United States is the GeneSearch site we already examined for passenger lists. The quickest way to the

Naturalization Certificate Index
Oneida County, Idaho
1907 - 1929

Naturalization Records

Name	Age	Vol.	Page	Certificate #	Date of Order
Abter, Joseph	43	1	45	407963	3-Mar-1914
Abter, Julius	34	1	1	18241	17-Jun-1907
Ashworth, James	55			733958	15-Oct-1917
Beard, Herbert Charles	36	1	3	18243	29-Jun-1908
Buist, William	33	4	3	407967	18-May-1915
Burkhird, Frederick	64	1	14	107202	9-May-1910
Carlson, Nels Christian	38	1	6	18246	3-May-1909
Cock, George	72			407953	10-Nov-1913
Dahten, Anton Carl	33			107206	16-May-1911
Denneber, Johmies Andres	53			407960	10-Nov-1913
Dursteler, Rudolph	45	1	2	18242	6-Nov-1907
Evans, Philip John	30	1	20	107207	3-Oct-1911
Faveri, Fred	33	1	18	107204	
Feller, Felix	25			733953	9-Nov-1916
Fry, Arthur John	27			733961	20-Oct-1919
Fry, James	51			733959	15-Oct-1917
Fry, Joseph Henry	25			733960	15-Apr-1918
Fry, William James	25	4	20	407970	22-Oct-1915
Funk, George	48			733966	10-Sep-1923
Garker, Philly	34			733963	9-Feb-1921
Gibson, William	39			257011	11-Nov-1912
Gunther, William Richard Albert	38			407954	

Typical naturalization index—one of many online. This one was transcribed as part of the USGenWeb project. Indexes allow you to search online, and then order a copy of the original document. (Image copyright 2006 Oneida County Idaho GenWeb Project. Used by permission.)

right Web page is to Google "naturalization records indexes," which will offer you this link at or near the top of the search results:

http://home.att.net/~wee-monster/naturalization.html

The page is a list of online and searchable naturalization indexes and records. Again, don't expect to find a neatly catalogued federal system of immigration records. The list will point you to a wide variety of links that are mostly to county records and to a few state archives. In some cases you will find all there is to find online, while in others the index will allow you to send to the archive for the original record.

Another quick way to locate naturalization records if you know the location is to type "naturalization" and the name of the state or county into Google or another search engine.

By now you will have become accustomed to the fact that the family historian is heavily dependent on the efforts of volunteers who have transcribed most of this data. Sometimes the original documents from which these transcripts are made are virtually undecipherable. It's not just a matter of the handwriting, which can be difficult enough. Variants of foreign names, spelling or interpretation of names, or damage to the original documents are all factors. It's well to remember that the absence of a name of your ancestor doesn't mean he or she is not in the record. Try every conceivable spelling or variation of the name before you conclude that it wasn't recorded.

The National Archives

The National Archives Web site at **www.archives.gov** has a search box at the top of the home page. Type in "naturalization" for an extensive list of resources, including several online name indexes.

The National Archives collection of online naturalization indexes is limited. A better reason for going to this government site is to understand more clearly how immigration and naturalization law has undergone many changes in the United States. Be prepared to do some reading if you have hit a barrier and need to understand more about naturalization.

Typing in "women naturalization" into the same home page search box presents you with a list of related topics. Browse down the list until you see "Prologue: Selected Articles." The two parts of an online article by Marian L. Smith are listed separately. They provide a detailed explanation of the challenges that women faced in gaining U.S. citizenship that will give you some grounding in this challenging but rewarding subject.

TIP: Understanding Soundex

If you've come this far and have been looking at a variety of genealogical Web sites, it's likely that you've come across the word *Soundex*.

As we have seen, the spelling of names can vary enormously, especially when we consider irregular spellings of a century ago and the Anglicizing of many non-English surnames to adapt to the American culture. The name *Sinclair*, for example, appears in my tree as *Sinkler*.

What was needed to overcome the confusion of multiple spellings was a phonetic system, and such a system was patented in 1918 by Margaret O'Dell and Robert C. Russell. It was called SoundEx. Over the years, there have been several improvements to the system, and the U.S. government applied one such improvement for U.S. census analysis which was called American Soundex. Even that system has been finessed, however. For example, see the Daitch-Mokotov Soundex System designed to accommodate Jewish names with German or Slavic origin, explained at **www.avotaynu.com/soundex.html.**

Soundex reduces names to an alphanumeric code consisting of a letter and three numbers. For most online work, it's not necessary to understand how the Soundex system works any more than you need to understand a car engine in order to drive a vehicle—just as long as you know what it's for. There are a few situations, however, when knowing how the code is compiled and applied is helpful or even essential. Fortunately, there are online tools that make the process simple.

For those interested in how the code is applied to names of people and places, one of the simplest explanations is in the Wikipedia online encyclopedia at **http://en.wikipedia.org/wiki/soundex.** Using the instructions on the page, you can easily work out the four-digit code that is the Soundex equivalent to any name.

Even more easily, the RootsWeb site has a Soundex converter at **http://resources.rootsweb.com/cgi-bin/soundexconverter.** Just enter the surname and it will deliver the code. So my Sinkler and Sinclair both appear as S524.

continued ➜

Understanding Soundex (cont.)

The system has limitations and anomalies. It is really designed to save having to search separately for similar names like Peterson, Petersen, Pederson, Pedersen, etc. Because it isn't foolproof, efforts are continuing to refine it. But understanding this root of phonetic searches on the Internet is useful when search engines don't always present the results you hope for.

11
ENGLAND AND WALES

Overview

Nowhere has the Internet made genealogical research easier than in Britain—specifically England, Wales, and Scotland. We'll treat Ireland as a special case, along with Scotland, in the next chapter. A multiplicity of Web sites has sprung up that has made researching British records from home a very attainable task.

For all practical purposes, English and Welsh research can be treated as if dealing with one country. The British government introduced a nationwide system of civil registration for England and Wales in 1837, taking over a job that had been performed by parish churches since the 1500s. The first census of genealogical value in England and Wales was undertaken in 1841 and continued every ten years after that.

Scotland's civil registration began soon after England's, in 1855. Scottish records need to be viewed as those of a different country, which they are.

The United Kingdom: What It Means

Americans sometimes have difficulty in grasping the nuances of the British governmental system. For clarity, consider the following:

- **British Isles.** This is a term used for England, Wales, Scotland, all of Ireland and the associated smaller islands, such as the Isle of Man and the Channel Islands. This is a geographical rather than political designation.

- **Britain:** This term is not interchangeable with "England" unless you want to offend the Scots, Welsh, and Northern Irish. Use "Britain" when you want to describe the whole of the political union of countries known as the United Kingdom of Great Britain and Northern Ireland. Whenever you refer to England, you should mean England only, and not all of Britain. The easiest way to think of it is that the individual countries of the United Kingdom are roughly equivalent to the states of the United States. Scotland in particular has its own parliament with significant designated powers, but the Parliament at Westminster in London enacts laws for the whole union just as the Legislature does from Washington, D.C.

- **Ireland** was one country until partitioned by the Government of Ireland Act in 1920. The six northern counties of Northern Ireland are now a constituent part of the UK and its citizens are British. The southern counties, comprising most of Ireland, form a nation quite separate from Britain or Northern Ireland. It is a self-governing republic. When people use the term "Ireland" they most usually mean the Irish Republic or Eire, which is predominantly Catholic. The term "Northern Ireland" is reserved for the mostly Protestant six counties of the north, or more specifically, the north-east.

- **Britain and Europe.** Britain, of course, is a part of Europe, but the physical separateness of that small group of islands from the large land mass of Continental Europe often leads to references to "Britain and Europe," as if they were distinct. The distinctions were acute in the days of the British Empire, when Britain's rivals for world power were just across the English Channel. An old joke in Britain refers to an English newspaper headline that allegedly read, "Fog in Channel: Europe Cut Off."

If the distinctions seem confusing or even arbitrary, consider the fierce independence of Canadians and their resistance to the inclusive term *Americans*. And think of how vigorously American citizens defend their identity as Texans, New Yorkers, Georgians, or Californians.

Why is this relevant? Because you need to understand exactly what you are looking at when you are on various Web sites that use these terms. If you are paying for access to an English census and expect to find Scottish addresses, you'll be disappointed.

Step 1: Search the Census Records—England and Wales

Several sets of census records are readily available online for England and Wales. The 1881 census is accessible free of charge, and most of the others between 1841 and 1901 can be viewed on a number of inexpensive pay-per-view sites. Ancestry.com's subscription site has all the England and Wales censuses for these years accessible in one place.

To demonstrate how they work, let's return to our old friend Henry John Smiles. In former chapters, we have touched on the family and descendants of this English immigrant in places as far apart as Mississippi, Florida, Alabama, and New York. In Chapter 10, we also found him on the ship *Britannic,* arriving at Ellis Island in New

York in 1893. Since the ship passenger list gave his age as twenty-three and his place of origin as Alnwick, we have a place to start.

Before logging on to our first census site, we need to find where Alnwick is.

Use the Genuki Gazetteer

1. Log on to **www.genuki.org.uk/big/Gazetteer/.** This is one case where the URL is case-sensitive—you'll need to type the capital G to get the correct site.

2. Type the name **Alnwick** into the **Place Name** box.

3. Click **Search.** The search comes up with four Alnwick names, all close to each other and all in the county of Northumberland, in the north of England.

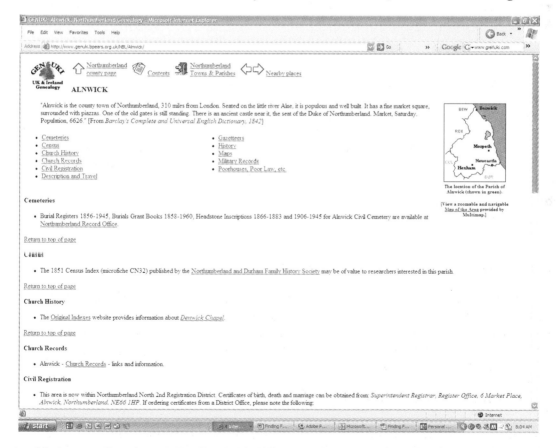

Genuki's Gazetteer shows not only details and a map of a location, but provides possible links of use to researchers. (Used by permission of the Trustees of Genuki. Home page: www.genuki.org.uk.)

4. Click the top choice on the list—the town of Alnwick. That leads us to a promising looking page with a number of possible links. At the top is this description of the little town written in 1842: "Alnwick is the county town of Northumberland, 310 miles from London. Seated on the little river Alne, it is populous and well built. It has a fine market square, surrounded with piazzas. One of the old gates is still standing. There is an ancient castle near it, the seat of the Duke of Northumberland. Market, Saturday. Population, 6626." [From *Barclay's Complete and Universal English Dictionary, 1842*.]

Place names in the Genuki Gazetteer provide a description of the place, often with accompanying links to sources of records if available. For this particular little town, there is a lot of information available, including the interesting fact that the local castle was used in the filming of the Harry Potter movies.

Ordnance Survey Maps

For really detailed, more sophisticated searches, the famous **Ordnance Survey maps** are available free online in as much detail you will need. Since the site delivers the precise location of a quarter of a million British place names, you can more easily identify the smaller places that family traditions often cite.

1. Rather than start at the home page, go to the user-friendly page at **www.ordnancesurvey.co.uk/oswebsite/freefun/didyouknow/.**

2. Enter a location in the **Start your search here** box.

3. When you see a table listing the matches with the place name you entered, click on the icon in the **All maps covering this area** column. This provides you with a number of different map types, so you see everything from topography to old maps from the historical archives.

Using the 1881 census

Now that we know where Alnwick is, follow these steps to search the 1881 British Census:

1. Log on to **www.familysearch.org.**

2. Click the **Search** tab at the top of the page.

3. From the menu at the left, click **Census.**

4. From the dropdown menu select **1881 British Census.** Because we know Henry was born between 1870 and 1873, according to U.S. census and Ellis Island records, we should be able to find him as a child of around ten years on the British census.

5. Enter the details that we know: "Henry" for the first name; "Smiles" for the last name; "England" for the country of birth; and "Northumberland" as the county. We should put the birth year as "1871" and then opt for a plus-or-minus five years search, to be safe.

6. Click the **Search** button.

Only one name is shown in the results, and it's a Henry Smiles, with the middle initial J.—and he was born in Alnwick in 1870. While this is not conclusive, it is a highly likely match. Alnwick is a small place, and Smiles isn't a common name.

To increase our confidence that we have found the right person, we can see how common the name was. Try another search, this time specifying all counties in England and not just Northumberland, and let's do a twenty-year span of birth years—ten either side of 1870.

This time we come up with five Henry Smiles names. One was born in London, which can be immediately discounted. Two were born in the neighboring county of Durham but are fully ten years earlier than 1870. Only one other was born in Northumberland County, but in 1878. That would have made him only fifteen years old if he was the same man that arrived in New York in 1893. Anyway, only one of the five Henry's was born in Alnwick. It looks like we have found our man. We have also learned that Smiles is a name that seems to be concentrated in northeast England.

We can now click on our Henry's name and then on **Household** to see his whole family, including his parents and two brothers. If we needed any additional evidence that we have found the right person, we can also see now that Henry named his first daughter in America after his mother, Eleanor. It seems Henry came from a fairly prosperous tailor's family, because we can see that his father employed four men, one woman and two boys in the drapery (tailor's) business at Bondgate Street, Alnwick. Whatever reason Henry had for leaving for America, it wasn't because his family was living in poverty.

The 1901 Census for England and Wales

By 1901, Henry Smiles was already living in America. But we can see what became of those he left behind, twenty years on. The 1901 census became available in 2001—the British government waits 100 years for privacy reasons, rather than the 72 in the United States. We'll have to move to another Web site to view it.

There are advantages and disadvantages of the 1901 census compared with that of 1881. For the 1901 census, the quality control of the transcriptions was not as high, and mistakes are quite common. On the other hand, as long as you can find the record you're looking for from the transcriptions, the original page images are viewable for 1901. This is not the case with the earlier census if you access it free on www.familysearch.org.

Log on to **www.1901census.nationalarchives.gov.uk.** One nice thing about this site is that you can do searches without charge, and the results of the searches are specific enough to give you a good idea of whether you have found the right person before you pay to see the details. You can pay by credit card online, and the cost is very reasonable.

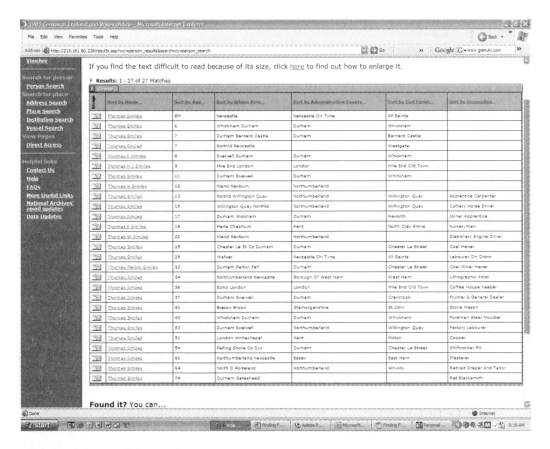

Original census data for Thomas Smiles and family. (Crown copyright, reproduced by permission of the National Archives, www.nationalarchives.co.uk.)

According to the census of 1881, when Henry Smiles was only eleven years old, the father in the home in Alnwick was Thomas Smiles, a draper or tailor, age forty-four, who was born in Dinnington in the same county. If Thomas was still alive twenty years later, we should find him on the 1901 census records, probably in the same locality where he had his business.

From the home page of the 1901 census, type "Thomas Smiles" in the search engine. A table of Thomas Smiles results is displayed (see this image on page 144). Just above the box, alongside "Results," is an indication of twenty-seven hits or matches. Looking carefully at the table, we can see that they are listed by age, starting at the youngest.

Click the **Next** button underneath the table until the names displayed correspond with a Thomas in his mid sixties. We find him on the third and last table, and the match is unmistakable. Thomas is sixty-four, a retired draper and tailor, and the civil parish of the census is the familiar Alnwick. Thomas's birthplace is listed as "North D Porteland."

Clicking on either the name of Thomas Smiles in red or the census page icon to the left of it will take you into a screen that allows you to buy a "session" for five pounds, or between $8 and $9 in U.S. currency. Unless you know you have a lot of searching to do, I recommend you buy the minimum session for five pounds, which credit has to be used up within seven days. You can always buy additional sessions if you spend your credit. Each census view of the original document—which is what you will want to see rather than the transcript—costs 75 pence (between $1.20 and $1.40).

Since I don't expect you to pay 75 pence to see the next stage, let me show you on the next page what you would have seen if you had done so.

There is some interesting information here. Thomas has retired, as might be expected. We can now see from the original record that his birthplace was in the county of Northumberland, town of Ponteland. The transcriber had rendered the Northumberland abbreviation "North^d" as "North D" and Ponteland as "Porteland." Transcription errors are inevitable when transcribing century-old documents, but the careless transcriptions on this site are often evident, and can be attributed partly to poor quality control in the transcription process. Good transcription practices require two independent transcribers to come up with the same rendering, and an experienced arbitrator to adjudicate any differences. This error was not crucial, but poorly transcribed names can prevent them from being found on the indexes altogether.

Crown copyright, reproduced by permission of the National Archives, www.nationalarchives.co.uk.

What else do we learn from this census? Of the three sons who were listed in 1881, only Charles is living at home. We know Henry emigrated to America, and we'll have to look elsewhere for the oldest brother, Ralph. At only thirty years old, Charles is already a widower, and there are no young children listed. We can sense a sad episode here, which we may be able to discover with more digging.

Charles is also listed as an employer in his occupation of tailor, and has clearly taken over the family business. Further down on this same census page (not shown in our partial-page view), we can see two other men whose occupations are tailors, and one draper's errand boy. Since they are described as "workers" and not "employers" it's possible they were working for the Smiles' family business. Such clues in old documents provide the "flesh on the bones" and begin to give us a sense of what life was like for our ancestor families. We might also notice that living on the same street as the Smiles and their tailor's business is a family whose father is described as a "rabbit catcher." This was rural England in 1901.

Other England and Wales Census Records Online

Ancestry.com. It's possible to view every England and Wales census from 1841 through 1901 online at Ancestry.com. If you have substantial British ancestry to research—dozens of even hundreds of census page views—you might consider at least a trial or short-term membership so you can access everything quickly and conveniently in one place. Unlike the U.S. censuses, the UK censuses are not on the public library Web sites or accessible online from a single Web address. However, in weighing that decision, remember that you can now get online access to all or part of every England and Wales census from 1841 to 1901 through the sites described in this chapter for minimal cost. The few counties that have not been completed for some census years will be online very shortly—probably before this book goes to print.

BritishOrigins.com. British Origins is another subscription service. It offers short-term access to its databases, including a 72-hour package for less than $14. The downside is that while census information is available for 1841 and 1871, the census coverage is far from complete. However, if the county in which you are interested is listed, this may be an option. Log on to **www.britishorigins.com** to see a complete listing of their databases including census counties and periods covered. They are being improved all the time.

FreeCEN. As we'll see shortly when we take a look at UK vital records online, there is a volunteer network in Britain that is rewriting the old methods of genealogical data research. Back in 1999, a project called FreeBMD—short for Free Births, Marriages, and Deaths—was launched on the Internet by a group of not much more than 100 volunteers. The project's aim was to make primary or near-primary indexes of vital records on the Web, and to do it without charging researchers.

The project was enormously successful and has expanded dramatically. FreeBMD was soon followed by FreeCEN, for census records, and FreeREG for parish registers that date back for centuries. Together they form the FreeGEN family of projects.

By far the most advanced is FreeBMD, but FreeCEN is rapidly transcribing census records, and some 6 million entries had been completed by the end of 2005. Since the information is free, you should certainly check FreeCEN's data for your ancestors. Its completeness will accelerate rapidly so it's also worth checking back every couple of months. The good news is not only that the project covers 1841, 1851, 1861, 1871, and 1891 censuses, but that Scottish counties are also included. Some Scottish counties are already 100 percent complete for some censuses.

You can access the FreeCEN site at **www.freecen.org.uk.**

Census-online.com. This site was examined in Chapter 7 when we looked at U.S. censuses. Its UK equivalent pages are just as easy to use. Log on to **www. census-online.com/links/England/** to see a county map of England as well as an alphabetical list. Click on the county in the list to see all the census databases online. These usually consist of censuses of workhouses or specific parishes. A few links are to subscription sites. It's worth checking here if you know the locality where your ancestor lived. It will be like looking for a needle in a haystack otherwise, and a national search on one of the subscription sites mentioned earlier in this chapter will be your best option.

1837online.com. This is a commercial service that we'll examine later in the chapter, because its greatest value is vital records. But it does have the 1861 and 1891 censuses of England and Wales and it's inexpensive to use because it's based on a pay-per-view model. See page 154 for more detail about the site.

Filling in the Census Picture

Before we start looking at vital records, and for the sake of efficiency, let's take it as a fact that we have now searched all the other census records between 1841 and 1901 to fill in our picture of the Smiles family, especially Henry's parents, Thomas and Eleanor.

What can we now deduce of the environment in which the Smiles family lived and worked in the closing years of the 1700s? Everything in the outline below was learned from online research, mostly from census records, ship passenger lists, gazetteers, and logical deduction. Sketching this picture now will provide additional context as we approach Step 2—our vital record search.

In the late 1700s, long before the Industrial Revolution boosted its population and transformed it, the village of Ryton nestled into the side of a richly wooded bank that rose steeply from the River Tyne, dividing the counties of Durham and Northumberland. In 1796, a baby boy was born into this picturesque rural setting. His parents named their new son John Smiles.

When he was 24, John married a Ryton girl, Mary Wilson. She was just 19. With the industrialization of England gathering strength, there was work to be had in the mines. Two pit villages or collieries, entirely populated by miners, were within two miles of Ryton. Working at a colliery brought housing and free coal—not a small consideration in that period. But it was a hard and sometimes dangerous life, and for whatever reason—work or some other factor—John and Mary turned their backs on that option and moved immediately north, across the county boundary into Northumberland. They settled in the farming community of Dinnington, population just a little more than 600. A year later, they added one more citizen to Dinnington—a baby boy, William.

John and Mary would eventually have a large family—six sons and two girls. The first four sons would all work on farms as agricultural laborers or husbandmen. The youngest, Stephen, would earn a living as a blacksmith.

Thomas, born in the economically troubled year of 1835, was the exception. He left home to become an apprentice tailor, later moving north to Alnwick, the county seat. There, he eventually established his own prosperous clothing business, married and had three sons of his own.

Of these three sons—Ralph, Henry, and Charles—the younger son, Charles, would take over the family tailoring business. There would be tragedy in Charles' life, however. His wife would not survive the second year of marriage. The eldest brother, Ralph, would eventually enter the mines, and marry late in life. Henry, with experience as a law clerk behind him, would choose to emigrate to America, boarding the ship Britannic *with a single bag and a head full of dreams.*

Such pictures can be pieced together from the scraps of information gleaned from a century or more of records. They always mean far more to the descendants than to non-relatives, of course. The picture of the Smiles family means a good deal to me because the baby born at Ryton in 1796 was my third great grandfather.

We're now about to see how the powerful combination of census data and online vital record indexes, together with accessible databases like the IGI, can fill in additional details and push back your research over generations very quickly.

Step 2: Search for Vital Records (England and Wales)

Those familiar with laboriously hunting from county to county for ancestors in the United States will think they've died and gone to heaven when they start looking for British vital records. For a start, there is an entire national index for England and Wales from the start of civil registration in 1837, right up to current years. Much of it is available online, and without cost or for very nominal fees. (You may encounter some problems with missing names up until 1875, when registration became compulsory and a fine was imposed for non-compliance).

In addition, many other vital record sources exist, including some at county level, and more are coming online all the time.

To work through this systematically and simply, let's make a list of some of the things we'd like to find out about the Smiles family. Again, even though this is not your own family we are researching I recommend following this process closely and clicking on the links indicated, since familiarity will help considerably when substituting your own ancestors' names. We'll now use online vital records to tackle the following questions:

- Charles, Henry's younger brother, is shown as a widower on the 1901 census, and no children are at home. Ten years earlier, the census shows him as then unmarried. Can we find out who Charles married and what happened to her?

- Can we find out if Henry's older brother, Ralph, had any children after he was married at age thirty-five?

- Can we learn more of the three sons' mother—Thomas's wife—including her maiden name?

- Can we get an exact birth date for Henry to clear up the three-year discrepancy on the U.S. censuses?

FreeBMD

Let's tackle the Charles Smiles problem first.

1. Log on to **http://freebmd.rootsweb.com.**

2. Scroll down until you see the horizontal row of red links, and click **Search.**

3. The search engine in FreeBMD is quite sophisticated, but easy to use. Click the following in the menu boxes: **Marriages, All Districts,** and **All Counties.**

4. Enter "Smiles" and "Charles" in the **Surname** and **First name** fields.

5. In the **Date range** field use the dropdown menus to enter "March 1891 to Mar 1901." This will generate a ten-year search for any marriage of a Charles Smiles anywhere in England and Wales. We could easily narrow the search by specifying the registration district (in this case, Alnwick is such a district), but it's safer to cast a wider net in case there are other possible matches.

6. Your screen should now look like the image on page 151. Click the **Find** button at the lower left of the screen and wait for the search engine to do its job.

It's clear immediately that we have a match. We already know that Charles' initial was W, and the place of the marriage was at Alnwick. We have now just learned that the "W" stands for Wilson, which was the maiden name of Charles' grandmother Mary. Remember that we searched all of England for this name, so we can be very confident that this marriage in March of 1898 is the right one. (Actually, "Mar" refers to the March quarter of January through March, just as "Jun," "Sep" and "Dec" refer to three-month periods ending in the named month. This is a universally used convention in British civil registration so you will encounter it time and again).

There is also an important code alongside the indexed entry: 10b 579. This is crucial information, and we will see shortly what it means and how it is used to order a marriage certificate.

But we are not finished yet with the results screen. Alongside the code is an icon of a pair of spectacles. Clicking on this link will take you to a view of the original index so you can check that the transcriber didn't make an error.

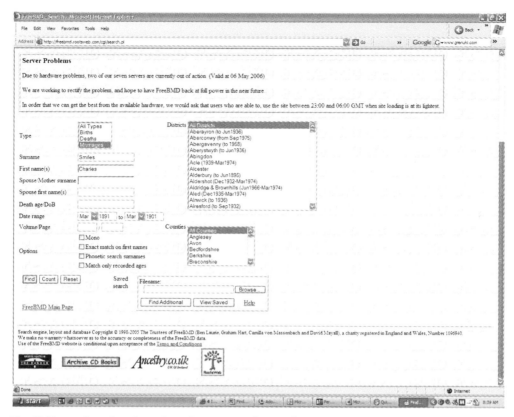

The FreeBMD search engine, shown here, is easy to use but gets busy. US users have an advantage because of the time difference if accessing the site in the evening, when British users are asleep! (Image copyright 1998–2005, the Trustees of FreeBMD. Used by permission.)

Now to the code. The 10b refers to the volume number in which the entries are recorded. Experienced researchers can tell very quickly which part of the country each volume refers to. The volume numbers changed over time, and in this period 10b refers to registrations in the counties of Cumberland, Northumberland, and Westmorland. However, this is not essential information as long as you have the volume number, since the registration district of the event is already written right alongside. The adjacent number—in this case 579—is the page number on which the entries are written.

Click the page number. It shows our Charles Wilson Smiles, one other man's name, and the names of two women. Which woman was Charles' wife? She is not necessarily the one whose name is next to that of Charles, but it's usually possible to figure it out by using a combination of census and vital records index searches. Of course, we could just order the marriage certificate, but let's see if we can work it out online first.

Marriage search results example from FreeBMD. (Image copyright 1998–2005, the Trustees of FreeBMD. Used by permission.)

The two women in this case are Ann Jane Stephenson and Christina Whillis. Since we know Charles' wife died between the marriage date of March 1898 and the census of March 31, 1901, let's search for each of these names during this three-year time period. Of course, the surname will now be Smiles and not Stephenson or Whillis, so we are looking for the death of an Ann Jane Smiles or a Christina Smiles.

Return to the FreeBMD search screen and enter the surname Smiles but leave the given name blank. Make sure you highlight **Death** instead of **Marriage.**

One name results for Ann Jane Smiles, and it looks like a match. According to the screen, Ann Jane Smiles was just twenty-seven when she died in the December quarter of 1899 at Alnwick, less than two years after her marriage. There are no deaths listed for a Christina Smiles. We now definitely have Charles' wife's maiden name, and a confirmed death in the December quarter of 1899.

Ordering the death certificate would give the cause of death, but let's look for clues anyway, since we may not need to incur the time and expense of ordering the certificate. Noting the code as 10b 279 and the other information exactly as recorded, we can leave that for a moment to test a theory as to whether death was in childbirth.

We now need to see if there are any Smiles child births or child deaths in Alnwick in this immediate period from the death of the mother to the 1901 census.

TIP: Choosing Between Search Engines

FreeBMD was developed independently by volunteers, but is now supported by RootsWeb and Ancestry.com. The non-negotiable principle with these volunteers is that the data must always remain free. That was the raison d'être for the original project. So while Ancestry has access to the same data on its site there is no charge to use it.

Ancestry's search engine is sometimes a little faster, especially when the FreeBMD site gets busy. However, one thing that the FreeBMD site offers uniquely is a view of the original index as well as the transcribed data. Since researchers should always get as close as possible to the original records, this is a significant benefit.

We can return to the search engine and this time specify Alnwick as the **registration district** for the search. Specifying a district prevents you from highlighting a county, so just highlight "All counties" in the county box. "Smiles" is entered as the surname, but the given names box is left blank.

This time, the search comes up empty, apart from the death of the mother that we found a moment ago. There are several possible reasons. Of course, our theory could be completely wrong and Ann might have died of a disease or an accident. Perhaps she had a miscarriage and no birth was recorded. Or, the transcriptions for the year in question may not be complete. Perhaps a child was born but died later.

Let's pursue a few of these possibilities as a means of demonstrating some other online resources that prove very helpful.

1. How do we know if the transcriptions for the year in question are complete?

Fortunately, FreeBMD has made this question easy to answer. Drop down the screen until you see the FreeBMD main page

TIP: Remember Notes and Sources

As you undertake any kind of research, remember to keep a note of each step you take. A search of a database or an index that is unsuccessful is important to record, too—just as successful ones are. To avoid backtracking and duplication of effort, and also to remind you of how you arrived at a conclusion, use the notes and research log in your software program constantly. In addition, record sources every time you add data to your tree.

link at the bottom. Back on the main page, click on the red **Information** link. Click the **Coverage Charts** link found under the Statistics heading. Select the **Deaths** link. You can scroll down the screen to see the graphs representing the state of completion of each year. As it happens, the crucial year for us of 1899 is 100 percent completed. This doesn't guarantee the childbirth theory is wrong because non-registration is still a possibility, but the theory is looking less likely.

2. Are there other Vital Records Indexes?

FreeBMD itself recommends caution when interpreting results. Interpreting "nil" results is particularly tricky, since the absence of something in a database could be the result of a number of factors.

Is there another way to check the entire, original death indexes for this year for any Smiles babies? The answer is "yes," and it's time to leave FreeBMD for the moment.

Log on to **www.1837online.com.** The odd name of this site is taken from the year of 1837, in which civil registration in England and Wales began. As mentioned earlier, non-registration was a bit of a problem at first until people got used to the idea—their memories helped, no doubt, by a government fine. But the early records are still valuable if you can read the handwriting. Later records are typed and are more likely to be complete.

From the 1837online.com home page, you'll need to register. It costs nothing to do so. The new visitor registration is at the very top of the page. Once in, you should click on the home page button that reads **1837–1983 Births, Marriages & Deaths.**

Viewing images of the original indexes costs 10 pence per view (less than 20 cents), and five pounds or 50 views is the minimum payment. You have three months to use those views before they expire. Views of the 1861 and 1891 census pages cost three units, or 30 pence each.

To save you spending anything to look at Smiles names that aren't on your own tree, take a look at the image on page 155. This is what you would have seen from a look at the December quarter of 1899. To be sure that the FreeBMD transcribers didn't miss anything, we would want to check every quarter from December 1899 through March 1901—six views, or 60 pence in all. The equivalent of roughly one U.S. dollar isn't bad to eliminate the possibility of a mistake and for peace of mind.

The images can be saved right from the Internet onto your hard drive, and you should always do so, whether it's an index like that on page 155 or a census record.

From the Web site at www.1837online.com. (Original document Crown Copyright, published by permission by the Controller of HMSO and the Office for National Statistics.)

The views on 1837online.com can also be enlarged on screen. Unfortunately, you can only search names on this site by the page on which the surname appears. You can't ask for a listing of similar names from different quarters or years because you are looking at graphic images of alphabetized names.

Since our search of any other Smiles deaths that could match a child of Charles and Ann has come up empty, what's next? We could ignore the issue and just consider this branch as one that ended prematurely. Personally, I don't like loose ends such as not knowing why a twenty-seven-year-old woman died, so we'll see now how to order a death certificate. It's the same process for marriages and births.

3. How Do We Order a Birth, Marriage, or Death Certificate?

You can order certificates from some local counties, as well as from the Government Record Office for the whole of England and Wales. Because the cost is the same and the national indexes are so accessible, it makes sense to use the national government facility. Here's how to do it.

The General Register Office for England and Wales maintains an efficient site that will dispatch certificates within a few days of receiving the order. Everything can be done online.

1. Go to **www.gro.gov.uk/gro/content/certificate** and have your credit card handy.

2. At the top right of the home page, register to log in. You won't have to pay anything until you are ready to order a certificate.

3. The first screen is headed "Certificate Choice." Since I'm ordering Ann Smiles' death certificate, I'd obviously click on the circle that designates death certificates, and enter the age of 27 in the box alongside it. The only other information required on this screen is the answer to the question: "Is General Register Office Index known?" This is the code we referred to earlier, and the answer is "yes." We also need to enter the year of the event—in this case, 1899. Pressing the **Submit** button now takes us to a self-explanatory page asking for address delivery details.

4. The next page is where we enter the code we picked up earlier on the FreeBMD Web site or 1837online.com. The "District" name is the place name alongside the person's name on the index. In the case of ordering a death certificate for Ann Smiles, I would enter Alnwick as the District name, 10b as the volume number, and 237 as the page number.

    The other boxes marked with a red asterisk are self-explanatory. Few certificates are so urgent that it's worth spending more than three times the amount to save three days, and you can ignore the boxes about reference numbers at the foot of the page. They are useful only to professionals who are ordering certificates in large numbers.

5. Press the **Submit** button and proceeded to the checkout. That's all there is to ordering an English birth, marriage, or death certificate. No requests for IDs, no having to demonstrate relationships, and no hit and miss searches through a multitude of counties with dozens of different rules.

Would I also want to order the marriage certificate for Charles Smiles and his wife Ann Jane Stephenson? It all depends on whether I'm interested in tracing Ann's line back through her parents. A marriage certificate would give the name of her father and make it more likely that we could find her easily on an earlier census before she married. If that line isn't important to me for now, I already have the marriage date and place narrowed to a three-month time period.

As it happens, when the death certificate for Ann Jane Stephenson Smiles arrives

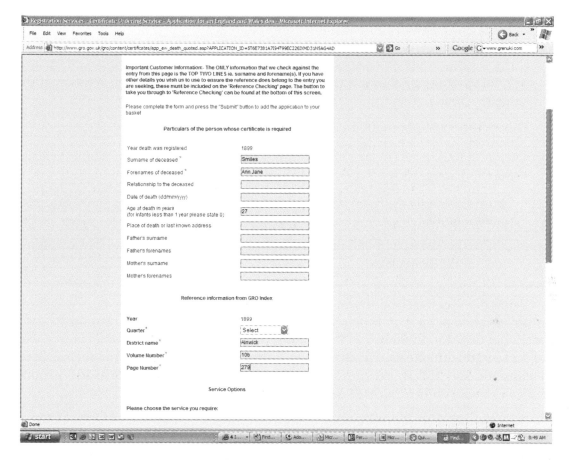

Forms like this one are also available for births and marriages and can be ordered online from the General Register Office, a central location for the entire country. Once a researcher has the numbers from the registration indexes, ordering a certificate is simple.

through the mail, I note the cause of death at age twenty-seven as a cerebral tumor. This family had its share of trials.

Loose Ends

With what we've covered in this chapter, you should be able to use the FreeBMD indexes to fill in a lot of gaps and answer many questions about your own British ancestors in the period after civil registration began in 1837. A little bit of imagination, a little detective work, and common-sense deduction, combined with registration indexes, can work wonders. This is particularly so if you are using the results of searches in connection with online census records.

By way of review, let's go back to the four questions we asked in Step 2 (pages 149–50). They were:

- Charles Smiles is shown as a widower on the 1901 census, and no children are at home. Can we find out the name of Charles' wife and what happened to her?

This question has been answered, but the three others remain:

- Can we find out if Henry's older brother, Ralph, had any children after he was married at age thirty-five?

- Can we learn more of the three sons' mother—Thomas's wife—including her maiden name?

- Can we get an exact birth date for Henry to clear up the three-year discrepancy on the US census?

Using the FreeBMD indexes in exactly the same way as before, we can easily find Ralph's marriage by searching all marriages in England between 1891 and 1901, specifying only Ralph Smiles as the groom. It takes four or five seconds before we are presented with one match only, in the June quarter of 1895, and the reference is Tynemouth, 10b 318. By clicking on the page, we can identify his wife as the former Mary Jane Simpson (we already knew the name Mary from the 1901 census).

Next, we want to see if there are Smiles children who were born but may have died between this marriage date in 1895 and the 1901 census, by which time we know they were childless. By doing a name search for births first, and then for deaths, and matching the two with any likely-looking names, we can advance our knowledge of this family still further.

In these two searches, two names jump out of the screen at us. An Eleanor Mary was born in 1895 and died in the March quarter of 1896. And a Thomas Ralph Smiles was born in the March quarter of 1897 and died six months later. Here are names of children that match precisely the name of the mother and grandmother, and father and grandfather, and they are born in the right time frame and in the right registration district of Tynemouth. These are undoubtedly children of Ralph and Mary, but we must prove it by ordering the birth certificates. (Subsequently, the birth certificates confirm our supposition).

The give-away clues here are the children's names. Ralph is not a particularly common name—as indicated by the fact that only one Ralph Smiles seems to be on the English marriage indexes for a whole decade. But what of even more children?

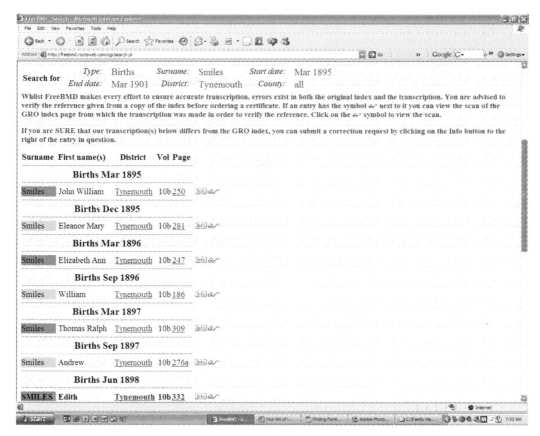

Birth indexes from FreeBMD show several children, at least two of whom could belong to Ralph and Mary Smiles. (Image used by permission of the Trustees of FreeBMD.)

The indexes show a number of other possibilities, and it's likely that Ralph and Mary Smiles had the misfortune to lose more than two.

Researching online, the only sure way would be to look at the other possible births and order certificates for those that look like a match from the spacing of the births and corresponding deaths. It is also worth checking the IGI (International Genealogical Index) on FamilySearch.org, since it's possible the parish records where the christenings took place could have been microfilmed and the names extracted. That should be standard operating procedure since such searches are quick, easy, and free.

As a side note, a search of the FreeBMD death indexes up to 1910 reveals that Ralph Riddle Smiles, the father, himself died at the young age of forty-three. This was a tragic branch of this family. Possibly other children survived, but it's beyond our scope to explore that further.

The final two questions we posed early in this chapter can be addressed now. The maiden name of the mother of Charles, Henry, and Ralph turns out to be Eleanor Riddle—not a surprise because it's Ralph's middle name. We can find it very easily, once again, by searching for Thomas Smiles and Eleanor's marriage. In this case we are also in luck because the 1871 census also lists Eleanor's seventy-six-year-old father—also a Ralph Riddle—living in the home.

Yet, after gathering all this information, we can never pin down Henry's birth. The future American immigrant does not appear on the FreeBMD indexes, nor can we find him in a systematic search of the original indexes on 1837online.com.

Explanations are speculative. Sometimes people failed to register a birth or other event. Sometimes there were mistakes by the registrars, or the spelling is so unrecognizable that the computer search can't find the person. Still, two census records and a ship's passenger list point to a year close enough to satisfy us. That little mys-

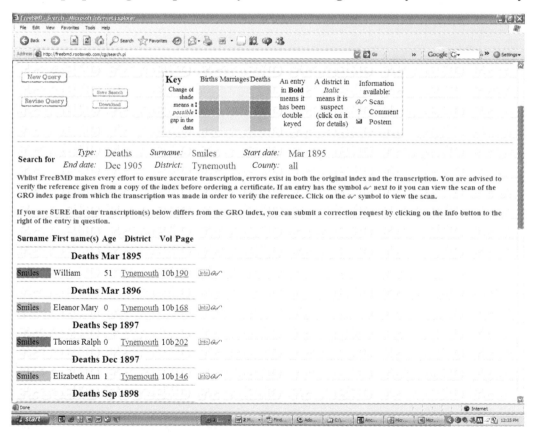

The apparent deaths of the same children listed in the previous image at only a few months old. Indicators like this must be followed by ordering birth or death certificates to verify what might seem obvious but could prove to be an incorrect deduction. (Image used by permission of the Trustees of FreeBMD.)

tery will have to be one that remains unsolved for now. Be prepared for this kind of situation, where someone disappears from a census or other record without explanation.

Other Options for British Research

We have far from exhausted the possibilities for researching your family tree in England and Wales. But because many of the British options also apply to Scotland and Northern Ireland, we'll take a look at those other parts of the United Kingdom first, and then devote a final British Isles chapter to the wealth of other information available online, and methods of cooperation.

12
SCOTLAND AND IRELAND

Scotland Overview

In recent years, a huge amount of Scotland's data has come online, and it's possible to do a great deal of searching for censuses, vital records, and other genealogical resources from your home computer relatively inexpensively. Scotland's own laws, conventions, and customs mean that research in this country is significantly different from that in England, although there are also many similarities. Scottish vital records offer more information than those from England and Wales. The most readily available and easily used online resource is that of the official genealogical Web site of the government of Scotland, called ScotlandsPeople and found at **www.scotlandspeople.gov.uk.** There are also other Internet sites with valuable information on Scottish genealogy, including FreeCEN mentioned on page 147 (**www.freecen.org.uk**).

Step 1: Register with ScotlandsPeople

If you are sure you have Scottish ancestry and you have at least a name and a rough date to begin with, your first stop after mining information from any extended family members and old papers should be ScotlandsPeople, the official government site for genealogical information. This is a very well-constructed site—easy to use, with powerful search engine, display and download options, and a charge system based on pay-per-view which isn't designed to break the family bank account.

Because of these factors and the wealth of information on this site, we'll spend some time looking at it closely.

Log on to the home page at **www.scotlandspeople.gov.uk** and you will be met with a clean, well-laid-out home page on which you can see all the essential components at a glance. In theory, the free surname search allows a user of the site to see if his or her surname is included in the various databases before committing to payment. However, all a search will show you is a list of statistics on how often

ScotlandsPeople home page. (Crown copyright. Image reproduced with the permission of the Registrar General for Scotland and the Queen's Printer for Scotland.)

the name appears in the various databases. You will still have to enter the site to see any first names and view the data.

ScotlandsPeople charges an initial fee of six pounds minimum (about $10 U.S.), which gives you thirty "page credits." In effect, your six pounds buys you access to the databases of census and vital records, which are considerable. It then costs one credit to view an index of the results generated by each search. Up to twenty-five names are listed on a single page of results.

To view the record itself costs five credits. This works out to be a little more expensive than viewing an image from the 1901 England and Wales census on the British site we discussed in Chapter 11, but considering the wealth of information and the range of years you're searching, this site is a good value. Make sure you narrow the search so that you get only one or two names in the index, if possible. Otherwise you'll have to view more of them to identify the name that may be your ancestor. That could end up being expensive.

For more on the payment system and how it works, click the **FAQs** link at the top of the home page.

Step 2: Review the Databases and Help Guides

From the home page, you can see that the available records fall into four types:

1. **Statutory registers of births, deaths, and marriages** began in Scotland on January 1, 1855. ScotlandsPeople has viewable government vital records from this date. Birth records more recent than 100 years, marriage records for the past 75 years, and records of deaths for the past 50 years are only available from a separate site (see page 170).

   The valuable element of ScotlandsPeople is that you can see the original handwritten record, not just a transcribed index or transcribed text. In other words, you don't even have to wait for a certificate—you get to see the actual register images online.

   Scottish vital records contain a wonderful amount of detail. When civil registration began in 1855, they contained even more than they do now. A birth certificate, for instance, included not only the usual details of the child but the age, birth place, and marriage dates and birth places of both parents. There was even a column indicating whether there were other children, and how many. Sadly, such a wealth of data proved difficult to sustain, and the registry information was much reduced the next year. Birth registers after 1861 still include parents' marriage information. Marriage and death registers include a correspondingly generous amount of detail. To see what each registry contains during any year since 1855: Click **Births 1855–1905** under the **Statutory Registers** heading on the home page. Right above the **Search** button on the next page is the link, **Click here for more information.** After a couple of paragraphs of text you will see another link to **Images**. If you have a lot of Scottish research to do, it's worth book marking this page because it will tell you exactly what you can expect before you pay to view a register.

2. **Old Parish Registers,** sometimes called Old Parochial Registers, include births/christenings and marriage banns and marriages from 1553 to the start of civil registration. There are no burials. The amount of information in an individual entry varies significantly, because there was no government supervision or uniform standard. Still, these records contain tremendously valuable information. It will probably be several years before all the parish records of neighboring England become available in this way.

3. **Census Records** were taken in the same years as in England and Wales, and are viewable online from 1841 to 1901.

4. **Wills and Testaments** from 1513 to 1901 can be searched free of charge, but it costs five pounds to view one of these documents regardless of the length. Since wills can go to several pages and contain a substantial amount of valuable data, the reason for the difference in price is obvious.

All of these records have limitations, but that's nothing new to family history researchers. For instance, the handwriting in some records may be poor, or the paper faded through moisture or misuse. The Old Parish Registers were compiled by the Church of Scotland, and so do not typically include the members of other churches. There are also gaps in the records, sometimes of months, sometimes of years, depending on the locality.

If you have substantial Scottish ancestry, I strongly recommend that before you go very far you browse the excellent **Help and Resources** section on ScotlandsPeople. It's written for people unfamiliar with Scottish research but in a way that delivers the details. It's one of the most comprehensive yet lucid Help sections I've seen anywhere. For instance, the section on surname variants is fascinating reading if you want to understand Scottish surnames, including the one-time practice of patronymics (see Tip box, page 170). It costs nothing to access the Help files.

Step 3: Enter the details of your ancestor

You'll need a full name and a rough date for any meaningful search. Because you can do national, multi-county searches, a location may not be critical, but will certainly help if you need to distinguish between people of the same name.

Where you start—with a census record, statutory vital records, or the Old Parish Registers—obviously depends on the time frame you're searching. Let's take a look at what you will see on screen for each of the major sources we've just listed.

The screen image below shows the results of a search in the **Statutory Records**

Crown copyright, reproduced with the permission of the Registrar General for Scotland and the Queen's Printer for Scotland.

for the birth of Lavinia Pickles in the Glasgow area. In this case, the unusual name helped, because only a single person resulted from the search.

Remember once again that the data you are seeing is transcribed information, and the transcriber may have misread some of the original handwriting. Also, indexes usually contain only the minimal information required to identify a person. Don't cut corners by settling for this partial information when one click can deliver a primary record. And since you can view and save or download the original information, there's no need to spend ten times as much by ordering an extract. Ordering an extract is a logical choice when online images are not available, such as in most Old Parish Registers.

The original record for the person on this index can be seen by clicking **View** in the **Image** column. If you have already viewed the image, the words "View (paid)" appear, and you can view the record as often as you visit the site.

The original image brought to the screen shows a lot more. Now we have the occupation of the father, the maiden name of the mother, and the place and date of

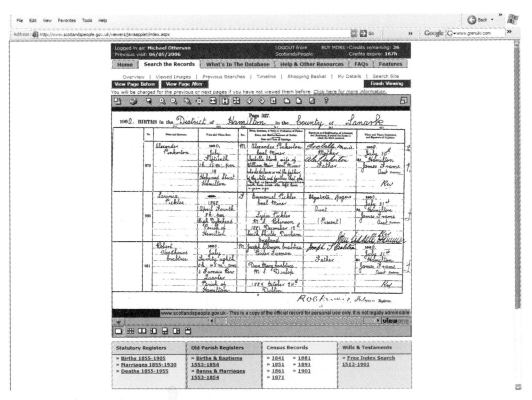

Example of an original record—the same person represented in the transcribed text on page 166. (Crown copyright, reproduced with the permission of the Registrar General for Scotland and the Queen's Printer for Scotland.)

marriage of the parents. Even the **Informant** column delivers the name of an unknown aunt.

However, take a look at the entry just above that for Lavinia. This is a good example of the unexpected information that can sometimes be found on such records. Under the column heading that normally specifies the names of the parents and their marriage details, the registrar has written that Alexander Pinkerton is the father, but then adds: "Isabella Clark, wife of William Muir, coal miner, who she declares is not the father of the child and further that she has had no personal communication with him since she left him 11 years ago." This is a genealogical gem, a piece of knowledge that will solve all kinds of problems for someone researching this line and hunting fruitlessly for a non-existent marriage. It also adds that crucial element of real life into what otherwise could be mere names and dates.

What if you were looking for an ancestor's **census record** instead of a statutory birth, marriage, or death? Then the page view would look like the image below. This is typical of British census returns and looks very much like those for England

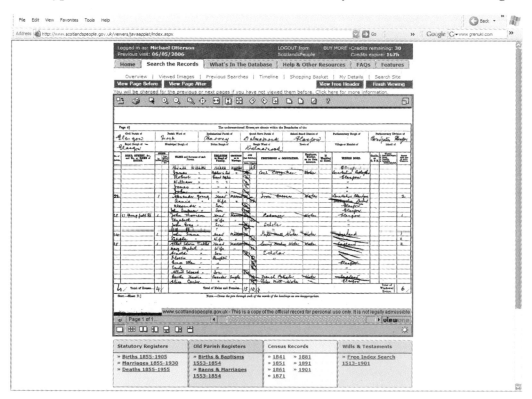

Example of a Scottish census record. (Crown copyright, reproduced with the permission of the Registrar General for Scotland and the Queen's Printer for Scotland.)

and Wales. On-screen tools allow for magnification of all or parts of the image, and the record can be saved to your hard drive.

The **Old Parish Registers** start in the late 1500s and cover an estimated 60 percent of Scotland's population before registration began in 1855. This is more than 10 million people, making them the best source of data for your family history before civil registration. The registers were kept by the Church of Scotland (Presbyterians), so don't expect to find Catholic or other denominations here.

In the case of these old registers, you are likely to encounter a "No Image" message when you generate an index from clicking on the **Search** button. This just means that the image isn't yet available, and you might want to consider ordering a certified extract. The $10 to order an extract is within the range paid for certificates in Britain and in various parts of the United States. Ordering online is like ordering from any commercial Web site, with orders transferred to a shopping basket that you pay for on checking out.

Below is an example of what you will see from an Old Parish Register search for a birth or christening.

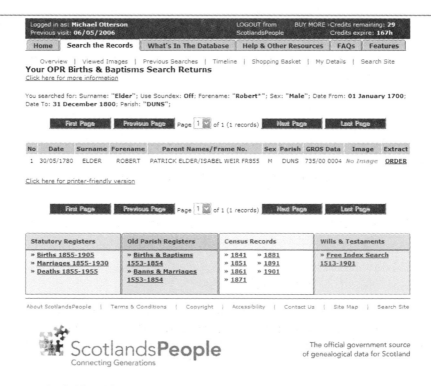

Results from a search of Old Parish Registers. (Crown copyright. Image reproduced with the permission of the Registrar General for Scotland and the Queen's Printer for Scotland.)

The **Wills and Testaments** indexes on ScotlandsPeople can be searched free and are self-explanatory. Because each view of a will costs five pounds, whether it's two pages or ten, you'll want to be sure you have identified the right ancestor before clicking the **View** option. Wills can be enormously helpful in yielding information about immediate family and for creating some of that human picture we have talked about. They can also yield almost nothing. It's all part of the uncertain element that is often so challenging about family history.

Ordering More Recent Scottish Certificates

Certificates for births within the past 100 years, marriages within 75 years, and deaths within 50 years must be ordered directly from the Scottish Government Records Office.

There is no facility on the Government Register Office for Scotland (GROS) for ordering these more recent certificates online. The options are a letter (allow two weeks for them to dispatch a certificate after they receive your letter), or you can phone. Of course, you can also make a personal visit to Edinburgh or one of the local register offices if you are planning to be in the area.

The GROS will do limited searches of their registers if you can be fairly specific on the details of your ancestor. The wider the search, the more expensive the cost. They won't search at all if you can't provide specific identifying information beyond just a name. The certificates themselves, aside from the search fee, are slightly cheaper than on the ScotlandsPeople site.

Frankly, it's disappointing that the GROS doesn't have the same online services for these more recent records that exist on ScotlandsPeople site, or even the General Register Office for England and Wales, where more recent certificates can be ordered with ease. The contact information for New Register House is:

- Mail: New Register House, 3 West Register Street, Edinburgh, Scotland, EH1 3YT

- Phone: International code + 44 131 314 4411. You will need to quote your credit card details and expiration date.

- Web site: Learn more about the procedures and the services offered by visiting the Web site at **www.gro-scotland.gov.uk.** From the home page, click **Family Records** and then follow the links you need.

TIP: Help with Scottish Surnames

Scottish surnames can seem complicated to those familiar only with English surname conventions. Many different ethnic groups and migrations have contributed over at least eight centuries to the mosaic of names seen in Scotland today. Some of the main points to bear in mind when looking for surnames in earlier periods are:

- Mac, so common to Scotland and Ireland, is the prefix to names of Gaelic origin and denotes "son."

- If in the earlier Old Parish Registers you also come across "Nc," or even "N" standing alone right in front of the surname, this isn't a mistake. This is the female equivalent, meaning "daughter of."

- Because there are numerous variants, always write the name in your genealogical program *exactly* as you see it written in the original record, whether or not the spelling is consistent elsewhere in the family.

Patronymics

Patronymics aren't likely to be a problem unless you are researching surnames in the Highlands of Scotland or perhaps the Northern Islands in the 1700s or early 1800s. The practice of using patronymics had mostly died out by that time in the rest of the country.

Those familiar with Scandinavian genealogy won't find this unusual. Patronymics involves using the first name of the father and adding "son," so John Danielson's son William would be William Johnson, and his father might have been Daniel Peterson. This means the surname name changes every generation. The system was also applied to females. You may see this in some of the Old Parish Registers when you find a surname ending in "daur" or some other abbreviation including just "d." This is very Scandinavian.

Deliberate or accidental changes

Added to the complexity of deliberate name changes for political reasons—such as clan protection or to avoid discrimination—was the simple fact that most people were illiterate. Names could not usually be spelled out to those compiling registers, and accents still vary greatly in Scotland as they do in England.

For a more detailed treatment of Scottish surnames, refer to the **Help and Resources** section on ScotlandsPeople.com.

Ireland Overview

Researching family history in Ireland isn't easy. Opportunities for online research lag substantially behind England, Scotland, and Wales. The key data that makes great strides possible in a short time—searchable census records and digitized indexes of births, marriage, and deaths—isn't available for reasons that will be explained. Still, neither is the quest impossible. As more and more searchable data for family historians comes online, it will break down huge roadblocks for researchers.

The history of Ireland that causes headaches for family historians includes:

- Centuries of religious and political conflict and social unrest, including the civil war of the early 1920s that led to the creation of a Republic of Ireland separate from Northern Ireland

- The deliberate destruction by government order during World War 1 of the 1861, 1871, 1881, and 1891 census records

- The fire in the Public Records Office in Dublin in 1922, which destroyed the earlier census records for 1821 to 1851, along with wills, marriage licenses, and many Anglican Church records

- Massive waves of immigration and emigration, especially during the famine era of the mid-1800s, much of it undocumented

The absence of original census records is a major handicap, but attempts have been made to bypass the gap by utilizing other contemporary records.

Significantly, Irish civil registration indexes on microfilm of births, marriages, and deaths are available for ordering at your nearest Family History Center, even though they are not yet available online.

A number of Internet sites now specialize in providing Irish genealogical data, usually for a fee.

Step 1: Read the Ireland Research Outline on FamilySearch.org

Probably no other organization has invested more time and effort to advance genealogical research in Ireland as The Church of Jesus Christ of Latter-day Saints. The titles and descriptions for their collection of microfilmed records for Ireland can be examined online in the Family History Library Catalog, and many can be ordered at local Family History Centers near you.

TIP: What Do You Do with Scanned Images?

At various stages of research, we have captured original images of census records or vital records from the Internet. Once you have extracted all available data from them, what do you do with them? Most people archive the images to a CD or other storage medium and forget about them. We have already seen that you can also save an image on your hard drive and "point" to it as part of your source citation.

If your genealogical software program displays photographs, consider also pointing to the image just as you would to a photograph. Since you will not have photographs for most people on your family tree, you can at least display a mini-image of key sources when you highlight a name. In programs such as PAF that allow you display a scrapbook view of several images, you might have a whole succession of census records at a glance every ten years. You can enlarge any of these on-screen for a detailed view.

This has practical, not just aesthetic value, especially if you have everything loaded on a laptop for when you visit family or travel for research. Your key source documents will always be a click away.

Before attempting any Irish research—unless you are well beyond the beginner stage—I recommend that your starting point be the Ireland Research Outline on FamilySearch.org. *Read this entire outline before going further*. It will be worth the time investment. To get there:

1. Log on to **www.familysearch.org**.

2. Click the **Search** tab.

3. Click **Research Helps** on the blue bar at the top of the screen.

4. Select "I" from the alphabetical lists.

5. Scroll down to **Ireland: Research Outline** and click the link. At the bottom of each page you will find a **Next document** link from which you can work through the other pages as time allows.

Significant Irish data is available from The Church of Jesus Christ of Latter-day Saints in one way or another, as we'll see later when we return to this site.

Step 2: Preview and Bookmark the Irish Ancestors Site

A site called Irish Ancestors is sponsored by the *Irish Times* newspaper at **www.ireland.com/ancestor.** Despite the usual drawbacks of a commercial site (occasional or frequent offers for professional searches that are not cheap), this is actually a very good site. On the home page, look for the horizontal bar of links across the page just under the Irish Ancestors masthead, and click on **Sitemap**. I

Site map for Irish Ancestors, sponsored by the Irish Times. This single page is an excellent reference source and jumping off point for seeing what's available in Ireland. (Image copyright 2005 Ireland.com. Used by permission.)

suggest you bookmark the resulting page, which is an excellent overview of Irish genealogical resources that you can see at a glance on a single page.

Clicking on most of these links gives you a succinct summary of the source and its relevance to Irish research.

Step 3: Check Census Information for 1901, 1911

It will serve you well to start with available census records, since they provide the most complete information on families.

As mentioned earlier, many Irish censuses have not survived through the years. The 1901 and 1911 censuses are the exception. Both are mostly intact, and the originals are held in the National Archives of Ireland in Bishop Street, Dublin. Both are available on microfilm from Family History Centers of The Church of Jesus Christ of Latter-day Saints. At the time of writing they have not been digitized, but it's certain they will be before long because the church is planning a massive effort to digitize its films (see Chapter 17). Indexes are already available on microfilm, as are lists of the townlands and towns of Ireland that appear in the censuses.

To see which films to order:

1. Log on to www.familysearch.org.
2. Click the **Library** tab.
3. Click Family History Library Catalog.
4. Click the **Place Search** button.
5. Type in **Ireland.** A long list of resources, including the census titles, will appear.

In addition to the censuses of 1901 and 1911, you will see in the list some references to other censuses. You can click on any one of these for more details, but note that some of these sources are books, while others are microfilm. They are not the full census, of course, but merely fragments or aids to research.

The publication of the 1911 census is an exception in the British Isles, which otherwise follow a 100-year privacy rule before publishing census information. The rule was suspended for the 1911 census because of the unavailability of other censuses—the result of an earlier government blunder in ordering the destruction of census data from the 1800s.

If your research interests fall in the period covered by these two censuses, you can also log on to **www.rootsweb.com/~fianna/guide/cen1.html.** This RootsWeb-sponsored site is Fianna Guide to Irish Genealogy. Much of the site is in serious need of updating, but this page has a number of shortcuts for ordering some of the films from the Family History Library Catalog just mentioned. It's worth scrolling down the entire page.

Step 4: Assess Other Census Links and Substitutes

The **Census-online.com** Web site that we have examined for other countries also proves helpful for Irish census records. A map of Irish counties and a parallel, alphabetical list shows the number of online databases available. These databases

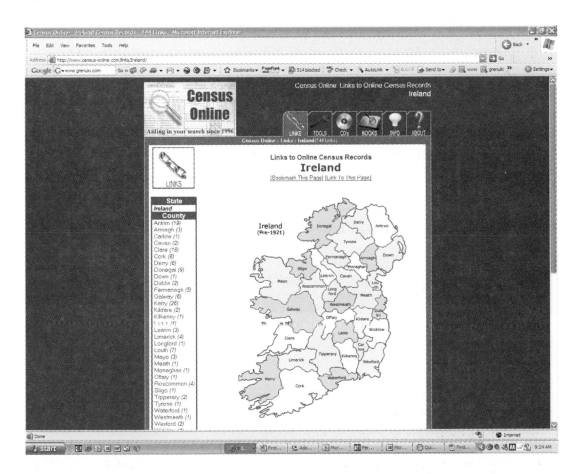

This page is a good starting point for supplementary Irish census data. (Image copyright Census Online. Homepage at www.census-online.com. Used by permission.)

are not complete indexes for the counties. They are partial lists of some towns and villages, for the most part. But they are better than nothing and the collections are expanding all of the time. Start at **www.census-online.com/links/Ireland** and follow the logical steps for your area of interest.

Another way to get at similar data is through the link at **www.genealogy branches.com/irishcensus.html** to the **Online Irish Census Indexes & Records** page. None of the collections at the other end of these links is exhaustive, although some of the independent Web pages, such as that for County Clare, are quite sophisticated. Some of the links on this site take you to subscription services, such as Ancestry.com or Genealogy.com, where there are limited collections of various Irish records online.

Irish Origins—part of the Origins Network—has **Griffith's Valuations, 1847–1862** online. This is sometimes described as a census substitute, although it delivers nothing like the amount of data of a census.

Griffith's Valuations, named for its director Richard Griffith, was an ambitious project to evaluate the property of each taxpayer, whether owner or occupier of the land. This allowed assessment of local taxes. Every property in the entire country was included in the evaluation, which was undertaken and completed between 1847 and 1864.

TIP: Finding Where Your Ancestor Lived

If you are clueless as to where your ancestor may have lived in Ireland, try this page: **www.genealogybranches.com/irish.html.**

It gives a number of ways for Americans to find information in alternative records.

Griffith's Valuations don't include the names of the family—just the occupier who paid the rent and the name of the lessor, or the person to whom he paid it. Because of the absence of Irish census records for this period, however, Griffith's Valuations have taken on more importance than they would have otherwise. They can help pinpoint where your ancestor was living. If you can definitely identify an ancestor's name, the record will show you the name of the parish and townland, as well as the county. Irish Origins allows viewing of the original image of the record and a map. You may have to download a tiff viewer to see the images, but a link to a free download is given on the site.

Although Origins is a subscription site, it allows short-term access for 72 hours for the equivalent of $6 or $7 US. Log on to Irish Origins and its associate sites at **www.originsnetwork.com/Welcome.aspx.** The site also has an **1851 census of Dublin City**, with accompanying Ordnance Survey maps so you actually see an address, and the site managers say they are adding Irish data continually. The site is not particularly intuitive to navigate, but you can use the search engine (e.g. *Search by Name*) to pull up a search screen that then lists all the databases. A search goes through all the databases and then lists the hits alongside each one, where you can then click **View Records** for details.

Step 5: Check the IGI Data on FamilySearch.org

Before you look at government sources for vital records (births, marriages, and deaths) in Ireland, you should check the online data on FamilySearch.org. The most

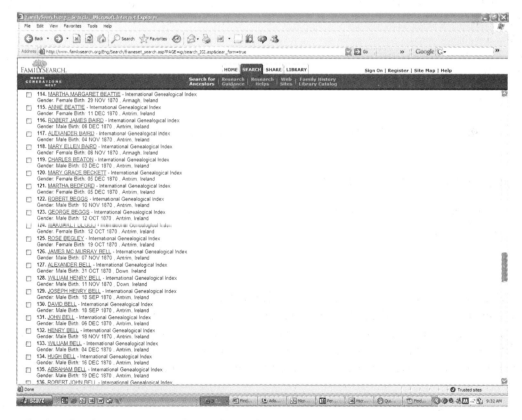

Example of results of an IGI name search in Irish records. Use the onsite search engine to narrow your search. (FamilySearch.org, image copyright 1999, 2005 by Intellectual Reserve, Inc.)

significant data drawn from vital records for Ireland that can be viewed directly online is found in the International Genealogical Index. The information for some localities is quite extensive. For instance, you can enter just a surname and a county in the search engine to generate a considerable list of names that you can then examine one by one to see if they correspond to the details of a known ancestor. You can narrow the search by specifying a time period from forty years down to an exact year, and you can ask to see records containing any event or specifically a birth or christening, a marriage or death.

The IGI, as mentioned earlier, consists of records that have either been submitted by members of The Church of Jesus Christ of Latter-day Saints or have been "extracted" by the church from microfilmed copies. Consequently, there is not necessarily uniform coverage of all countries or parts of countries. Nevertheless, as was shown in Chapter 8, the IGI is a huge source of information of births, marriages, and deaths that is valuable if it's used thoughtfully. It's even more useful in the absence of online indexes of births, marriages, and deaths from official government sources.

Step 6: Vital Records in Ireland

Official registration of all births, deaths, and marriages in Ireland began in 1864, although state registration of non-Roman Catholic marriages began earlier, in 1845.

There is no facility as yet for accessing the indexes or the data from Irish vital records on the Internet in the same way that those from Scotland or England can be found—that is, in a complete national index. However, that day may not be far away. Microfilmed copies exist in the Family History Library of The Church of Jesus Christ of Latter-day Saints, and because Irish ancestry is so significant in the United States it's a reasonable assumption that national indexes will be a priority for digitization.

That does not mean that no vital records at all exist on line. Although the collections are not yet extensive, you can check several Irish genealogical sites that offer on-line indexes or data.

The page at www.from-ireland.net/gene/civilregistration.htm has an excellent explanation of the Irish civil registration system. At the bottom of the page is a link to Civil Registration Districts and extracts on the site that have been transcribed from the indexes in those districts.

Check out also:

www.groireland.ie/about_us.htm This is the General Register Office for the Republic of Ireland, and if you have the date and locality of the event from your ancestor's life—birth, marriage or death—this is the place to order certificates. Start on the page found through this link, but also click on **Apply for cert** from the menu. The site shows how the Irish government is already busy digitizing its vital records.

www.ireland.progenealogists.com includes valuable resources for the researcher in Ireland, including several Irish databases. This is a particularly well laid out site.

Throughout this book I have concentrated on providing Web addresses for substantial on-line help and data, rather than refer the reader to hard-copy books. One exception is a helpful little book that is part of a series published by the Federation of Family History Societies in England. *Irish Family History on the Web* by Stuart A. Raymond is essentially a directory of Web addresses for Irish research. You'll find everything from introductions to Irish genealogy to message boards to gravestone inscriptions, census and vital record data. You can order it online at **www.samjraymond.btopenworld.com** for about $10.

Until more vital and parish records come on line, the best option is still to visit a Family History Center of the LDS Church to examine the microfilms or order the films you want if they aren't already in the center. The church has copies of not only the General Register Office indexes but the registers, too. This means a researcher can get as much from a Family History Center as they can from a visit to the General Register Office itself, and for a lot less money.

The ability to search the registers themselves in a Family History Center is a huge plus. Most governments allow only a search of indexes and then charge fees for producing an official certificate. If, for example, you were to visit the General Register Office of Ireland in Lombard Street, Dublin, you could search the indexes for a reasonable fee. The GRO holds the master indexes to all 32 counties up to 1921 and to the 26 counties of the Republic of Ireland after that date. Technically, you would be searching copies of the indexes. If you then wanted a printout from the microfilm, you would be charged another fee for each entry—around $2 to $3, U.S. equivalent. These printouts contain everything you would find on a government-produced certificate—they just have no legal standing, which shouldn't be a problem for family historians. The benefit of being able to do all these searches in a Family History Center without incurring more than a small shipping fee for the films, is obvious.

A Note about Northern Ireland

If you are looking specifically in the counties that now comprise Northern Ireland, the General Register Office for Northern Ireland (**www.groni.gov.uk**) is the place to apply for birth, marriage, and death certificates.

For Northern Ireland, the indexes and registers from 1921 are held at Oxford House, Chichester Street, Belfast. Unfortunately, none of the indexes are searchable online.

The only conclusion to draw from visiting the GRONI Web site is that the office is focused entirely on its statutory obligations for civil registration, and is oblivious to the enormous public interest in family history research

In order to obtain a certificate, you have to fill out an extensive form that requires virtually every detail that you would find on the certificate. The fields are mandatory, so if you are lacking a single piece of information you may conclude that you can't submit the form. For instance, a death certificate application requires not only the usual address of the deceased, but the post code (zip code) as well. This is absurd. Few people are likely to know the zip code of someone who has died. If other countries can do limited searches with a reasonable amount of identifying information, it seems strange that Northern Ireland can't. The GRONI will do limited searches—two years either side—if you submit an approximate date, and you can pay for wider searches, but you still need all the other information, such as mother's maiden name. The whole point of needing certificates, of course, is to find such information in the first place. If the details are already known, a certificate isn't necessary except as primary source verification.

GRONI is looking at simplifying this process, according to correspondence I had with them early in 2006. Additionally, here's a tip. Typing "unknown" into any of the mandatory fields usually works, though there is nothing on the site to say so.

Click the **Historical Records** link in the menu on the left of the home page to see a complete list of what is available at the GRO in Belfast, and on the link at the bottom of that screen for more details about the search facilities and procedures for people visiting.

Northern Ireland Public Records Office

The Web site of the **Public Record Office of Northern Ireland** (**www.proni.gov.uk**) is a good source of information for what's available on microfilm and for background explanations of what these records contain. Log on to the home page and select **The Records in PRONI** link from the left-side menu.

Scroll down and read this entire page, and then link to the indexes for microfilms for the Church of Ireland and the Presbyterian Church. Again, these are simply pointers to microfilms, not to the names of people.

At the top of this same page there is a link to **Records Held.** This gives you a list of everything held in the Public Search Room. On this page you can also get background information on such things as the census records that were destroyed, and census substitutes for the eighteenth and nineteenth centuries.

13

DIGGING DEEPER IN THE BRITISH ISLES

Overview

Most of our efforts in previous chapters have been focused on censuses and vital record indexes and registers, which provide the maximum amount of information in the shortest time. Efforts to transcribe genealogical data for the Internet have quite properly concentrated on these key sources first.

But the genealogical research world is much richer than this. In the course of a lifetime, an individual may leave many more written traces of his or her existence than a line on a census every ten years, or a handwritten name on a birth, marriage, or death register.

There may also be interactions with government agencies of one kind or another, such as schools or courts. There may be property records, military records of service, references in newspapers, or registers of employees kept by companies. Then there are poorhouses, correctional institutions, postal directories, probate records or wills, professional association lists, tax records, and travel documents.

Genealogists have learned that virtually any document that contains an identifiable name is of use to someone. The four suggested steps in this chapter are not exhaustive, but will cover some of the easiest online places to access for these additional resources.

Step 1: Explore GENUKI

The British Isles are a good place to introduce some of the other online sources that we have barely touched so far. So how do we know what to look for and where? There are some excellent starting points, one of which is the Web site of GENUKI (short for Genealogy of the United Kingdom and Ireland). GENUKI isn't a collaboration site that tries to link people doing similar research but is more of an online reference library for primary historical material. Run by volunteers, the site is free to use. It even has a section devoted to researching from overseas.

Go straight to **www.genuki.org.uk/big,** which I find the most useful launching point for exploring this site. The map breaks the British Isles into its constituent parts, with separate maps for Ireland and even the Isle of Man and the Channel Islands. Below the maps is a list of resources that apply to the British Isles as a whole. Clicking on one of the maps brings up a list of genealogical sources for that specific country, and the lists are substantial.

Once you are ready to go beyond census and vital records, these lists are worth browsing slowly and looking for possible sources of relevance, including online data. There are many of them. A sampling of the more unusual:

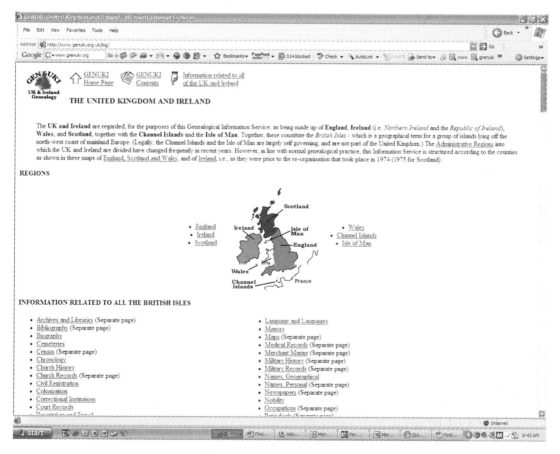

Genuki's site is an excellent place to explore the less usual avenues of research. (Image used by permission of the Trustees of Genuki. Home page: www.genuki.org.uk).

- A photographic collection of the churches of Britain and Ireland
- A site where you can access 90,000 birth, marriage, and death certificates that have been contributed by users—with a month's free trial
- The Black (and white) Sheep Index—names from 350,000 reports, including victims and villains, extracted from newspaper reports of court cases and inquests from 1865 to 1900.
- Passenger Lists on the Internet (leading to extensive links)

Step 2: Look for Parish registers on FamilySearch.org and British-Genealogy.com

After census and vital records, the biggest single source of information for England and Wales is from the parish registers compiled by clerics and bound in volumes from 1597 (we already covered the Scottish equivalent in the last chapter). Some such records date back as far as 1538, but were loose pages not bound in registers, and few now exist.

One fortunate break for researchers in England and Wales is that from 1597, clergymen were required not only to compile registers of baptisms, marriages, and burials, but to send a copy to the supervising bishop. There are therefore sometimes two sources to choose from, or one may have survived while the other has been lost.

Bishops' transcripts are now held in government offices, usually at the county level, but The Church of Jesus Christ of Latter-day Saints' microfilm copies of these records are extensive. All can be accessed at a local Family History Library as well as County Record Offices, but many of the records have also been extracted and names can be searched for online.

Because of the way the FamilySearch site is structured, there is no option to cherry-pick specifically from a menu of bishops' transcripts or parish records and then go straight to the names on the register. But you can use the Library Catalog to search for the place names in which you are interested, since it will tell you whether your targeted locality has been filmed. In effect, any use of the search engine for your British ancestors before 1837 is going to draw on this source of parish registers or bishops' transcripts because there was no civil registration before that date.

The process of getting to the names is similar to what we saw in Chapter 8.

1. Log on to **www.familysearch.org.**

Listing of the extensive British Record Collection on FamilySearch.org, including parish registers. Access the detailed lists, including some online data, through the Library tab. (FamilySearch.org, image copyright 1999, 2005 by Intellectual Reserve, Inc. Used by permission.)

2. Click the **Search** tab.

3. Select **International Genealogical Index** from the left-hand column.

4. Type in the known first and last names of your ancestor (without the parents or spouse information unless the list of results is unmanageable).

5. When you are presented with the list, click on the desired name to bring up the IGI Individual Record.

6. The key information will be under the **Source Information** section at the bottom of the screen. Click on the **Source Call No.** and you'll be taken to the Library Catalog description of the records. You'll find the name of the registers by parish, plus the years the registers cover and any missing pages or dates. There may be several quite different parishes on the same roll of microfilm, but this will be clearly indicated.

7. Click on the **Batch no.** in the same section and you'll be returned to the search engine with the batch number already entered.

8. Click on the **Search** button to see an alphabetical list of everyone in the parish register, which you can browse at your leisure.

Because the online records are not the original films (at least, not yet), you will want to check the original film at a Family History Center or local facility that holds such records, usually the County Record Office. It's much easier to do so when you've found a name online and just need confirmation.

British-Genealogy.com

An excellent, comprehensive site for explaining parish records is found at **British-Genealogy.com.** From the home page on **www.british-genealogy.com,** click **Church Records** from the menu on the left of the screen. This presents you with a wealth of information on the development of parish records, including an explanation of the contents that can be expected for each time period. Everything on British-Genealogy.com is beautifully and clearly laid out and also free. However, it is not in itself a source of online data. It's an information site with background and pointers to data sources.

You should also check out the explanation of British counties and subdivisions on British-Genealogy.com. You get to it directly from the **County Resources** link on the home page menu.

Step 3: Check Boyd's Marriage Index

Checking the Boyd's Marriage Index is such an easy thing to do that it shouldn't be omitted. Boyd's Marriage Index is an index of English marriages from 1538 to just after civil registration began in England in 1837. Between 6 and 7 million entries cover perhaps 15 percent of all English marriages over three centuries. The indexes are drawn from marriage registers, bishops' transcripts, and marriage licenses. While Boyd's coverage of some counties is sparse, it is almost complete in others.

Percival Boyd also undertook a burial index, although it's restricted to about 243,000 entries in the London area from 1538 to 1872, and contains mostly adult males. You can search by surname, forename, year of death, and the burial ground.

Boyd's indexes are online at **www.originsnetwork.com.** As mentioned in Chapter 11, this is a subscription site, but short-term access is possible.

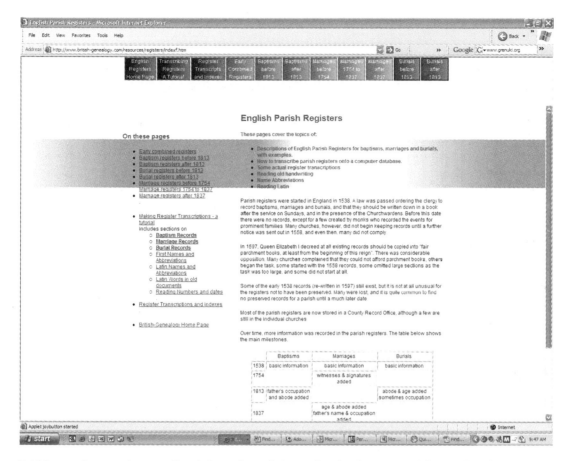

British-genealogy.com is an excellent information and signposting site. (Image copyright www.british-genealogy.com. Used by permission.)

TIPS: Early English Searches

Go back far enough and you'll begin to find parish registers written in Latin. Don't be deterred. It's harder to read the handwriting than to translate the Latin. Relatively few words are used in these registers, and speakers of European languages can figure them out with a little practice. Some are obvious—you know that "baptizavi" has something to do with christening (I have baptized) and "matrimonium" sounds like marriage. "Filius" is close to the French for "son." However, if you get

continued ➔

Early English Searches (cont.)

stuck on "in comitatu," British-Genealogy.com has a section called **Latin Words to recognize** under its Church Records section. "In comitatu," by the way, is "in the county of."

What are Marriage Banns?

Sometimes you'll come across a reference in online sources to *marriage banns* rather than the registration of the marriage itself. The term is used widely around the world, even in more recent times. *Banns* comes from an old English word meaning *to summon*. Essentially, it's a summons of people privy to the marriage to lodge any legal impediment, such as a previous marriage or a marriage to a close relative. Under a different name, the practice of issuing marriage banns in this way probably dates back to twelfth-century France. By virtue of the Marriage Act in England of 1752, banns were supposed to be read from the church pulpit on three successive Sundays before the wedding occurred. Neither the reading of banns nor the issuance of a license to marry is necessarily proof that the marriage took place.

Before civil registration, a bridegroom and a friend could also enter into a marriage bond, in which they made a declaration that a sum of money was to be forfeited if any impediment to the marriage came to light.

A marriage license was a way around some of these formalities. Obtaining a license from Church authorities to marry made it unnecessary to have banns called. The Library Catalog on FamilySearch.org has a list of records, including marriage bonds, banns, licenses, and related records.

Lady Day

Dates can be a bit of a problem before 1752 if the event fell within the first three months. Until that year, the New Year began on Lady Day, March 25, not on January 1. Because the year therefore begins on March 25 and continues until March 24 of the following year, you will need to make adjustments. If you are reading a microfilm of the original record, you can adjust the date yourself, or write something like 5 Jan 1711/1712. You should make a note attached to the individual in your genealogy program that you have made that correction. If you are using later transcripts, the date may have already been corrected. Look at the start of the film for any such annotation.

Step 4: Search Military Records

Some of the sites listed in this chapter are good pointers to the less usual sources of information mentioned in the overview. But one set of records stands out because of its ease of online access. A long history of British military tradition shows itself in numerous Web sites, some created by descendants of those who served. The **Commonwealth War Graves Commission** site at **www.cwgc.org** provides free searchable indexes to 1.7 million men and women who died in British Commonwealth forces in the two world wars.

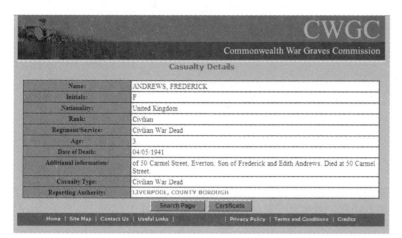

Record of civilian death in the bombing of Liverpool, 4 May 1941. (Reproduced with thanks to the Commonwealth War Graves Commission for original material.)

The database covers 23,000 cemeteries worldwide. Also useful is the inclusion of the names of 67,000 civilian war dead. Often, the record includes names of a spouse and parents, and even an address.

Additional information on British military records can be found at:

- "British Military Records," by Jay Hall, on the GENUKI site at **www.genuki.org.uk/big/BritMilRecs.html**.

- British Isles Military Records, Wars & Conflicts, with several useful links, at **www.genealogy.about.com/od/uk_military/**.

- FamilyRecords.gov.uk is an official government site, with a good section on military records and how to find them at **www.familyrecords.gov.uk/ topics/military_1.htm**

- Use Google or another search engine with the name of a regiment, specific conflict, and/or the name of an ancestor.

World War II cemetery in France, overlooking English Channel at Normandy beaches. Many indexes exist for military cemeteries for fallen soldiers of many nations.

Step 5: Check the National Archives

The British National Archives in London has one of the largest archival collections in the world, representing nearly 1,000 years of history, from the famous Domesday Book of 1086 to recent papers.

There are two things to know about the National Archives. First, they have a very enlightened attitude to public access—in fact, they *want* to make the information they have available to the public. That includes anyone, from anywhere in the world, not just British citizens. Even for records that have not yet officially been released, the British Freedom of Information Act—akin to that of the United States—ensures that everything is available unless there is an exemption attached to the records. Exemptions usually only apply where some harm might result if the information is released. So, the assumption is that information is available to the public from the outset unless one of the exemptions applies.

The second thing to know is that the National Archives prides itself on being on the leading edge of digitizing records to put them online, and access is free. (If the information isn't yet online, they will do searches, but the searches are expensive).

The National Archives Web site is at **www.nationalarchives.gov.uk** and its home page has options for researching family history, military history, and history in general. However, there is no all-name index. If you want to search the family history records you will have to do so by looking at PDF files on-screen.

The section offering online records access is called DocumentsOnline and can

be accessed directly at **www.nationalarchives.gov.uk/documentsonline.**
Many of the searches will lead you only so far. You may still have to ask for a search
of a particular record that you find in a catalog, but the wealth of records is staggering. There are indexed name files of various sorts, including a huge collection
of wills.

An example of an indexed name search appears on page 191. These are from a
list of soldiers who received medals in World War I. To illustrate the database here,
I entered the uncommon name of Otterson. The resultant list of seventeen names
includes five members of my own family—my grandfather among them. A fee of
around $6 is payable for each image ordered. An attractive feature of the site is not
just that you can pay online by credit card, but that the image is then available
immediately for download in Adobe PDF format.

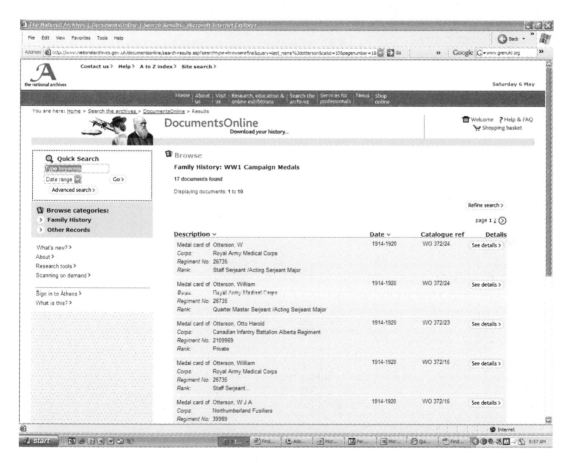

Results of a search for military campaign medals ast the British National Archives. (Crown copyright, reproduced
by permission of The National Archives, www.nationalarchives.gov.uk).

Step 6: Use Google and Other Search Engines

Simple as it may sound, using an Internet search engine with a specific name, combined with a date or a location, can yield good results. One of the most enjoyable aspects of family history is what can turn up from such efforts to dig a little deeper.

Early in 2006 I received an email from my cousin Margaret in Wales, who had discovered a short paragraph in a British government report from the 1840s. The report was compiled by the Royal Commission into the Employment of Children in Mines, and included evidence taken from children working in the horrific conditions below ground. The twelve-year-old John Otterson—who describes in his boyish way and yet so graphically that terrible life for a child—was the younger brother of my second great grandfather. He began working in the mines at the age of eight or nine. Most of my ancestors from that period in England were coal miners, but Margaret may have never come across this genealogical gem if it had not been for the Internet.

The route to this was actually quite simple. **4schools** is part of Durham University Library's effort to encourage the use of primary source material by students and teachers. The university has compiled some amazing resources to help discover what life was like in the past. Once on this site, it was a short step for Margaret to find a section on work practices during that part of the nineteenth cen-

English miners with pit pony at an unidentified colliery in County Durham in the 1800s. Some of the miners are boys still in their teens. (Reproduced by permission of the Durham County Record Office.)

tury. Young John Otterson's testimony to the Royal Commission virtually jumped out of the page.

Interestingly, if you simply type "John Otterson Durham" into the Google search engine you go directly to this report—a reminder of what powerful allies the Internet search engines have become to the family historian.

> **No. 116.—*John Otterson.***
>
> I am 13 the 15th April, 1841.—I became a door-keeper on the barrow-way four years ago. I got up at four o'clock, took breakfast, walked to the pit by half-past four; began work at five. I had no candles allowed at all, except my father gave me any; he gave me four, which burnt about five hours, and I sat in darkness the rest of the time. I liked it very badly, it was like as if I was transported. I used to sleep; I could not keep my eyes open. The overman used to bray us with the yard wand; he used to leave the marks; I used to be afraid. The putters sometimes thumped me for being asleep. They never gave me any money. We loose at five and come home. I got my dinner—washed; I took off all my clothes, and then went to bed about eight. I did not go to play; the more we play, the more we sleep in the pit.

Extract from the Royal Commission Report into the Employment of Children in Mines, 1842. (Reproduced by permission of the Durham County Record Office.)

Step 7: Register with GenesReunited

GenesReunited at **www.genesreunited.co.uk** is worth mentioning because of the significant success it has enjoyed. Much of the activity on this site comes from people looking for lost relatives—in fact the site makes a point of advertising those features. It is also characterized by a huge majority of its users being beginners. There is little genealogical information of an instructional or resource nature here—for that, you have to go elsewhere.

That said, GenesReunited generates a significant amount of email. The process is to upload your family tree in a GEDCOM file. The site translates that to a list of names which are then posted. Anyone researching any of your surnames can write to you via the site (your own contact information remains confidential). When people write to you, you have the facility to allow them to see the tree you have posted—otherwise, it remains invisible. You can also request to see their tree on the site.

GenesReunited will email you periodically with a list of "hot matches" drawn from a comparison of the names and dates you have posted with the names and dates of others that appear to be the same. Like other sites offering the same capabilities, most hot matches are lukewarm at best because the matching criteria are so broad.

Recent improvements have made the site more serviceable, but it is still somewhat cumbersome and by far the best course is to ask someone to send you a GEDCOM of their family tree so you can view it in your own software program rather than getting bogged down on the site. While there are certainly experienced researchers on GenesReunited, expect to find many of the site's users unfamiliar with even basic protocols, such as sending GEDCOMs.

Because so many users are beginners, you will also find that many of them have compiled their trees from unquestioning acceptance of other users' research. Nevertheless, one of the great values of the site is its ability to fill in gaps with living relatives. I have added hundreds of names to my extended family tree using this site, just through contact with distant cousins. If you want to cast your net that wide and you have significant British connections, GenesReunited is worth taking the time to register. The annual fee is minimal.

14
OTHER
INTERNATIONAL
RESEARCH

Overview

The estimate that 70 percent of Americans trace at least some of their ancestry to the British Isles—and the fact that so much is now available online—justifies the closer look we have taken at online British and Irish records in the past three chapters. Nevertheless, there are growing collections of records available throughout the rest of the world. While you shouldn't expect to find the breadth and depth of U.S. or British records in every country, there are still some excellent sources, from Norway to Australia.

The starting point for a global overview is the online library catalog at FamilySearch.org. A million and a half microfilms and nearly 300,000 microfiche contain genealogical records of over 150 countries, making the library in Salt Lake City by far the largest family history repository in the world. For some countries, records are already online, such as the civil registration records for Mexico and Scandinavia. In most cases, however, it will be necessary to visit the nearest Family History Center until the records are digitized, indexed, and placed online (see Chapter 17).

For a simple overview of the vast LDS international records collection, go to **www.familysearch.org** and click the **Library** tab, then choose **Record Collections** from the menu on the left. Clicking **International Records Collection** will give you the collection highlights for over thirty countries where significant records have been microfilmed. These include collections found nowhere else. The library has the largest collection of Korean family histories anywhere in the world, for example.

Because the types of records that yield the most data have already been examined extensively in previous chapters, this chapter will focus on listing prominent online resources country-by-country, rather than looking in detail at how to examine each site. If your ancestry reaches into these countries, use the principles we have covered in previous chapters to drill down further. Because of the vast amount of data coming online, no single book could adequately cover all of it. My purpose here is to point you in the direction of those Web sites that have significant amounts of online data (that is, the names of people and associated events), instructional materials that are exceptionally clear, or those that provide a large number of links specific to a country.

Canada

A vast amount of Canadian genealogical data is already online, with more being added daily. Here are some of the major sources:

FamilySearch.org. The 1881 census of Canada is accessible on FamilySearch.org without charge. It is one of the most valuable genealogical resources freely available online.

To access the census:

1. Log on to **www.familysearch.org**.

2. Click the **Search** tab on the menu at the top of the page.

3. Click the **Census** link on the menu at the left of the screen.

You'll find a wealth of other Canadian sources that you can access at a Family History Library by clicking the **Family History Library Catalog** tab on this same page. Enter "Canada" as a place name and then select **Canada** again from the top of the list. You will see a list of well over 300 sources at the library. Pay special attention to census records (especially the indexes), emigration and immigration indexes, and vital records. A great deal of material is background or reference information, but

> ### TIP: Locating Canadians on FamilySearch
>
> Use the search engine under the Search tab on the site to simply type in a Canadian ancestor's name with "Canada" and "All provinces" as the only other criteria. If the resultant list is too long, narrow the search by filling in other fields. This search will cover all Canadians in the indexed databases, including, for instance, people born in Canada but on the censuses of the United States.

HOME

British Columbia Lists

CENSUS	VOTERS LISTS, NEWSPAPERS, DIRECTORIES & STRAYS	GOVERNMENT SOURCES	PETITIONS	STORIES and PICTURES

CENSUS

1871 City of Victoria Census	1881 Vancouver Island Census	1891 Vancouver Island Census
More Material Continuously Added	1901 CENSUS of the VICTORIA CITY and Southern Vancouver Island over 26,300 entries	Items below also include b, m, d, bios, obits & marriage notices

VOTERS LISTS, DIRECTORIES, NEWSPAPERS & STRAYS

BC Voters List 1875	Obituaries of British Columbians from The Yukon News obituaries, 1960 to 2000	Directories 1882 - Victoria & Nanaimo 1892 - Victoria
BC Voters List 1898	1909 Geographic Names and Clubs, Associations & Churches of Vancouver Island	Victoria Directory 1868
	Genealogical Extracts (BMDs & misc.) from BC Newspapers, 1861 - 1875	
	Genealogical Extracts (BMDs & misc.) from The Canadian News (pub. in London, Eng) 1858 - 1861	

GOVERNMENT SOURCES

TOP

SCHOOLS

BC Public School Teachers & Trustees 1888-89 & 1889-90	Public Schools Report 1890	Public Schools Report City of Victoria, 1894	Provincial Roll Of Honour, 1889

POSTAL

BC Post Offices & Postmasters, 1893	Unclaimed Letters Victoria Post Office 1863	Unclaimed Letters Victoria Post Office 1870	Unclaimed Letters New Westminster Post Office, 1871

PRISONS & INCOME TAX

Deaths of Convicts B.C. Penitentiary, 1875-1916	Report On Gaols & Rules For Prisoners 1888	Prisons of BC 1884	Income Tax B.C. people, 1889

JUSTICE OF THE PEACE & CIVIL SERVICE

These British Columbia lists at www.rootsweb.com/~canbc/bc.htm are a good example of data produced by the Canadian GenWeb Project. GenWeb sites are a good place to browse for records like this, but you can also sometimes get to them by typing specific interests into an Internet search engine. (Image: copyright BCGenWeb. Reproduced by permission of the Coordinator.)

many names have been extracted and are on the IGI. Other name collections are on CDs, details of which are in the catalog.

CanadaGenWeb. The role of the CanadaGenWeb Project is to help Internet researchers get to the Canadian data they need if it's already online as part of census extracts, vital record transcriptions, or more unusual sources. The project is based on USGenWeb, and the information is grouped primarily within the various provinces. The site's volunteers also add continually to the data already online.

As with the USGenWeb Project, each provincial site is very individual, offering data and information specific to that locality. Searching for record types is easy, and none of the lists is so long that it can't be browsed. Finding a database that has exactly what you want for your time period is another matter. Nevertheless, CanadaGenWeb should be one of the first places to look for your Canadian ancestors.

Automated Genealogy. Take a close look at this site and bookmark it. Those who operate the site are not only transcribing census records but are linking various sources mentioning a single individual. So, if you find a name on a census, you may also find links to other sources mentioning the same person. Look especially at the Illustrated Index to the 1901 Census Project, where actual photographs are being linked to names. This is the way of the future, so keep an eye on this site. Transcription projects include Canadian censuses of 1901 and 1911, and the three prairie provinces of 1906. Find the site at **www.automatedgenealogy.com.**

Canadian Genealogy. This is a very nice Canada-wide site, with lots of links to online resources. Indicators show whether the data is free or not, and what's new to the site. Find it at **www.canadiangenealogy.net.**

Ancestry.com. The premier subscription site arranges its Canadian collections by province, and they are significant. Of course, you can also do a global search for a specific name and then pull the most likely Canadian sources from the results list. Concentrate first on Canadian immigration records, censuses, and vital records, which are all searchable. You can get more details for some of what you see on-screen by paying a fee.

Library and Archives Canada. Log on to the main site at **www.collec-tionscanada.ca,** then click **Canadian Genealogy Center** on the right of the screen. Click **Databases** on the menu across the top of the page.

The digitization process is always further advanced than the indexing process, and it shows here at the Canadian National Archives. Searches of some sources take much longer than others. One of the most useful databases is the 1901 Canadian census. There is a nominal index but not for the entire census, so read the FAQ section to get the most out of using it. You can also view the 1911 census, although again only by geographical location. Since no name index is available, you will have to search the pages as you would a microfilm.

Online data is also available for immigration and naturalization records, marriages and divorces in certain periods, and land and military records. All are listed under the **Databases** section.

Internet Search Engines. To find provincial public archives and records offices, type the name of the province and "public records, vital records, or archives" into a search engine like Google. What's available online on these provincial sites varies considerably. Some have virtually nothing, others can be surprising. For instance, Nova Scotia has a Halifax City deaths database, indexed, that allows not only a free view of the index but views also of the original handwritten images.

Military records. Canada's equivalent site to the Commonwealth War Graves Commission site discussed in Chapter 13 is on the site for VAC (Veterans Affairs Canada). Go to **www.vac-acc.gc.ca/remembers/** and look down the list of links until you see **The Canadian Virtual War Memorial.** Click on this link for access to the data.

Unlike the British site, photographs have often been contributed to these memorials. The **Commonwealth War Graves Commission** Web site also includes Canadians. An excellent site for background and context—one that claims to be the oldest and largest of its kind on the Web—is **Land Forces of Britain, the Empire and Commonwealth** at **www.regiments.org.** Click on the **Nations** tab, and then select **Canada** from the world map.

Cyndi's List, Genealogylinks.net. It's very easy on these signposting sites to get caught in unproductive links to other sites where the listed links are outdated or where you end up facing a subscription invitation. Nevertheless, patience can pay off. Focus on census and vital records, and on the specific localities you want in order to find sources of all types. For the home pages of these sites, type the required country and the type of records you're seeking into the search engine.

Mexico, Central, and South America

Mexico

This is not a treatment of Mexican-Americans or Hispanic sources within the United States, but a look at what's available outside the United States.

FamilySearch. By far the most significant online data for Mexico is on FamilySearch.org. The Church of Jesus Christ of Latter-day Saints has microfilmed and digitized a large collection of vital records and church records for Mexico, and has also filmed the only publicly available census—that of 1930. The census, however, is presently available only on microfilm.

Start with the **online research guide** for Mexico. To get to it:

1. Click the **Search** tab at FamilySearch.org.
2. Select **Research Helps.**
3. Select **M** from the alphabetical list and scroll down to Mexico. You can see descriptions of a number of Mexican online resources.
4. To start, click **Mexico Research Outline.**

Look down the list for anything that applies to your particular search. The list is long and varied, and you will find nothing this comprehensive anywhere else. Note the section on censuses. Census records in Mexico are both less accessible and less reliable than in the countries we have examined so far, for many reasons. Vital records and Church records are more dependable sources.

Civil registration began in Mexico in 1859 and had become general by 1867. For periods before that, you will have to rely on mostly Catholic Church records, which are excellent sources. There is no national repository for all church records in Mexico, but the Family History Library's collection of church records before 1930 is extensive, and goes back several centuries.

The recent addition of Mexico vital records to the online databases on FamilySearch.org brought a significant step forward for Mexican research. Access the vital records by clicking on the **Search** tab from home page, and then **Vital Records** from the menu.

The MexicoGenWeb Project. This site is far behind comparable projects, where volunteers have been working for much longer and in much greater numbers. Links on the site also tend to be out of date. But it should be checked periodically for additions of new data. You can find it at **www.rootsweb.com/~mexwgw.**

Cyndi's List. This signposting site has noted some Mexican links in the Hispanic section at **www.cyndislist.com/hispanic.htm,** but the paucity of sites with online data is obvious from how thin the list is. Sometimes help can be found from the message boards on **RootsWeb.** There are several devoted to aspects of Mexican research where you can post queries.

Ancestry.com has a number of Mexican parish records between 1751 and 1880 on its site.

Central and South America

Web sites for online data in Central America and most of South America are still in their infancy. Some GenWeb sites exist, and others are looking for hosts. The **FamilySearch** Web site is the only significant source of data at the time of writing. Consult the online research guides on FamilySearch.org, specific to each country, for the latest information.

Europe

European Internet resources are much further advanced than anywhere else in the world outside North America. The WorldGenWeb Project divides Europe into four parts—the British Isles, Central Europe (which actually includes the Nordic countries), the Mediterranean, and Eastern Europe (mostly the countries of the former Soviet bloc).

The Nordic Countries

Scandinavian genealogy is different from anything we have done so far, and a little familiarization is essential before beginning to look for records.

Norway is a good place to start our look at the Scandinavian countries since a number of significant databases have recently come online. This includes a number of census and other records pioneered by the **Norwegian Historical Data Center** at the University of Tromsø, and vital records now on the FamilySearch.org site.

Norway's GenWeb site at **www.rootsweb.com/~wgnorway/new.htm** is also useful. Log on and read the link suggested in the opening paragraph, **Research Tips: Before you Research in Norway**. (Another good beginner's reference is the Norway guide in the **Family History Research Helps** on FamilySearch.org). With a little background knowledge, the online databases will make much more sense. But remember that these guides, good as they are, are not updated every day and do not necessarily cover the most recent additions to the growing number of resources online.

Because much depends on whether you can find out where in Norway your ancestor lived, the recent additions of Norwegian census data that allows nation-wide searches is a huge help.

The University of Tromsø—which, incidentally, claims to be the most northerly situated university in the world—is doing fabulous pioneering work not only in making census data available but other records also. The Norwegian Historical Data Centre (NHDC) is a national institution under the university's Faculty of Social Science. Its objective is to computerize all of the Norwegian censuses from 1865 onwards, together with the parish registers and other sources from the eighteenth and nineteenth centuries. The home page is at **www.rhd.uit.no/indexeng.html.**

The site is in English and Norwegian, though not all the pages have been translated. It is still fairly easy to find your way around the site, however. One innovative feature is a database for the 1886 Land Register, with each locality downloadable in a zipped Excel file. Some parish vital records have been digitized and can be searched online.

The other significant single source of online data for the Nordic countries is the vital records collection on **FamilySearch.org**, which covers Norway, Sweden, Denmark, and Finland births/christenings and marriages (but not deaths).

The GenWeb sites for these same countries vary considerably in their layout and usefulness and the frequency of encountering broken links.

Sweden has also made substantial advances recently in making research tools, information, and databases available online. The next few pages will look at four particularly helpful Swedish Web sites.

The **Federation of Swedish Genealogical Societies** is the umbrella organization for 150 genealogical societies covering the whole of Sweden. Their Web site is at **www.genealogi.se** and a menu on the left of the home page offers an English translation. While not an exact English-language replica of the Swedish site, it contains all the key links to important information and to several online databases.

If you have not engaged in Swedish genealogical research before now, your starting point is the translated English-language home page. Find it by clicking on the **Swedish Roots** link below the "In English" heading when you first log on to the Swedish site.

Read through the menu and explore the links top-to-bottom, starting with **The First Steps.** Here you will find guidance on the basic requirements for Swedish research, including the necessity of knowing your ancestor's Swedish name and the parish he came form. There are tips on how to uncover that information if you don't know it already.

The next heading is the **Anbytarforum.** This is the society's discussion board, and part of it allows discussions in English. Here, you can post queries on a variety of topics and interests and get responses in English. However, you should read through the rest of the menu options before you start posting queries. Without at least a basic orientation to Swedish records, you'll risk wasting people's time.

Read everything under the heading **Swedish Records.** The Swedes have some of the finest records in the world because they date back for several centuries. The Lutheran Church had enormous power through much of Sweden's modern history, and there was no civil registration at all until fairly recently. Even censuses—or their equivalent—were done by the church. Church records thus take on an even greater significance than they do in many other European countries.

For our purposes, we're primarily interested in what's online. Since the main menu stays visible with every page view, look under the menu heading **Useful Knowledge** near the bottom of the list, and click on **Links.** One section of the links

Swedish genealogy site Genline, where you can access original images of Sweden's rich collection of parish records. (Image copyright Genline AB 2000–2006. Used by permission.)

page is **Swedish Databases Online,** which include several parish record and census databases.

However, for a more substantial collection of parish and census data and the ability to search original record images online, go to a different Web site, **Genline**, at **www.genline.com.** You have to love the Scandinavians for their anxiety to share everything in English. All four of the Swedish sites that we'll look at here have their English-language counterparts.

Genline was created in the mid-1990s with the purpose of digitizing Sweden's rich historical church records and putting them on the Internet. These are the same records that Mormon microfilmers photographed in the 1950s and 1960s, then gifted a copy of the films to the Swedish National Archives. The information dates from 1500 to 1860. Additional information up to 1900 comes from other sources.

Genline is a subscription site, but there are options for short-term access and you can buy a 24-hour demo subscription for about $10 U.S. The half-yearly and annual subscriptions equate roughly with the cost of similar subscriptions with Ancestry.com, but watch also for special offers that can cut that cost substantially. You can make an intelligent judgment on what works for you once you have narrowed your ancestors down to specific parishes and dates. Genline's Web site tells you clearly which parishes are already available and what's in preparation.

The **Swedish National Archives** site (SVAR) at **www.svar.ra.se** is another way to access Swedish church records online. You can make a three-hour exploratory visit for 50 Swedish kronor, or between $6 and $7.

On this site you will also find the complete 1900 census, extracted from the household examination rolls that were made by the Swedish State Church. The record shows the home parishes where the information was recorded, with name, year of birth, parish of birth, gender, occupation, and marital status. Census data for some earlier censuses is available online, can be ordered on CD, or is in preparation. Additional databases on this site include one for seamen, and even one for convicts.

Now let's take a look at a different kind of Swedish site, one based on volunteered data from GEDCOM files. **DIS** is **the Computer-Genealogy Society of Sweden,** and a place for volunteers to share information. The data drawn from submitted GEDCOM files can be searched for a small annual subscription cost. The data is secondary material and therefore should be checked against primary sources before being accepted. DIS is found at **www.dis.se.** Click on the small British flag to go to the English-language version.

Again, always look at **FamilySearch.org** when exploring a new country. After hitting the **Search** tab, click on **Research Helps** and then click **S** as in "Sweden" and scroll down the page. As mentioned earlier in this chapter, there are now significant Scandinavian vital records online at this site.

Denmark is not yet as Internet-rich in data as Norway and Sweden. But one site stands out. At **http://ddd.dda.dk/kiplink_en.htm,** the Danish Data Archive site seems deceptively simple at first glance—quite empty of the splashy text typical of some new sites. The top three links are all gateway points to key data, however. The remaining links lead to other Scandinavian sites and sources, including an almost out-of-place link to census information on the U.S. Virgin Island of St. Croix. This is offered because of ownership of the island by the Danish West India and Guinea Company from 1733 until it was sold to the United States in 1917.

On the home page at the Danish Data Archive site, you can search across all counties and for a period from the 1700s to the 1900s by clicking on **Search for**

Individuals. Since it's not immediately apparent what data you are drawing from, or how much, read everything on the page carefully and click on the dropdown menu arrows wherever they appear. Extra information is in the vertical color bars on the right side of the page. The next menu item on the home page, **Expanded Search for Individuals,** is a variation of the first and provides more specific search options.

By clicking on **What's in the database** you can also look at the individual counties, parishes, and towns, and the periods the records cover. For instance, just entering the name of a parish without any other information and then hitting the search button shows a list of all the towns in the parish and the periods spanned.

There is an active **Iceland** genealogy mailing list on Genealogy.com, at **http://genforum.genealogy.com/iceland/.** Iceland has a wealth of genealogical data in its long history, and virtually everything has been filmed. Getting at it is best done through a local Family History Center. Census records back to the early 1700s include indexes for about every fifty years or less. Emigration and church records are also

```
Iceland - Census - 1703
Iceland - Census - 1703 - Indexes
Iceland - Census - 1762
Iceland - Census - 1762 - Indexes
Iceland - Census - 1801
Iceland - Census - 1801 - Indexes
Iceland - Census - 1801 - Indexes
Iceland - Census - 1801 - Indexes
Iceland - Census - 1816
Iceland - Census - 1816 - Indexes
Iceland - Census - 1835
Iceland - Census - 1840
Iceland - Census - 1845
Iceland - Census - 1845 - Indexes
Iceland - Census - 1850
Iceland - Census - 1855
Iceland - Census - 1860
Iceland - Census - 1870
Iceland - Census - 1880
Iceland - Census - 1890
Iceland - Census - 1901
Iceland - Census - 1901 - Indexes
Iceland - Church directories
Iceland - Church history
Iceland - Church history - Biography - 1746-1869
Iceland - Church records
Iceland - Church records - Indexes
Iceland - Church records - Inventories, registers, catalogs
Iceland - Colonization
Iceland - Court records
Iceland - Description and travel - Guidebooks
Iceland - Directories
Iceland - Emigration and immigration
Iceland - Emigration and immigration - Indexes
Iceland - Folklore
Iceland - Gazetteers
Iceland - Genealogy

Numbers 1-50 of 95 matching topics for this place.
```

Extensive Icelandic record collections are shown in this partial list from the Family History Library. (FamilySearch.org, image copyright 1999, 2005 by Intellectual Reserve, Inc. Used by permission.)

often indexed. This will be a gold mine for those with Icelandic ancestry when the films are eventually digitized and put online. To see the list, use the **Library Catalog** tab at **www.familysearch.org** and enter Iceland as a place name.

Netherlands

The early association of the Dutch with North America, particularly their influence in New York and Pennsylvania, make the Netherlands a key country for many American researchers.

The Dutch started early to keep civil registers in the home country. The official national Civil Register began in 1811 (some parts of the Netherlands were even earlier). Now, the Dutch National Archives and various regional history centers have joined forces to create **Genlias** at **www.genlias.nl.** The site is in Dutch and English, so look for the English translation button at the top of the page.

The online search engine gives you access to nearly 200 years of births, marriages, and deaths. But the really powerful element to this Web site is the search engine's capability of matching two name searches together. So by searching for a "first person" who you know is associated with a "second person" you can greatly reduce the number of results with common names. Other search options allow you to reduce searches down to specific towns.

If you read Dutch, the Genlias site has a number of links to other genealogical sources for those doing research in the Netherlands. Check out those at: **http://genealogie.startpagina.nl** and **www.stamboomsurfpagina.nl.**

If you don't read Dutch, check the research guide on **FamilySearch.org** by clicking the **Search** tab, then the letter **N** and choosing the Netherlands. While the research guides tend to lag behind in noting the online services that are now available, they provide excellent content and background for understanding the history of the country and the types of records that family historians should search for.

For a list of other significant online Dutch databases, go **to www.dutchgenealogy.com.** This site offers products for sale, but it has access to free information, too. Click on the **Learn** tab, then look for the last menu item—**Links to other favorite Dutch genealogy websites.** Several of these are in the Dutch language only.

Ancestry.com also has significant databases that include Dutch settlers in the United States.

France

French interest in genealogy began to build rapidly some twenty or thirty years ago, and the French have taken to it with a passion. As evidence, take a look at the **FranceGenWeb** home page at **www.francegenweb.org.** The impressive list of France-based GenWeb projects down the left side of the page is evidence of how deeply this activity has reached into the French community. Unfortunately, the value of the site is diminished by the fact that it doesn't have an English version.

If you read French, start with this site to familiarize yourself with the various links that interest you. Even basic French will be useful to look at the FranceGenWeb-related projects on the left of the home page. If you don't have that ability, an Internet translating tool probably won't be enough. You'll need the assistance of a French speaker to make any progress with such a wealth of instructional materials at your fingertips. Or, you can fall back on the instructional materials on **www.familysearch.org.**

The pros and cons of researching in France are fairly clear cut. France is a very old country and despite its many wars and social upheavals a lot of records have been preserved. On the other hand, the French government restricts access to vital records within the past 100 years. It's also important to know the precise town in France where your ancestor was born. Before making any serious attempt at research, read the online research guide for France on FamilySearch.org. There are some language helps in the guide for common terms in French, as well as an explanation of the various forms of local government and their terminology.

The **IGI** contains well over 3 million French names in its index, and the library collection of French records extends to 100,000 rolls of microfilm. As with other countries, check the **FamilySearch Library Catalog** with France as a place name. The list of options is huge.

Germany

The country that even vaguely resembles modern Germany was not established until 1870. Before that, the states of Germany existed in various forms going back many centuries. German history, and its location in the middle of Europe, has included frequent transfer of territory to the east and west, so an understanding of the geography of the country is unusually important. Your German ancestors may have come from somewhere that is now in Poland or France or elsewhere. In addition, many original records have been destroyed, and others are restricted. Church Records, civil registration, and emigration or shipping lists will form the nucleus of any research for German ancestors. It is important to know where in Germany your ancestor came from—meaning the town or parish, not the state. Knowing the religion also helps.

At first glance, the **Germany GenWeb Project** doesn't have much to offer. The two links you are most likely to click on first when entering the site at **www.rootsweb.com/~wggerman/index.htm** are **Databases** and **Resources**, but neither of these lead to significant information. Instead, click on **States of Germany,** which leads to much better possibilities. There are some helpful shipping lists and maps, including the home page link to the Map of Civil Registration, which shows the date that civil registration began in the various states that now make up Germany.

The **FamilySearch.org** research outline for Germany is the best source of online step-by-step help. In addition, the FamilySearch Web site shows a list of more than 250 matching topics in the Library Catalog for Germany, many of these leading to additional listed resources. Browse the list once you know what you are looking for by way of location and type of record.

A German Web site worth a visit is **Genealogienetz.de** or **Genealogy.net.** It contains mailing lists, the names of German genealogical societies where you can write for help, and links to a number of databases. Some of the databases are in German, and some are American sites specializing in German ancestry. These include ship and passenger lists. The facility for exchanging GEDCOM files and collaborating with other German researchers may be helpful. The site's home page is **www.genealogienetz.de/genealogy.html.**

Other recommended checks:

- **Genealogylinks.net** at **www.genealogylinks.net/europe/germany**
- **Cyndi's List German references** at **www.cyndislist.com/germany.htm**
- German forums/mailing lists on **RootsWeb, Ancestry.com, Genealogy.com** etc.
- **Google and other search engines** deliver many other possibilities. Combine a place name—at least a state if not a town—in your search criteria, using German words and spelling. Set the search options for German language as well as English.

Italy

The **Family History Library's** collection of Italian records is less extensive than that for parts of northern Europe, but still amounts to 65,000 rolls of microfilm. FamilySearch has now filmed more than half of the civil registrations of Italy—births, marriages and deaths from 1809 to 1910—and has done an especially good job in the southern provinces. Attention has now shifted to the central and northern provinces. These are not yet all online, of course, but many Italian records have also been extracted for the IGI and can be searched quickly and easily.

Researchers of Italian records will encounter the same problems found elsewhere in Continental Europe. You stand a better chance of getting further if you know not only the full name, but the town or parish and a date. You will encounter "Comune" or "Municipio"—villages and towns—frequently. Because there is no central repository for Italian vital records, you will have to work at the local level.

Knowing the locality also makes possible a much more intelligent search of the online data at FamilySearch.org via the IGI, and also in the search for vital records from the same site. The Vital Records Index for Western Europe is also available on CD for purchase or can be viewed at a local Family History Library. It contains extracted data birth, christening, and marriage records of Italy and several other western countries over several centuries.

First, familiarize yourself with the best approaches to tracing Italian genealogy by reading the online research guide. The screen image below, for Italy, is typical of those available for most major countries.

After exploring both the research guide and online data at FamilySearch.org, check out these additional sites:

- **ItalyLink.com** is a site for Italy-lovers in general, but it has a genealogy link on the home page that's worth using. Some of the sites that are listed aren't worth the time spent to click your mouse, but there are also valuable resources. If you can't see Vital Records in the list, then enter the following into the address line on your Internet browser: **www.italylink.com/vital-records.html.** The information was prepared by staff in the American Embassy in Rome to help people with Italian origins write for birth, marriage, and death certificates. Read the information carefully, and definitely use the

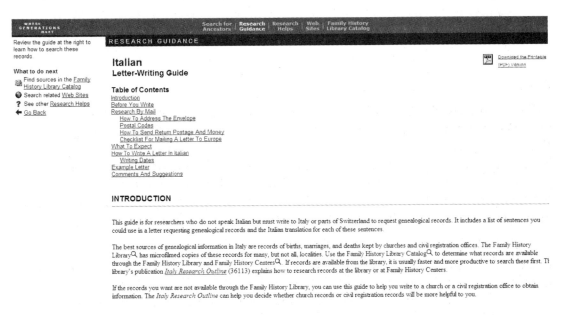

Italy research guide at FamilySearch.org. (Image copyright 1999, 2005 by Intellectual Reserve, Inc. Used by permission.)

online **Letter Builder,** which not only shows you how to lay out a certificate request letter but also translates it for you. Embassy staffs don't come any more helpful than this.

- **Italy GenWeb** is mostly a site of general information, but some of the links to the provinces are helpful. There is a limited amount of data online—for instance, ship passenger lists with names of migrants.

- **Italian Genealogy Online** at **www.italiangenealogy.atspace.com** is worth a visit. I tend to avoid sites that scream at me in multiple colors and bold type, but this site has a lot of valuable information. This is mostly methodology and Italian genealogy forums, but also includes some good guidance on writing letters to Italian authorities for vital record information.

- **Cyndi's List** contains quite a lot of links if you type Italy in the search engine from the home page and then click on the first item on the list. However, many of the links are very light on substance. Rather than browse unproductive links, including a lot of general information pages, look for list headings that seem to describe specific locations or online databases that interest you.

TIP: Italian Census Isn't the Best Source

Censuses—so often a boon to family historians—have been taken in Italy every ten years since 1871, but are not the readily accessible treasure trove that such records are elsewhere. Until 1911, Italian censuses usually listed only the head of the household by name, simply referring to the others by a collective number. After 1911 the censuses take on the appearance of those we have referred to in other chapters—names, relationships to the head of the household, birth places, and occupations.

Unfortunately, very little of the census records have been microfilmed. The records are generally held in the relevant Italian state archive.

An added problem is that the Italian census records are less reliable than those found in, say, the U.S., England, or Scotland. The census taker could accept information from someone else in the family—or even a neighbor—if the head of the household wasn't at home. Different cultures also have varying degrees of acceptance of officialdom. In some cases, information was unquestionably falsified.

Australia

Turning our attention to Australia brings us into another country where there is a wealth of genealogical data available, although there are also some conspicuous gaps. The similarities of Australian and U.S. history are striking. This vast country, first named New Holland by Dutch explorers, later became Australia when it was settled primarily by the British. It was not, as popular myth suggests, one vast penal colony. Certainly Australia was seen as a place for England to deport its criminals, but so also it was a place of dreams for settlers and fortune seekers—some of them soldiers after their term of service had ended.

Like the colonies of the United States, Australia's first century or more saw immigration that was primarily British. The various colonies that they established later became states or territories. Immigration from the mother country eventually broadened into waves of migrants from Europe and, more recently, global immigration that has changed the ethnic makeup of much of the country. Some Australians even immigrated to the United States, and vice versa.

Perhaps it's this relatively recent migrant history that infuses Australians with a love of genealogy. There is a certain romanticism about those early years that has led Australians with convict ancestry to be somewhat proud of that fact. Much effort has gone into unearthing the records of the early settlers. That, combined with huge penetration of the Internet into ordinary homes, is providing increasingly fertile ground for family historians working on the Web.

Conversely, the researcher of Australian family history is immediately struck by the obstacles imposed by more modern governments. Records such as censuses and birth, marriage, or death registers—so crucial to research the world over—are sometimes difficult or even impossible to obtain in Australia. Census records have been destroyed by government edict for privacy reasons—an unjustifiable act of official vandalism, in my view. Archiving census records for over a century before they are released to the public would take care of the privacy issue without destroying a nation's priceless heritage. In addition, restrictions on access to Australian birth, marriage, and death registers or indexes have prevented them from being microfilmed even for the famous Family History Library in Salt Lake City.

Still, there is much information available, and more is coming online continually. In fact, there are so many Web sites on the Internet dealing with Australian genealogy that the enthusiast who is also a novice can find himself or herself buried and bewildered in unproductive searches. Many sites simply contain links to other pages, including international databases that are of little use in Australian research.

Those listed here are characterized by genuine focus on Australia, including clear instructional materials and online data.

The **National Library of Australia** in Canberra maintains Web pages specifically for genealogists, with links to every state library. Start at **www.nla.gov.au/oz/genelist.html** and browse the list. Look for the links to **Australian genealogical or family history societies**, which are listed by state and found in dozens of Australian cities and towns. Where online sources are not available, many of these societies will do local searches for quite reasonable fees.

The most productive of the National Library records for online research are those listed under **Immigration** and **Convicts.** Many of the databases are substantial collections of indexed names, including the convicts carried in the "First Fleet" of ships (with over 1,000 convicts and military) that arrived in Australia in January, 1788. The **Military/Service Records** section also contains some productive links.

Web Sites for Genealogists is a gateway site with links to a variety of sources. Find it at **www.coraweb.com.au/index.htm.** It's a good, clean site and the list of links is not so exhaustive that you can't browse it in its entirety. There are some

IMMIGRATION

Indexes and lists of immigrants to each state are available in a variety of formats including microfiche, microfilm, book and electronic formats. Some are available on the internet. Local, state and family history libraries may hold material relevant to that state and other areas of Australia. The National Archives hold records on immigration after 1923 when immigration became a Commonwealth Government responsibility.

  ▸ NSW - Index to Assisted Immigrants 1839-96 - New South Wales 1844-1896, Moreton Bay, 1848-1859, Port Phillip 1839-1851
  ▸ NSW - Index to Unassisted Immigrants 1842-1855
  ▸ Mariners and Ships in Australian Waters - primarily New South Wales, unassisted records from the 1850-80s, incomplete
  ▸ National Archives of Australia - post 1923 immigration records
  ▸ Queensland Assisted Immigration 1848-1884
  ▸ South Australian Passenger Lists up to 1848
  ▸ Victoria - Index to Registers of Assisted British Immigrants - 1839-1871
  ▸ Victoria - Index to Unassisted Immigration to Victoria - 1852 -1923
  ▸ Victoria - Outward Passengers to Interstate, UK, NZ and Foreign Ports 1852-1861

CONVICTS

Indexes and records of convicts are available in a variety of formats including microfiche, microfilm, book and CD. Some indexes and guides are available on the internet and generally provide information for further research in material in State Archives and libraries.

  ▸ Convict Records at State Records NSW
  ▸ Convicts to Australia - A Guide to Researching your Convict Ancestors
  ▸ First Fleet Online
  ▸ Irish Transportation Records
  ▸ Irish Convicts to NSW 1791-1830
  ▸ Ships of the First Fleet
  ▸ South Australian transported convicts 1837-1851
  ▸ Swan River Convicts 1850-1868
  ▸ PRO Victoria - Convict Records
  ▸ Index to convict applications for permission to marry 1829-1857 - Tasmania
  ▸ Proceedings of the Old Bailey 1674-1834
  ▸ Claim a Convict

Part of the list of Web sites and links under the Australian Family History and Genealogy Section of the Australian National Library in Canberra. (Image copyright National Library of Australia.)

excellent jumping-off places here for people who have already read some of the beginner material on FamilySearch.org. The most productive links are to convict and early immigration sources, and vital records. The least productive are those to census records.

The Web site has a helpful table listing the names and addresses of the registrars of birth, deaths, and marriages in each state and territory of Australia and showing the current cost of certificates. Australian vital records certificates are not cheap.

The NSW Registry of Births, Deaths and Marriages maintains a site at **www.bdm.nsw.gov.au.** NSW stands for New South Wales, which is not only the most populous state but by far the most important for early convict records (the next being Tasmania). This site has good online facilities for ordering certificates. Other states are less helpful.

Certificates are only made available to the person named on the certificate if the birth was within 100 years or a marriage within 50 years. However, the Registry has a separate classification that it calls "unrestricted records" for family historians wanting certificates before these dates, and for deaths more than 30 years ago. Online indexes and application forms are available. The dollars shown on the site are Australian dollars, so American buyers typically will pay a little less than the prices shown.

FamilySearch.org has a substantial list of Australian resources in its Family History Library Catalog, but check the film notes because some valuable records in the main library are not available for distribution to Family History Centers. The IGI contains significant numbers of Australians from a variety of sources. As always, the ease of checking the IGI should place it high on your list if you know who you are looking for.

Footnote to International Developments

Several factors are aligning to bring more and more genealogical data online in countries where it has never been available before:

- The continued penetration of computer technology and the availability of the Internet to consumers

- Recognition by governments of their obligations to safeguard the vital records of their own people through microfilm or digitization

- Rapidly developing technology that is enabling digitizing and indexing of records to proceed at an ever-faster pace

- A huge increase in the number of people around the world interested in their family history

- Increasing numbers of volunteers willing to spend time to transcribe data and put it online, as evidenced by the spread of WorldGenWeb projects

If the country in which you are interested isn't listed in this chapter, check the Library Catalog at FamilySearch.org that covers dozens of countries. From the 1903 census of the Philippines to an alphabetical guide to gravestones in South Africa, microfilmed records are already available through Family History Centers. Digitized records are not too far behind, and commercial organizations like Ancestry.com are looking closely at international areas. To be sure, some of the materials are still sparse. But the trend is encouraging, and in most countries it's just a matter of time before online research from home will become part of standard practice.

15
MEAT ON THE BONES

Overview

No one knows for sure where the Internet is going. Neither will we know when we get there—whatever "there" is. For now, we have something approaching a vast, bewildering, and random assembly of digitized knowledge, experience, opinions, and culture from most parts of the world and in dozens of languages. It might be described as organized chaos, except that there is, at present, little about it that's truly organized. Search engines help us find our way through the maze, as a powerful magnet might help locate a needle in a haystack, but that isn't the same as organization.

Whatever the trends might be and however our children and children's children will access the world's accumulated knowledge (see Chapter 17), the Internet that is here now can still be of enormous help to us. Whatever our expertise about a subject, there is always someone, somewhere, who knows more. By drawing on real-life examples, this chapter shows how to harness the amazing resources of the Internet to flesh out the picture of your family that has begun to emerge from dates and places.

In previous chapters we touched briefly on a few individuals—the widow who ran the boarding house in pre-Depression Alabama; the children before the age of ten who worked in the pitch black of English coal mines for 12 hours at a time; the family wiped out as a city's dockland is bombed in the darkest days of World War II; the young man who rejects the family's tailoring business and leaves for the uncertain new world of America. This is what makes everything come alive. Now, by looking at one or two individuals, you can see how to turn genealogy—the names, dates, places, and relationships—into true family history, what is often called the "meat on the bones." For people who enjoy sleuthing, this can be a particularly enjoyable and rewarding activity.

A Personal Story

I never knew my own father. He was killed in a motor bike accident when I was nine months old. I grew up knowing only that he was a professional soldier and that he had been in a POW camp for a few years in World War II. These bare bones were supplemented with a very few anecdotes. I was vaguely aware of his old tool box—a musty wooden box that had once been dark green, kept in the bottom of the same cupboard as the water heater. And, I had learned of the existence of a war-time log book.

It wasn't until the age of twenty that a previously unarticulated need to know more about his life turned me to an interest in family history. Always, as I've pushed back the generations and lifted the curtain on the lives of hundreds of my ancestors, there has been that desire to know more about my own father.

In the 1980s, on a visit to England and Denmark, I took the trouble to capture on audio tape the childhood memories of his elder brother and sister. From my own generous sisters I obtained copies of photographs, his World War II medals, a collection of letters written during the war to my mother, and the now-prized war-time log book. It was as far as I could go.

Sgt. Robert Otterson, 1911–1949

With the rapid development of the Internet, however, I was able to dramatically expand my knowledge, adding context and circumstances to the events which shaped his life and—subsequently—mine. The following are some examples which I hope will stimulate you to explore the world of resources that is waiting to be tapped for your own forebears. However rich or poor your collection of "family papers," there is almost always something more to be learned.

From pages 1–4, war-time log:

[The engagement] had taken place about thirty miles south east of Mersa Matruh, in the desert. We had been encircled by the enemy and were attempting to fight our way out. After experiencing an inferno of shells and bullets during which the flames from burning vehicles illuminated the bodies of dead and wounded sprawled on the sand, I received the coup-de-grâce.

I had been riding on the running board of the vehicle in order to direct the driver to avoid boulders and other obstacles, when something seemed to clutch at the flapping tail of my greatcoat. This was followed immediately by a terrific crash. The truck swerved violently, and I was flung to the ground. A moment later I felt an intense pain in both of my legs as the rear wheel passed over them, grinding the flesh among the rocks and sand. I remember German stretcher bearers arriving shortly afterwards and carrying me into a wadi filled with wounded. My legs were roughly dressed, and I spent six long hours before the dawn listening to the battle raging on the escarpment above me.

[The] scene was seared on my memory by a burning June sun, under which I lay for the remainder of that day without any shade, and tormented by a myriad flies attracted by the smell of blood.

Several vital pieces of information were in this passage, beyond the description of the battle itself. He gives:

- A date (June) in 1942 when he was captured

- A location—thirty miles south east of Mersa Matruh on the North African coast

- He describes the engagement as "fighting our way out" of an encirclement

- He refers to an escarpment

All of that was enough to find on the Internet a precise description of the raging battle between June 21 and July 4—two crucial weeks in North Africa that finally stopped General Erwin Rommel's second offensive. The key article was one written by journalist and historian David H. Lippman and posted on a site named for a ship and called **www.usswashington.com.** This includes a detailed description of the military maneuvers on both sides. It allowed me to copy into my father's history with some confidence the following extract from Lippman's historical narrative:

> *As British troops withdraw from Mersa Matruh, Field Marshall Erwin Rommel orders a concentric attack on the town, to cut off the British retreat. The British pull out slowly, but with skill—one column zips through Rommel's own headquarters—but the Germans claim more than 7,000 POWs.*

Then I added*: Sgt. Robert Otterson is among them.*

The next step was to find photographs. By entering "Mersa Matruh" into Google and clicking on **Images,** I found a Russian map that had been translated into German and housed in the military publishing house of the former German Democratic Republic since 1975. The map showed the coastal area from that time period, including the arrows of the advancing Afrika Korps that end at Mersa Matruh. German copyright "fair use" policy readily allowed the use of the map not only for my own files but for publication in this book. I also found a precise map of

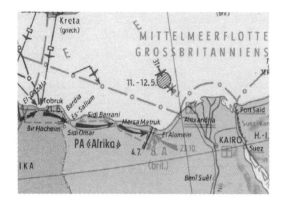

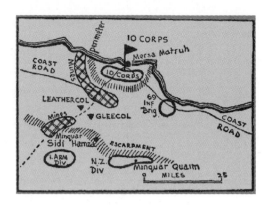

the battle area, showing the escarpment mentioned by my father in his log. The latter was on the University of Kansas Web site and appeared to be taken from a book—probably W.G.F. Jackson's "The Battle for North Africa, 1940–1943," published by Mason/Charter, New York 1975.

Photographs of the weaponry used in the great tank battles of the North African desert—tanks, long-range guns and aircraft—were easy to find.

Incidentally, Sgt. Robert Otterson could not have known it, but two weeks before his capture, his wife's brother, Sergeant Arthur Dix, was also taken prisoner in North Africa—at Bir Hakeim, Libya. He was not so fortunate. He died of wounds soon after.

The amount of detail and the degree of insight that can be gleaned from the Internet is often surprising, even to experienced searchers. Later, in a succession of prison camps ending in Germany, Sgt. Otterson described camp life and its toll, particularly on the mentally undisciplined. Some prisoners read everything they could get their hands on. Others wasted their time playing "crown and anchor." I had no idea what that was, but a few minutes on the Internet showed me—together with pictures of the dice that were used in this simple but addictive gambling game in which the "bank" always has the edge.

What did the prisoners use for currency? Usually, cigarettes or food, sometimes clothing.

When the soldiers were transferred to Italy because of the approach of the British counter-attack, my father helpfully mentions the name of the cargo ship—the *Ugo Foscolo*. From the Internet I now learn that the ship was one of the first in

From a ship modeling Web site, the aft section of the merchant ship *Ugo Foscolo*. (Image copyright Steve Backer, www.steelnavy.com.)

the eleven-ship *Poeti* class, named after Italian poets, which entered the merchant fleet for Italy in 1942. She was immediately pressed into service for transportation of military equipment and supplies. With a little searching, I find not only photographs but reference to the actual voyage to Naples that carried my father and so many other prisoners, now suffering badly from disease and malnutrition. Three weeks after discharging its miserable human cargo at Naples, the ship was caught by RAF bombers out of Malta, and sank in flames with its load of gasoline. I even find a site that shows me models of the ship for purchase—the aft hatch where my father spent three cramped nights is clearly visible.

As I read, I feel I would like to visit these places, walk these streets. The journal captures mood as well as event. One passage in particular strikes me. It's a scene in the Adriatic coastal town of Bari. The prisoners have de-trained and formed up on the platform, ready to march the five kilometers to their new camp. The march will take them through the town.

> *As we passed through the city, the doors and windows of every house were filled with curious spectators. There were giggling girls, mocking youths, grave-faced men and an old lady who watched while tears ran down her furrowed cheeks.*
>
> *Truly, our appearance was more to be pitied than laughed at, but ragged, unkempt, dirty and half-starved as we were, we unconsciously held our heads erect, got into step and gazed defiantly back at the mocking faces, while the war songs of 25 years ago burst from our lips and echoed through the street.*

By the time Sgt. Otterson is transferred to Germany, it is the latter part of the war and the invasion of Normandy has already taken place. His journal is scanty by this time, for reasons I have never discovered. But I can supplement it with a remarkable amount of detail from World War II Web sites. I type the name of the prison camp—Stalag IVB—into a Google search and find myself looking at a long list of personal stories by Allied veteran soldiers on www.pegasus-one.org.

There are diaries, stories, and even photographs. When my father talks of walking out of the gate after the camp was "liberated" by the Russians, I can see a photograph of the same gate, and of the "theatre," the shower block, the watchtowers, the latrines with zero privacy, the church during a worship service, and laundry hanging on a barbed wire fence. I look at the hundreds of faces in those photographs and realize that my father probably knew some of these men. What I am seeing is phenomenal. Everything comes alive because countless people load batches of data onto the Internet for who knows what reasons? But the result is a knowledge and feeling for my own father than I could not have obtained in any other way.

What if there had been no wartime log book? Then I would have fallen back on letters, looking at the dates and checking on history sites to find out what events were occurring on that day. I would still have had the taped interviews I did with his elder brother and sister. I would still have had the stories of him from older family members—stories telling of him waiting as a boy, with his brother, at the bottom of a steep hill in the English industrial town of Sunderland to help women up the hill with their heavy baskets of still-wet laundry from the

The main gate at Stalag IVB. (Image copyright Rijksmuseum Amsterdam. Used by permission.)

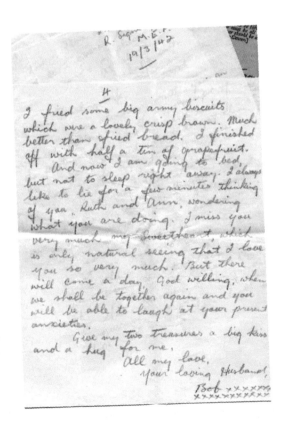

public washhouse. It would still give me a glimpse into that other time that now seems like another world. Almost any subject that can be named of a historical nature has some contribution by someone or other on the Internet. To find out more about public washhouses or laundries in that era, for instance, I could have consulted a lengthy article on that very subject on the British History Online Web site!

Fact and Fiction

One of the cautions in drawing history from the Internet is to choose reliable and authoritative sources. Resist the temptation to add color where there isn't any, or to stretch the facts to fit a pre-conceived story or to embellish an account because it fits a family legend. When dealing with history, there are many excellent Web sites belonging to universities, major public libraries and museums, government archives, and even major news media organizations—especially government-sponsored media such as PBS, the BBC, or the Canadian Broadcasting Corporation. Museums that specialize in the history of the region can be especially useful, as can local genealogical or family history associations. Content from Web sites written by individuals without qualifications or expertise should be verified elsewhere.

Sometimes we may find things that challenge popular myth. We like to think of Europe's "huddled masses yearning to breathe free," flooding into New York and other cities in the 1800s and finding both liberty and opportunity. And indeed there is much in Emma Lazarus's famous poem to the Statue of Liberty that deeply stirs us. Yet as any historian knows, the truth is much more complex. To an Irishman walking off the boat in New York in mid-July of 1863, there wasn't much that felt like the Golden Door. Instead he would have smacked right into the Draft Riots— the worst mob violence in New York of any time before or since. Other New Yorkers were being set upon by enraged mobs—an easy target for Irish and other poor immigrants driven to frenzy by draft laws which conscripted them for the Civil War, but allowed those who could afford $300 to buy themselves out. The supreme irony is that the mob anger in this northern city turned on the African-Americans, whose plight was at the very core of the Civil War

New York, 1892. (Picture in the public domain.)

itself. The New York draft riots were just ten days after the Union victory at Gettysburg.

Look for such events and context in every date that you record for your ancestors. For New York in the second third of the 1800s, the terrible squalor and poverty of the tenement buildings as thousands of immigrants poured into the city, the lack of decent sanitation or even minimum standards or rent control for urban housing, all provide us with context for an ancestor's experience—unless they were wealthy.

New York City Tenements, 1900–1910. (Library of Congress: Touring Turn-of-the-Century America. Photographs from the Detroit Publishing Company, 1880–1920.)

Henry's Arrival

Henry John Smiles came too late for those more turbulent times. When he disembarked at Ellis Island, it was September, 1892. The *Britannic's* ship manifest shows that he was bound for Chicago, so his stay in New York may have been short. In that next year—1893—Chicago played host to the World's Fair. The city was transformed. We wonder what this tailor's son from rural England thought of it all.

How Family Can Help

Several years ago, I received an unexpected email from Henry's great granddaughter in Alabama, Suzanne Smiles Barkdale. It was one of those emails family historians love to receive, because it filled in many gaps and answered many questions about what happened to Henry and his descendants beyond what I could find in the written record. I was able to do the same for Suzanne for the years before he arrived in the United States.

Suzanne had not researched the family before, and was in the early exploration stage. But among the things she was able to tell me that I didn't know was the sad fact that Henry died very young—in his late thirties, probably in Iowa. His death came after traveling around many parts of the country and trying his hand at a variety of enterprises, from working heavy machinery in Alabama to growing oranges in Florida.

TIP: Easy Access to Historical Events

To find out what was happening in the world in every year for the past 2,000 years, go to **www.brainyhistory.com.** Type your year in the search box, and select the circle that says Brainyhistory.com before clicking on the **Search** button.

All of this points out something we alluded to earlier. Family sources and family legends can provide much that is interesting when fleshing out the skeleton family tree. Most of it is available nowhere else. Near the beginning of the book, I advised readers to focus on the names and dates and places that were genealogically significant. That's the right starting place when you are looking for names and dates and places to positively identify ancestors, but additional material about school, work places, attitudes, and beliefs is exactly what you should try to ferret out when you're ready.

Gather everything you can from living relatives, and try to tape or video the conversation. At the beginning of the tape or digital recording, note the subject of the interview, who is asking the questions, and the date and place.

If there is a family box of papers, whether it's a shoe box or an organized filing cabinet, examine everything carefully. Throw nothing out. If you have a scanner, scan everything to preserve a digital image. Attach the more significant images to the appropriate individual in your family history software. And remember that photographs are the jewels to be most prized.

Use of facilities like email or instant messaging tends to be generational—many young people even now consider email "something old people use." But there are many exceptions, and if you and your elderly relative are really computer-savvy and live far apart, you can even hold your conversations through an online chat using a service such as AOL Instant Messenger, MSN Messenger, Yahoo! Messenger, Skype, or Google Talk. The advantage is that you can capture and archive entire conversations. However you approach it, the important thing is that you capture the details of a person's life and time that are locked away in someone else's head.

Probate and Wills

This is where wills and probate records come into their own. While wills often contain valuable genealogical information, such as names and relationships, they also provide what most other records can't. An indication of a favored son or daughter, an insight into the type of clothing or furniture, and even an understanding of what the family valued, are all obtainable from wills.

Probate is the term used to describe the court proceedings to settle an estate of a deceased person, while a will is the actual document that expresses the wishes or "will" of the deceased. A study of probate records is beyond our scope, but there is a great deal of instructional material on the Internet. We have already made reference to the substantial collections of wills that are now online in various countries, such as Scotland.

For more information on how to search probate records, see **Ancestry.com's** Learning Center (top menu bar) and type in "Probate." Read the articles listed on the first page. It's enough.

Places and Their History

So much of what our ancestors did—how they lived, where they worked, who they married—has to do with place. People then, as they do now, moved from place to place in search of productive work. Sometimes that meant a large industrial city that offered work opportunities but also brought difficult living conditions. Sometimes it meant wide open spaces and a chance to buy land and farm it.

A wealth of information about the villages, towns, and counties of the United States and other countries is available, and is often very easy to find. The easiest way to start is to type in the name of the town or city in an Internet search engine. Type in the name of the place and then run the *Image* search to show if there are photographs.

Sometimes the list of images that results includes old, historical pictures such as postcards. For example, if I'm looking for historical photographs of Bartow, Florida, at the time when Henry Smiles was there I can find a whole series of photographs on a Web site called Polkpages.com, and headed "Vintage Views of Bartow, Florida." There is also a summary of the beginnings of the citrus industry—helpful to round out my picture of Henry Smiles struggling with his orange grove. Unfortunately, this particular site contains no way of contacting the Web master and no way to verify copyright, so I can't reproduce any images here.

I had better luck finding a photograph of ancient Alnwick Castle, the most important landmark in the town where Henry lived in England. But it took a bit of digging before coming across a Finn whose passion is English castles, and who readily consented to let me use of one of his photographs.

The castle at Alnwick, Northumberland, England. The adjacent town is the birthplace of Henry Smiles and where his father set up his tailor's business. The castle has been used for some of the scenes for Harry Potter movies. (Copyright Risto Hurmalainen, www.castles-uk.com.)

There are countless sites that give more information about places, some of them very sophisticated. Those listed below are included because they are intuitive to use, not necessarily because they contain the most information. Of course, you also want to find sites that include history, so type "history" into the search engine along with the place name.

- **50states.com** for information about the 50 United States

- **Fallingrain.com** has information on the towns and cities of every country in the world—maps of various scales and perspectives, plus weather graphs and other links to the named city. Go straight to **www.fallingrain.com/world/US** for American locations.

- **Google Earth**. If you have not tried this site, you are in for an experience. The site displays aerial photographic images of any place in the world, down to the details of individual cars in the driveways of homes or on the streets.

Satellite photo of The Battery, New York, now a public park but once the arrival point for many US immigrants. (Used by permission from Google Earth's Web site at http://earth.google.com/.)

Find your own home to get an idea of how the site works. You have to download the program from the Internet, but you can do so free. Log on to **www.earth.google.com** and follow the screen instructions. Although these images are of today's places, you can still get an idea of terrain and permanent features, such as rivers and lakes, and it's much better than looking at a map. The Google Earth image shown here depicts the southern end of Manhattan Island. I selected it because it shows the location of the Battery, which has so much significance for early immigrants to America.

Copyright Issues

Copyright law is complex, and the Internet has made it more so. You should always have the copyright issue at the back of your mind when extracting material from the Internet. Materials may be copyrighted even if they don't carry a copyright notice.

If you are simply using a picture in your own software program, for your own family with no intent to publish it or take commercial advantage of it, then you'll probably never have to deal with the problem. Many Web sites allow such personal use, and you can look at the footnotes attached to Web pages to see if there is a copyright notice that you can click on for further information.

Be extremely careful about copying images or text and then transmitting them to third parties. Most genealogy software programs will allow you to link images to the individuals in your tree, and when you send someone a GEDCOM those images are usually excluded. Software programs do give you the option to retain the links within your program when you create a GEDCOM, and of course you can send numerous images to other people as email attachments. Be aware that by doing so you may be in breach of copyright.

If in doubt, write to the copyright owner indicated on the Web site. If none is listed, find another image or a different article.

For a full explanation of copyright law, including its vagaries, see the Wikipedia entry under "Copyright," and read all of the associated articles (**www.wikipedia.org**).

So, with those few cautions and a little common sense, you can use the Internet in a multitude of ways to increase your understanding of the times in which your ancestor lived, and the forces and social mores both local and global that shaped their world. And it will only get better.

16
KEEPING A
PERSONAL JOURNAL

Overview

When I was a child, a common enough Christmas stocking present was a small diary with a pencil in its spine. To a child of eight or nine, a diary has little purpose as an appointment scheduler, so the idea, presumably, was for me to use the diary to write about what was happening in my life. I did so in occasional short spurts of a couple of nondescript sentences between very long lapses.

When we discuss in this chapter the idea of keeping a personal journal, this is not it.

Today there are all kinds of options to record the things in our lives that our descendants will find interesting and meaningful. The recording media through which we can tell and preserve aspects of our lives have reached a high degree of sophistication. Handwritten journals on lined paper are still preferred by some people. But there are also digitized records on a CD entered from a keyboard and including pictures and documents, electronic sound, or video files saved in a variety of formats, or sophisticated scrapbook binders with acid-free paper and page protectors that will last for centuries. All are options within most people's reach.

Why bother? It's reasonable enough to wonder why others would find our lives interesting, and to answer the question we need to take the long view. If you picked up this book because you had any kind of stirrings about your own ancestors, maybe you already know the answer. Your life will be fascinating to your grandchildren. Your world will seem strange to them.

Think of all that happens in a single generation. Even before the lifespan of my own children there were no health stores or fitness centers to speak of. There were no VCRs, and video stores were still in the future. So were desktops and laptops and email, DVDs and SUVs, the Hubble telescope, the Genome Project, and 9/11. The

Cold War, the moon landing, Vietnam, and Watergate are pulled from history books, not from their own experience or memory. It will be the same for our grandchildren.

There will always be that inner desire for people to make a genetic connection—to know who they are and where they came from. Maybe, too, there's a part of us that wants to leave our own trace—some indication that we lived and made some contribution, no matter how small that may appear to us sometimes. Like carving initials in a tree or like the graffiti-prone youth with a spray can, we want to proclaim that we existed, that we left something behind.

Here are some guidelines for recording your own history.

Step 1: Know What to Include

If you have a gift for writing or even a degree of talent, you may not need encouragement. Your creativity will find its own outlet. Some people are capable of writing their life story in a way that will interest or even enthrall others, but this chapter is also for the person who perhaps lacks the skill but could benefit from a simple approach.

So, know what you're looking for. Certainly, part of your objective should be to capture enough of your day-to-day life that a reader in the future—especially one of your descendants—can get a feel for where and how you lived. But it should be much more than that. Of course I'm greatly interested in my coal mining ancestors and the hardships they endured. But I also want to know about their values—about what they thought was important—and what their views were of the society around them. Much of that is now unknowable because those records were never made. Let's not leave our descendants wondering about who we were, what we thought, and what we valued.

Step 2: Choose Where to Start

Just as building a skyscraper involves first laying a foundation, then constructing a steel skeleton and pouring concrete floors at each level, there is a simple framework that we can use to build the picture of our lives.

This doesn't mean that you have to start when you were born and continue methodically to the present day. Sometimes that task can seem overwhelming. Rather, use the following list to stimulate your memory and to drive you to the keyboard or the writing pad. Start with what's most interesting or most fresh in your memory, or with some story that you want to make sure is passed on. If something comes to your mind that you think is relevant, then write it down under the subject heading and decide later how and in what order you will display or present it. Once you have decided on something you want to write, whether it's a sentence or two or several pages, capture the memories by mentally immersing yourself in the time and place. The following list should stimulate some thoughts, and then we'll give a couple of examples:

The Earliest Years

- Earliest childhood memories—your first home, the rooms, the décor, the outside yard or garden, even the sounds and smells of home
- The people from the early part of your life, perhaps grandparents on both sides of your family, favorite uncles or aunts, your parents—what you remember about them
- The food you ate, what you liked and disliked
- How you played, with whom and what
- Special memories, such as a Christmas or birthday or family vacation that stands out

School

- Teachers who had an impact
- Friends, recalled fondly or otherwise
- Favorite subjects—including what motivated you and why
- Sports teams, hobbies, and other interests
- School outings
- Achievements and awards
- Looking back, what you valued, and what you learned beyond the school books and exams
- Stories—especially those that make a point that would be of value to your descendants
- Class photographs, and pictures of the school itself, even if you have to go back and take a picture as it is today

Teens and Young Adulthood

- First dates
- College and thoughts of career
- The views you held—political, social, religious. These are hugely formative years for most people. Our opinions and views often change as we mature, but try to remember what you were passionate about. If you are still in those years as you write, so much the better.

Employment

- First job
- Bosses and coworkers
- Likes and dislikes
- Working conditions and environment, hours, salary
- Tools of the trade
- Plans for the future, career path, advanced education, other jobs
- Professional associations, clubs

Marriage and Children

- Capture your feelings—your spouse, how you met, what attracted you, your first child
- Where you lived and why, setting up house
- Financial struggles and how you managed
- How you communicate with your partner and your children, how you solve problems and resolve differences
- How you teach your children values
- What you do together—free time, weekends, vacations
- Your feelings about your children—individually

Other Life Experiences

- Travel, business, or pleasure

- Recreation

- Obstacles—illnesses, loss of a relative, serious setbacks—how you felt and how you coped

- Religion and church life—where and why

- Politics—your interests, your views

- Books you have read that have made an impact, and why

- Your recollection of the great events of history—what you were doing during the first the moon landing, the assassination of President Kennedy, the collapse of the Berlin Wall, or the attack on the World Trade Center in New York. Recall your feelings.

Step 3: Assemble Your Memories into Stories

Could this seemingly dull list of memories be made to sound interesting? Let's take just the first couple of bullets from the "Earliest Years" list and see what the resultant stories might look like when written down. Then start expressing your own memories in story form, one step at a time.

Example 1: Sounds and smells

My mother contracted polio when she was twelve. Polio was one of the great killers of children in the early 1900s, but she was lucky. She survived with an iron brace on her leg. It was an unwieldy and ugly thing that kept the bones straight but made social interaction with other children a trial. Later, the iron came off, but the shyness and self-consciousness remained. So did a slight limp. I remember sitting quietly in the tiny living room, perhaps reading or drawing while the bland music of the BBC Light Program played on the radio, and hearing my mother limp about the house. It did not sound the same as my sisters' walk. There was a clear "thump" with every other step as that house-proud widow, duster in hand, collected every speck from already gleaming hardwood surfaces.

The smell of furniture polish was always in our home, but sometimes it was overcome by the competition from the kitchen. On baking day, that might be from fresh apple pies or some treat, still hot on the kitchen counter. On wash day, it might be the steamy smell of the week's washing that had been soaking in what was called "the copper" before being squeezed through a hand-wringer, the steam condensing and running in rivulets down the kitchen walls and window.

* * *

Example 2: Christmas

Children really do see Santa Claus. I know because I saw him. I might have been four or five on that cold Christmas Eve, snug in my mother's big double bed where I slept until was considered too old, and my sister was forced to vacate her bedroom. But on that Christmas Eve, the last warning before the light was put out was that stern reminder that Santa didn't come to children who stayed awake to watch for him.

About two in the morning I awoke suddenly and peered over the covers in the pitch blackness. It was not distinct, but my child's over-excited mind was so certain even in the darkness of the red coat and hat and white beard that I immediately ducked back under the covers and held my breath tight, terrified of making a sound and being discovered. I have no idea how long I stayed like that, but I awoke again around 4 A.M. with instant recall, convinced that I had involuntarily banished Santa from our home and that, alone of all the kids in the neighborhood, I would be present-less on Christmas Day. I wiggled my feet as far down the bed as I could reach, where the pillow cases full of presents were supposed to be deposited. No sound of rustling paper, no dead weight on my feet. Horrified, I woke my mother and plaintively told her that Santa hadn't been. Patiently, she put on the light to show me the pillow cases, just out of my reach, then quietly turned out the light and went back to sleep. For years, I considered it a great injustice that my mother and sisters never seemed as excited about my seeing Santa as I was.

* * *

Example 3: Relatives

We lived a long way from my uncles and aunts, and visits were rare. When my eldest sister was married, it brought a flock of strange adult visitors into my eleven-year-old world whom I knew only as a collection of names preceded by Aunty-this or Uncle-that. I was mortified when a strange woman introduced only moments before as Aunty Bessie planted a very wet and overly generous kiss right on my mouth. I'm certain nobody noticed my instinctive recoil, but years later when there was a prospect of a reciprocal visit, I appealed to my mother: "She won't kiss me, will she?"

* * *

These stories are triggered simply by reflecting on the topic headings and spending a few minutes in thought. It doesn't matter if you struggle to express yourself in written form. That's not at all unusual. Just write it down any way you can. The important thing is to capture as many of the memories that are important to you as possible.

The three examples have several things in common. These all happen to be my memories, drawn from the deepest recollections of childhood. Perhaps my sisters might remember things differently or have drawn different conclusions. It doesn't matter. These are *my* memories, and this kind of narrative tells as much about the writer as about the people who are the subject of the stories.

Stories have an intrinsic importance. They are passed on from parents to children, and they give a family a common thread that links generations. A brief recitation doesn't do the next story justice, but recently I read an account from an elderly lady who, as a child of about five, had broken a bowl at the dinner table. Expecting to be scolded, she was grateful when her father pointed out that it was an accident, and acknowledged that she had not meant to do it. She said that incident came to mind throughout her own life and she never scolded her children for anything they did accidentally. That family principle or value continued on and now spans six generations.

Neither do the stories have to be about the past. Many people find it easier to write about the present, especially if the stories are about their own children. Again, when you write, try to draw a conclusion as to why the incident or memory is significant to you. Remember that your audience is your own posterity and they'll want to know what you *think*.

The following example from Australia is a good one not just because the writer has a sense of humor and writes in a conversational style, but because she reveals her private feelings in drawing her conclusion.

Example 4: Girls Are Soft

My Mum visited us from America a few years ago. I have a great relationship with my Mum; I think she has so much patience. She bore and raised eight children, six girls and two boys. On top of that she is just an innately good person.

Needless to say, when she visits, she is well aware of how kids act, but not wanting her to think that we live a chaotic, frantic, undisciplined existence, I begin pep talking the boys about their understanding of the way we should be living.

It's kind of like when you go to the dentist and you want to make sure your child gives the correct answer when asked how many times a day they should brush their teeth. While we run from the car park to the dentist's office I ask, "How many times a day should you brush your teeth? Yes, after each meal, but no less than twice a day. Good boy. Remember that when the dentist asks you."

We do the same when Mum visits. I begin reminding them that perhaps the sign on their bedroom door 'ENTER AND DIE' may be a little harsh for Grandma to see, saying, "Remember, you guys are brothers and are best friends." Along with this I reintroduce the job chart to them and explain the theory of how each member of the family contributing will develop a sense of pride and satisfaction in their contribution, to which I am met with "How much money do we get?"

I start realizing that kids can't cram for good behavior and wish I had been more consistent sooner.

"Look boys, I want Grandma to be proud of you and think you are lovely boys, so please be kind to each other." I just wonder if we can hold up the facade for a few weeks.

Within minutes of Mum arriving, I give up and realize that she cannot be fooled. We are not perfect. The boys do not ask politely to go to bed and read once their homework is finished. Nor do they speak lovingly to one another at each interaction. They spend each half an hour preceding bedtime trying to justify to me why they should be able to stay up later, and will go out of their way to humiliate, tease or inflict pain upon one another at any opportunity. Mum looked weary and said, "Maybe a little girl would have softened your family a tiny bit." Defensively I replied, "Mum I am sure there is some reason God gave me four boys." Her reply was, "But what would that be?"

I have pondered that question to this point.

Why do I have four boys? What am I supposed to learn from them? Maybe tenacity, or maybe strength. Perhaps I am meant to learn to think quickly on my feet. A sense of humor?

The other day I looked out the window to see the boys in the front yard with their youngest brother who had his swimming pants pulled between his buttocks, sumo style. He and the next door neighbor boy, several years his senior, were engrossed in a sumo wrestling bout, trying to bring each other down. My initial reaction was to call out for them to stop, but seeing his three older brothers barracking for him and patting him on the back for pulling out tricky moves, made me change my mind.

The scene went from hell-raising to heartwarming in seconds and I silently cheered on my little cheeky-bottomed, sumo son from behind the blinds.

Who cares about the answer to the question? I am just glad that those four loud, hungry, adventurous, young boys are mine. In addition to that, somehow I can't imagine a little girl enjoying her big brothers making her adorn sumo attire in the front yard, whether it softens us or not!

Liesa Wilson

Emu Plains, New South Wales

Step 4: Decide How You'll Display Your Journal

There is a wide range of choices when it comes to how you want to record the stories for your journal, and much of it is simply a matter of personal preference. Some people think that a journal isn't a journal unless it's in the handwriting of the author. My daughter-in-law complains to me that virtually all of my journals are typed. I counter that if they were handwritten, no one would be able to read the writing. She isn't satisfied, and insists that the occasional notes or messages I write to her children are written in the old-fashioned way. She's probably right, but I still prefer legibility over authenticity in this case, and have settled for just a few hand-written entries.

Some journals are almost all text, with separate photograph albums. Wherever you decide to put pictures, remember to identify everyone in the photograph in a caption next to it. You may be well aware of who's who, but your children and grand-children won't be.

My personal preference is to mix the narrative or stories with documents, photographs, letters, or other materials that add interest and depth to a page. Because original documents are often two sides and can be damaged by permanent mounting, I sometimes scan an item I want to include. That also allows me to size it on the page and build text around it just as in a magazine page. Then I keep the original safely in storage, properly identified.

Since my own journals fill several volumes, I've also taken to making the first double-page spread of each volume a simple list of the major events that were occurring in the world during the years covered by the journal. I believe this adds context to a life. We are all affected by the events around us, directly or indirectly. Listing the events of a decade or two on the wider national or even world scene is a way of painting your life against a backdrop.

	1960				1966	
•	May:	USSR shoots down American U-2 spy plane. The incident wrecks the Big Four summit in Paris.		•	Aug:	Mao Tse-tung launches "Cultural Revolution" in China to purge non-Maoist thought.
•	Jun:	Kruschev publicly criticizes China.			1967	
•	Nov:	John F. Kennedy wins US presidential election.		•	Jun:	Israel defeats combined Arab armies in Six-Day War.
	1961				1968	
•	Apr:	Russian Yuri Gagarin becomes first man in space.		•	Jan:	Viet Cong launches Tet offensive in Vietnam.
•	May:	Alan Shepard becomes first American in space.		•	Apr:	Martin Luther King assassinated in Memphis.
•	Aug:	East Germany closes Berlin border, begins construction of Berlin Wall.		•	Jun:	Senator Bobby Kennedy shot dead in Los Angeles.
				•	Aug:	Soviet troops and tanks invade Czechoslovakia to crush democracy movement.
	1962					
•	Oct:	Cuban missile crisis ends with Soviet backdown.		•	Nov:	Richard Nixon defeats Hubert Humphrey in US presidential election.
	1963				1969	
•	Feb:	Beatles record their first LP - "Please Please Me."		•	Mar:	Soviet and Chinese troops clash at Ussuri River.
•	Jun:	Russian Valentina Tereshkova becomes first woman in space.		•	Jul:	Neil Armstrong steps onto surface of moon.
•	Jun:	John Profumo, British Secretary of State for War, resigns at height of "Profumo Affair" and almost brings down British government.		•	Aug:	British troops deployed in Northern Ireland.
					1970	
•	Jun:	President Kennedy makes "Ich bin ein Berliner" speech in West Berlin.		•	Oct:	Anwar Sadat succeeds Gamal Abdel Nasser as President of Egypt.
•	Aug:	Britain learns of Great Train Robbery.			1971	
•	Aug:	Martin Luther King makes "I have a dream" speech in Washington, DC.		•	Mar:	Lt. William Calley found guilty of murdering Vietnamese civilians at Mylai in 1968.
•	Nov:	President Kennedy shot dead in Dallas, Texas.		•	Dec:	India defeats Pakistan in two-week war.
	1964				1972	
•	Feb:	Cassius Clay defeats Sonny Liston for world heavyweight boxing title.		•	Jan:	Britain signs Treaty of Brussels to join European Economic Community from January 1, 1973.
•	Aug:	US Congress approves President Johnson taking "all necessary action" against communists in Vietnam.		•	Feb:	President Nixon makes surprise trip to Communist China.
•	Oct:	Leonid Brezhnev deposes Nikita Kruschev in USSR.				
•	Oct:	Harold Wilson elected Prime Minister of Britain.				
	1965					
•	Jan:	Winston Churchill dies, age 90.				

Part of a double-page spread at the start of a volume, listing the major events in the world during the years covered by the journal. The list appears over a watermark of a significant event - in this case a moon walk. Set your life against a broader context so those who read it will have a sense of time and place.

If there are major events that occur outside your own family, record them and your reaction to them. I have several pages with the graphic newspaper photographs that followed 9/11. Those who read my journals after me will know this was important to me, that I felt a personal connection with what was going on even though I was thousands of miles away at the time.

Use the Internet to pull some of these materials together. The site mentioned in the previous chapter—**www.brainyhistory.com**—gives a highly detailed summary of the events throughout the world on any day. Scanning through this list and pulling out those items of significance to you can provide you with the list. You might consider displaying that list, perhaps with a watermark behind it, depicting one of the events listed. I've done that with the 1969 Apollo 11 moon landing, for instance.

Tip: Protecting Digital Files

You can print out your own digital photos, but those done in a professional photo shop will probably last longer. It's all to do with the type of ink used. The difference could be five years for your own print, or twenty for a professionally printed photo. Prints from film last much longer, but you can't reprint them from a digital file.

The storage life of digital files is a constant concern. You can't just save images on a disk or CD and forget about them. To begin with, storage mediums change all the time. No one works with the large, old floppy disks any more, and even the smaller floppy drives are hard to find. Even zip disks have given way to jump drives and other high-capacity storage devices, and while CDs are used widely, we can expect continued upgrades in technology. You could be left with hundreds of photos on a storage medium that you can't access or copy.

It's wise to save your files to a new medium—even if it's the same type—about every three years. If you have the discipline to do that, fine. If not, there are now Internet sites where you can store your images, which is good practice because even in a house fire or other calamity your irreplaceable photos are protected. If you have a lot of pictures and space is a problem, then at least select the very best that you couldn't bear to be without.

Modern software allows anyone to be a graphics designer and publisher, as long as they have a reasonable eye for layout. Detailed design principles are beyond our scope, but a couple of basics are warranted. First, don't mix multiple fonts just because you can. Stick to a family of just a few fonts, and use all-capital titles and multiple colors in titles sparingly. Colors should complement and enhance, not blind the reader from the main subject matter, which is the text and the pictures.

The term that is generally used for the kind of journal activity I'm describing is *scrapbooking*. I've never liked the term because I don't consider what I put into a journal as scraps. But whatever you call it, there are companies that now specialize in protective binders, acid-free-pages, tape and tape applicators for fixing items in the page, clear plastic page protectors, templates for drawing designs, and a host of other items. Scrapbooking shops are becoming common. If you are a man and think that these are just cutesy places to buy stick-on petals in pastel shades, think again. Some of the most impressive journals I've seen have been compiled by fathers with an eye to design.

Find out more from these Web sites:

- www.creativememories.com
- www.scrapbooking.com
- www.scrapbooking.about.com.

Keeping a modern journal, then, is more than writing in a diary. Even an audio or video CD, or a DVD, can be slipped into a sleeve on a page and pulled out to play. Public domain pictures can be copied from the Internet to illustrate some of your entries—pictures of places, events, and people.

How you want your journal to appear is limited only by your creativity. Journals can be simple or elaborate, modest or very impressive, but they will always be one of the most valuable things your family will own.

17
THE EXCITING FUTURE

Overview

In December 2004, Google announced that it had an agreement with five of the world's greatest libraries to digitize their collections and make millions of volumes searchable on the Internet. The scope of the Google Library Project was beyond anything previously announced—perhaps 30 million volumes scanned from the New York Public Library and the libraries at Harvard, Stanford, Oxford, and the University of Michigan.

The plan called for the scanning of books in the public domain for which the entire text would be displayed. For copyrighted works, inserting a text string into a Google search engine would deliver to the user brief snippets that would appear both before and after the search string. Google said it would work with publishers to determine how much of the text of copyrighted works would be displayed.

The project almost immediately ran into probing questions from book publishers and authors, and intense debate and legal wrangling began about how to protect the interests of those who create the original works and those who want to promote public online access. That debate will continue. However it ends, the scanning of so many millions of volumes will take years. But the vastness of the project was in line with Google's stated mission "to organize the world's information and make it universally accessible and useful."

That mission statement has an echo in the slogan of another Web site, the Internet Archive. Their slogan reads: "Universal access to human knowledge." The people who since 1996 have been building the Internet Archive include some of society's brightest minds and most respected institutions, including the Library of Congress and the Smithsonian. Their aim is to build a massive freely accessible library of cultural knowledge—books, movies, music, scientific papers, photographs that have been digitized. In this case, everything on the archive will be free.

All this points to an inexorable process not only of making more and more information available online, but of helping to organize the present digital chaos so that researchers can truly benefit.

What is the genealogical equivalent of these developments? The great strength of the Internet for family historians is also its weakness. As we have seen, there are now unprecedented opportunities for sharing data and for cooperation with others. But there are no universally accepted standards of behavior, protocols, or controls that discourage people from exchanging unsourced and unverified material. This chapter looks at some of the initiatives already beginning to take shape that will address these weaknesses and also dramatically increase the amount of reliable data online. For this final chapter, we'll focus particularly on the two giants of the family history world—The Church of Jesus Christ of Latter-day Saints, and MyFamily Inc. and its suite of member organizations.

Young girl records data the old way—with pencil and notepad at gravesides. Such volunteer efforts to capture elusive data for digitizing will continue to ease the path for family historians everywhere.

The other great area of innovation is with the rapid development and increasing sophistication of search engines. Likely developments go far beyond refinements. Rather, they promise to fundamentally rewrite the way genealogists search for data online.

FamilySearch.org

Anyone who has spent any amount of time researching their family tree has, sooner or later, run into terms like *LDS, family history center, the Family History Library,* the *Genealogical Society of Utah,* or simply, *the Mormons.* Probably the most common term used on message boards and mailing lists is *the LDS,* which has become a kind of collective term for all of the church's available resources.

A little background will help explain why the Mormons have become such huge players in the world of family history. It will also explain why their continued presence is going to help shape the genealogical world of the future and dramatically expand the options for your family research and mine.

LDS Family History Library, in Salt Lake City, Utah—the largest of its kind in the world. (Image copyright Intellectual Reserve, Inc.)

Properly called The Church of Jesus Christ of Latter-day Saints, the church was formally established in 1830 in New York State. Before fifteen years had passed, the church's rapid growth and distinctive teachings about "Restored Christianity" had brought it national attention, and not a little opposition.

Church members soon became known as "Mormons" because of their acceptance of additional scripture known as the Book of Mormon. But the only issue of relevance here is the Mormon or Latter-day Saint belief in the family as an eternal bonding of parents and children. World religions vary hugely, of course, in their teachings about an afterlife and whether familial associations continue after death. For Latter-day Saints, conviction of the continuing existence of the family is a central tenet of faith. But in order for a family relationship to continue eternally, church members believe they must first identify their ancestors. Once identified, Latter-day Saints attend services in temples where they stand in as proxies for their ancestors, who are "sealed" or united together as husbands and wives. Children are also sealed to their parents.

In LDS theology the departed soul has the free will to accept this offering or reject it. The same is true of preliminary ordinances or ceremonies including baptism, again performed by proxy.

Why is this relevant? Because only by understanding the depth of that commitment does the investment of such enormous resources in family history by a church make any sense. The Genealogical Society of Utah was established in 1894 primarily to gather vital public records to help church members research their families. What it has since become is truly mind-boggling. More than a century of record gathering, greatly aided by the advent of microfilm in the 1930s, has led to by far the world's largest collection of genealogical records. The records themselves are not actually removed from their original repository. They are microfilmed or, today, usually digitally photographed. While the original records remain in place the copies are stored in a vast underground vault blasted out of solid granite, 700 feet below the surface of the Rocky Mountains in Utah. There they remain, safe from fire, flood, war, and accident—all of which have so often ravaged or destroyed irreplaceable records around the world.

Because the church has grown to more than 12 million members in more than 160 countries, the acquisition and preservation of records has expanded accordingly. While the large U.S., Canadian, British, and Scandinavian collections reflect the composition of early church converts, substantial acquisitions from other countries reflect an increasingly diverse modern church membership.

One of dozens of Mormon temples across the world, the final stage for church members wanting to "seal" their families. This one is in Monterrey, Mexico.

Conveniently for everyone else, the church has always made all of these records freely available to the public. At first, that was through the central Family History Library in Salt Lake City. When that proved inadequate, the church began to provide Family History Centers in its chapels around the world—more than 5,000 at last count. When the Internet arrived, the Church put millions of names, including the IGI and the 1880 U.S. census online, again without charge.

To give an idea of scale, consider that many genealogical Web sites at the county level post numbers of visitors to their sites numbering tens, sometimes hundreds of thousands. By comparison, the LDS FamilySearch.org site had three billion hits within the first year of operation after its launch in May 1999. Some 2,400 people a day visit the Family History Library in Salt Lake City in person.

So, as family historians look to increasing Internet resources and systems as the way of the future, what can we expect next from The Church of Jesus Christ of Latter-day Saints?

For the past few years, the Family and Church History Department of the church has been a frenzy of activity. The entire picture will not become clear until formal public announcements are made. But enough has been said at various genealogical conferences to set the genealogical community abuzz. Images of pages from a redesigned site were already online at **http://genealogy.about.com/b/a/201217.htm** in September 2005 following a Federation of Genealogical Societies annual conference in Salt Lake City. From what was disclosed at the conference and since, the church's plans amount to a quantum leap in Internet genealogy and the tools for research.

Scanning and Indexing of the Library Collection

Virtually the entire collection of films and microfiche in the genealogy vault is to be scanned and placed online—at least, everything for which digital rights can be obtained. That's nearly 2.5 million rolls of microfilm equivalent to 6 million volumes of 300 pages each. The process would have taken decades—or even longer—except for the fact that new high-speed technology has dramatically accelerated the process. Now, it appears that around a third of a million rolls of microfilm could be processed each year, with the entire project completed in six years.

The essential parallel project to the digitizing of the records is the indexing project that will make them all rapidly and easily searchable. The program depends on two pillars. The first is new indexing software that can be used by volunteers in their own home and which reduces the likelihood of transcription error. Thousands of volunteers were already testing the software by early 2006. The second pillar of the initiative is plans to recruit an army of volunteers.

A look at the home page of the FamilySearch Indexing Web site used in the beta test for this program (see the link above) shows the emphasis is heavily on people, not on names, dates, and places. The screen message, "In 30 minutes, you can save a life" is an appeal for volunteers everywhere to help preserve the world's heritage of human records. The text goes on to explain that the vital records of thousands of people are destroyed every day by floods, fires, earthquakes, war, and other disasters.

The way in which the volunteer indexing program is organized says much for the attention that has been paid to the issue of accuracy. When the program is beyond the initial testing stage and truly goes public, it's expected that a volunteer going onto the Internet site will register, download the software from the Internet to their home computer (a 15-megabyte file), and then have a chance to view a batch of scanned images on their screen. He or she will begin to type what they see on the record, but the new software will guide them to the appropriate field to make sure they are transcribing the correct data.

In the software being tested, whatever the transcriber interprets is saved, but it doesn't become final until a second data entry volunteer has entered identical information. That volunteer could be anywhere in the world, but the computer won't accept anything as firm until it has two independent and identical interpretations. In cases of discrepancy, the data field is referred to an experienced "arbitrator" who will determine the correct information. While this process doesn't entirely eliminate the possibility of human error—especially with very difficult-to-read handwriting—it greatly reduces that problem.

There are all kinds of built-in helps and dropdown menus for the transcriber, including such innovations as a locality look-up—a boon to anyone transcribing records from an unfamiliar area.

The first collections to go online for volunteer testing were death certificates from the state of Georgia, followed by records from Mexico and Ohio. Note that what is being displayed on the screen in this new program is images of the original certificates. The original images will be available to any family history researchers working online. This is the best of all worlds for the researcher. Volunteers with a few hours a month to spare will constantly feed indexed information into a vast digital pipeline, with the researcher at the other end able to view the original scanned image.

What the church is clearly hoping for in this effort is that it will reach far beyond LDS membership and into the realm of individual volunteers, family history societies, worldwide archivists, and the broadening commercial world dedicated to making data available online. Given past experience, there is every reason to believe this will happen. The scale of the effort suggests that it will galvanize the genealogical community in ways that have rarely, if ever, been seen before.

One of the most important implications of this development will be the establishment of higher industry standards for the sharing of data. When such a big partner in the genealogical community makes its indexing software freely available to organizations which want to partner with it—as the church has said it intends to do—it is certain to raise the bar substantially. Local family history societies are hoping that they will be allowed to have their own batches of data that they can then decide to extract. In effect, this would make a huge global partnership out of what the church is doing, together with the world of individual societies and USGenWeb and related projects worldwide. Again, the church hasn't indicated—and possibly hasn't decided—whether the indexing software will be available to anyone who asks

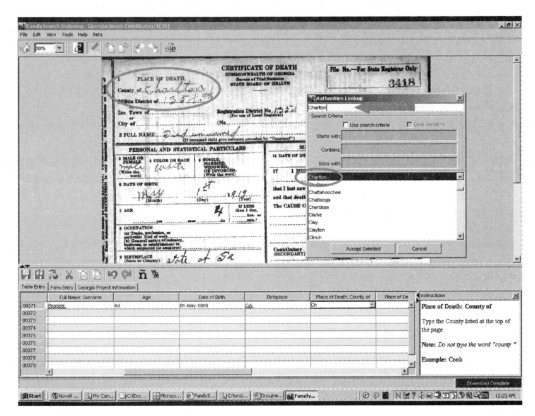

The FamilySearch Indexing program puts the original scanned record at the top of the screen, while the transcriber types in the columns at the bottom. A series of highlights prompts the user from field to field, and drop-down help menus provide additional guidance. Two independent transcribers have to come up with matching data before the information is accepted, thus dramatically reducing the risk of error. (Image copyright 1999, 2005 by Intellectual Reserve, Inc. Used by permission.)

or just to specific partner organizations in the genealogical world. But either way, the implications are enormous.

The other obvious beneficiary will be archivists at all levels. All archivists want indexing and publishing tools to increase patron participation and public accessibility of records. Whether these images are ultimately hosted on a county, state or national archivist's Web site or that of FamilySearch.org doesn't matter as much as the fact that they will be freely available.

The Launch of a Pedigree Linked Tree

The second big initiative expected from The Church of Jesus Christ of Latter-day Saints will be its own greatly improved version of a worldwide family tree that any one can access, contribute to, and within which they can coordinate and collaborate with others. But there will be substantial differences from those we have discussed already in previous chapters, because programmers are finally addressing some of the fundamental problems of bad data and inexperienced contributors.

At the time of writing, an outline of what the church is planning to put on FamilySearch.org has been shared at various genealogical conferences and with groups of church members worldwide who are testing the new systems. Whatever this family tree looks like, the emphasis will still be on coordination and sharing of information, but there will be a huge move to "make sources king." As described in detail in Chapter 4, sources are critical for any meaningful family history, yet they are mostly neglected or ignored by the members of the online community that use the popular genealogy Web sites, especially beginners.

The new LDS approach will work something like this. The appearance of the home screen will probably resemble the pedigree view first shared on page 38, with an option to shift to an individual or family view. Each name will include attached sources and information to justify the data that has been provided. The computer will be able to discriminate between the quality of those sources, for example selecting a birth certificate ahead of a census record ahead of a family Bible.

In addition, there will be a facility that will not only allow a contributor to add a note, but to dispute a source or a conclusion on screen with another contributor. The sources will therefore be ranked, and you will be able to make your own intelligent choice to determine which, if any, piece of information, belongs in your own tree.

Such innovations will raise the confidence and opportunities for serious contributors to coordinate and collaborate on their shared lines, with all that means for pooling knowledge of our forebears.

All of this will be a dramatic advance in improving the quality of family history on the Internet, but there will be many complexities to iron out. Will data without sources be displayed? Will people who are beginners or not passionate about getting their information right bother to look for sources or provide them if they don't have to? Time will tell.

MyFamily.com, Inc.

The expansion of the MyFamily.com group has been one of the great successes of the genealogy world in recent years. The genealogy community has benefited in two major ways—by the availability of key online data through Ancestry.com's aggressive acquisition program, and by its sponsorship of free sites.

MyFamily.com's ownership of Ancestry.com, with its particular collection of U.S. and British censuses, and its fairly recent acquisition of Genealogy.com, make it easily the leader in subscription services for online data. However, MyFamily.com's acquisition of RootsWeb positioned it as much more than that.

RootsWeb itself hosts most of the nonprofit genealogical groups on the Web. It is the backbone of the GenWeb projects discussed earlier. The appeal of RootsWeb is as a place where organizations can create their own mini-sites, where researchers of family history can talk and network with each other, post queries and access free data. Users of Ancestry.com's site tend to be more experienced, and are willing to pay for access to the special collections. In turn, Genealogy.com has its own, separate substantial collection of online data but is more targeted at beginners.

All of this puts the MyFamily.com Inc. group of companies in an ideal position to help shape the direction that new collaboration software—notably "world" family trees—will take in the future. Their people are already working to address the same kinds of problems that The Church of Jesus Christ of Latter-day Saints are wrestling with. They are just as aware as the LDS programmers that lack of sources and inability to properly discriminate between them is allowing the Internet to be flooded with questionable data.

The WorldConnect family tree on RootsWeb (see Chapter 9) allows contributors to post just about anything. It isn't monitored by Ancestry.com because it's a free site. You therefore "get what you pay for." But Ancestry has already attempted to address the issue of source reliability in a number of ways on its own site.

When you upload a GEDCOM file to Ancestry's OneWorldTree, the data is "scrubbed"—meaning that the software checks for illogical data or inconsistencies. This might be a child's death date before a birth date, or a wife's marriage date after a husband's death date. All good genealogy software programs do the same thing. If the Ancestry program detects errors like this, it will reject the data and the tree altogether.

Ancestry also has the facility for users of their site to attach a note in order to correct data, even if it's on a census record. Other people who disagree could, in theory, also post a note. This is a long way from the vision of programmers who want to genuinely rank sources, but it does show that the company is concerned with the same issue. The leading players in the genealogy world are all concerned with finding solutions.

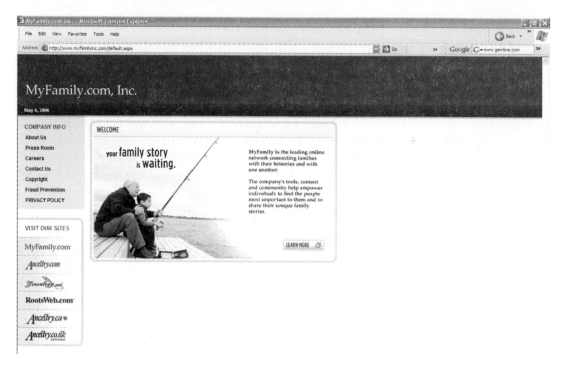

Image copyright 2005 MyFamily.com, Inc., and reproduced from MyFamily.com. Used by permission.

Internet Search Engines

Most of the references to search engines in this book have been to Google—a reflection of its dominance in the marketplace. Yet Google is not alone in experimenting with wholly new approaches to searches that will materially improve their effectiveness for family historians.

Search engines are constantly getting better. Because they are continually changing you should periodically read the search tips associated with each one. A few minutes doing so will save you that much time and more in inefficient searches.

Today's search engines are experimenting in a number of areas. Some of the innovations described below are already appearing on the Internet. Future search engines will include:

- **Personalized searches**. Your search engine will keep track of the things you look for. After a while it will accumulate a kind of profile of your interests. If it detects you are interested in genealogy it will return that type of result at or near the top of your list so you don't need to scroll down lots of pages. In fact, most people don't bother to scroll through dozens or even hundreds of results but choose to settle for just the first few. If you are one of those, this feature is likely to present you with results you wouldn't even see otherwise. You can try this now on Google, for instance. When you create a Google account from their home page, it automatically activates "Personalized Search" that then begins to monitor your search habits and look for patterns.

- **Federated searching.** Already operational on the Internet but not yet widely known, this allows you to broadcast a search to a number of different databases simultaneously, and returns merged results but with each topic listed separately, with the number of hits for each.

- **Cluster searching.** Clustering pulls up a designated word or text string on, say, several thousand Web sites but then examines each result to see if there are additional words that some of the listed sites have in common. If so, it clusters them together. A moment's thought will show how valuable this is to a genealogist. Looking for Harriett Johnson in a results list of thousands isn't practical. But if the search engine also brought together all the Harriett Johnson entries that also include Frederick Riley, you might be down to a list of 50 or 20. That's manageable. You can examine this relatively new Internet facility by checking the Web site at **www.clusty.com**.

- **Intelligent searching.** Another word for this is semantic searching, which is being hailed as the next generation of searching. The search engine doesn't just look for what you tell it literally, but also for what you *mean* or want. It tries to provide context. For instance, if you were searching on the name of a musician, you might also be offered information on his birthplace. If he was born in France you might also get a Paris weather readout. This has significant implications for genealogists. Suppose you were looking for a Friedrich Müller born in Germany in 1850, and you wanted to find his marriage. The search facility might return spelling variations even if you didn't ask for it if the result looked promising. It could also ask if you know a wife's first name so it can go through hundreds of records and reduce the list.

- **Genealogy market place.** One of the more interesting innovations is the possibility of paying a single fee to shop in a whole variety of places in the family history world. This would be much like paying an entry charge at a theme park and not having to spend more on individual rides. In effect, each user of the site would have an account, and whenever they accessed a paying facility their account would be debited. This is an attractive proposition for those reluctant to pay $200 or $300 a year for a single site subscription. Instead, a pay-as-you-go system would deliver benefits to both user and provider.

Vision for the Future

Aside from the technological innovations, what, then, is the vision for the future? There must be a much wider public recognition of the need to preserve existing records of the people who have gone before us, whether that's at a county level in the United States or in a village in Africa where the only records are oral histories. Governments in poor countries that are strapped for cash are unlikely to do this on their own, but the increasing availability of new software, along with technology that can be shared with minimal cost and a growing army of international volunteers, make the prospects look better than at any time in our past.

Questions in the minds of some members of the public, including some in government, have not entirely been resolved. There are issues of privacy and questions about transmission of personal data electronically across international boundaries. Solid lines need to be drawn between legitimate needs to protect the privacy of the living and the rights of people to research the preserved records of their own departed ancestors. Those distinctions are not always clear.

In addition to more attention to preservation, we will see a massive increase in indexing activity and the amount of online data will grow exponentially.

And finally, for you and me, the amazing technological breakthroughs we are now seeing will mean easier and more meaningful access to the lives and times of our ancestors, of their struggles and successes, their triumphs and tragedies, their hopes and dreams.

Instead of only a few shreds of perishable paper or the fading register entry of an individual long since dead, we will begin to expand our picture and better understand the lives of many of our ancestors. As living descendants each contribute their piece of the picture, there will be photographs and stories, timelines and lessons—all brought together, preserved for as long as history continues. We are already moving toward a truly collaborative effort to capture something of the footprint left by each person in their brief passage in time. For individual families, there will be greater appreciation for forebears, stronger identity and bonding.

Family history is about to enter a golden age, and for family historians, that day can't come soon enough.

APPENDIX: SPECIALTY AREAS ONLINE

Overview

Some areas of online research require specialist knowledge because the distinct methods of research and the availability of records fall beyond the standard approaches described in this book. Refer to the following sources for further reading on the Internet, and for sources of online data. Web sites and sources are listed in alphabetical order.

African-American research

Afrigeneas.com. A significant Web site where African-Americans can access an increasing collection of online data, surname lists, and message boards to coordinate and collaborate with others.

Ancestry.com. From the **Learning Center** page, enter "African Americans" in the search box. Many of the links are dated, but there is still valuable information on the basics of African-American research. Among the links, *Ancestry Magazine* is a good source. Select the more recent articles, because the picture improves constantly. At **www.ancestry.com/learn/**.

Christine's Genealogy Website. This site contains contemporary information helpful to African-American research, and links to some unusual online databases. At **www.ccharity.com**.

FamilySearch.org. From the home page, select the **Library Catalog** tab and enter "African Americans" as the subject. Several databases are listed, although little is yet online. However, the great breakthrough resource that the church produced was the Freedman Bank records, initially on CD at little cost. These can be accessed online at other sites (see below). You can also find out more about the significance of these records by simply typing "Freedman's Bank" into any Internet search engine. These records helped to begin breaking down a significant wall that poses obstacles to pre-Civil War research. At **www.familysearch.org**.

Freedman's Bank. See above, under FamilySearch.org. Access to the Freedman's Bank records at HeritageQuest Online is via libraries across the United States. This is the same process for accessing free census data. See pages 55–58. At various public libraries.

Military Records

Ancestry.com. Ancestry.com has by far the broadest collection of military records in one place on the Internet, including the American Civil War, the Revolutionary War, both World Wars and other conflicts. Some 16 million names are included in the databases. Military records can be particularly valuable because they often give detail unknown from other records—hair and eye color, scars, distinguishing marks and other detail. Record types include draft and registration cards, casualty listings, and even prisoners of war. Text descriptions with each database explain what the resource contains and, in some cases, what to do next with the search results. At **www.ancestry.com**.

Cyndi's List. This page contains links to military resources for U.S., Canadian, and British military conflicts (British Empire forces). Includes the U.S. Civil War. At **www.cyndislist.com/milres.htm**.

National Archives and Records Administration. A short but helpful explanation of how to begin research of military records, which records are held by the National Archives, and how to access them. Includes documents from the Revolutionary War or earlier. At **www.archives.gov/genealogy/military/**.

RootsWeb: United States Military Records. Instructional, with some links, but covers extensive military history, including even minor conflicts. Limited online data. At **www.rootsweb.com/~rwguide/lesson14.htm**.

Native American Research

Access Genealogy: Indian Tribal Records. An information-rich site with extensive links. Searchable databases include 1896 Census Applications, the Armstrong Roll, Dawes Final Rolls, Guion Miller Roll, Kern Clifton Roll, Reservation Roll, Old Settlers Roll, Ute Roll, and Wallace Roll. At **www.accessgenealogy.com/native**.

Ancestry.com. From the **Learning Center** page, enter "Native Americans" in the search box. The results include articles on Native American research, backgrounders on history, maps, and links to databases—including those on Ancestry.com. At **www.ancestry.com/learn/**.

Cyndi's List Native American section. Plenty of information to lay groundwork and orientation for research, and including an extensive list of online Indian census records, special rolls, cemetery, land, and other records. At **www.cyndislist.com**.

Dawes Rolls at the National Archives. The Dawes Rolls are the lists of more than 100,000 individuals who were accepted as eligible for tribal membership in the "Five Civilized Tribes" (Cherokees, Creeks, Choctaws, Chickasaws, and Seminoles) from 1898–1914. At **www.archives.gov/genealogy/tutorial/dawes/**.

Jewish Research

Ancestry.com. From the onsite search facility found under the **Learning Center** tab, enter "Jewish genealogy" and scan the links. Extensive list of useful background articles on Jewish research. Note especially "Jewish Immigration to the United States," by Gary Mokotoff, excerpted from "The Source: A Guidebook of American Genealogy." At **www.ancestry.com**.

JewishGen. Jewish research should start at this comprehensive site, which is a powerful resource for Jewish genealogists worldwide. It includes JewishGen Family Finder (a database of 385,000 surnames and towns), JRIPoland (a name index to thousands of Jewish records from Poland), and many other significant databases as well as the JewishGen Discussion Group which connects researchers with each other. JewishGen's "Family Tree of the Jewish People" contains data on more than 3 million people, and the JewishGen Holocaust database draws a million entries from multiple sources. The Stephen Morse search facility for locating Jewish immigrants through Ellis Island—a part of some subscription databases—can be accessed free on this site. Under the Research heading, click on JewishGen databases for a rich list of online data, including much from Europe. At **www.jewishgen.org**.

IAJGS. This is the official website of the International Association of Jewish Genealogical Societies, an independent non-profit umbrella organization coordinating the activities and annual conference of more than 80 national and local Jewish genealogical societies around the world. At **www.IAJGS.org.**

Yad Vashem. This is the Central Database of Shoah Victims' Names—some 3 million already and attempting to collect the other 3 million names of Jews murdered in the Nazi Holocaust. This database is remarkable for another reason—the fact that contributors are encouraged to provide not just names, but details, testi-monials, and photographs if possible to ensure the continued memory of those who died. At **www.yadvashem.org**.

New York Public Library. Many Yizkor (Memorial) books are accessible online as original images. The site contains good historical summaries and expla-nations. At **www.nypl.org/research/chss/jws/yizkorbooks_intro.cfm**.